The
SURVIVAL GUIDE
to
ARCHITECTURAL
INTERNSHIP
and
CAREER DEVELOPMENT

Grace H. Kim, AIA

WILEY

John Wiley & Sons, Inc.

Published by John Wiley & Sons, Inc., Hoboken, New Jersey
Published simultaneously in Canada

For general information about our other products and services, please contact our Customer
Care Department within the United States at (800) 762-2974, outside the United States at
(317) 572-3993, or fax (317) 572-4002.

Wiley also publishes its books in a variety of electronic formats. Some content that appears in print
may not be available in electronic books. For more information about Wiley products, visit our Web
site at www.wiley.com.

Library of Congress Cataloging-in-Publication Data

Kim, Grace H.
 The survival guide to architectural internship and career development / Grace H. Kim.
    p. cm.
 Includes bibliographical references and index.
 ISBN-13 978-0-471-69263-8 (pbk.)
 ISBN-10 0-471-69263-8 (pbk.)
 1. Architecture—Vocational guidance—United States. 2. Architecture—Study and teaching
    (Internship)—United States. 3. Architectural practice—United States. 4. Career
    development—United States. I. Title.
 NA1995.K56 2006
 720'.23'73—dc22

                                                                          2005019105

Printed in the United States of America

10 9 8 7 6 5 4 3 2

CONTENTS

FOREWORD:
Surviving Internship

For some, navigating through an internship can pose as many problems and create as much stress as architecture school. Some of the same mysteries occur in both: Why do certain things work and others don't? What steps should you take, and in what order? Where can you go to get answers to your questions? This book goes a very long way toward answering such questions and taking the mystery out of the intern process. It offers advice on how to get your first job, make your way through the Intern Development Program (IDP), and take the Architect Registration Exam (ARE). It also addresses how to protect your employee rights, receive a fair salary, continue your education, find a mentor, pursue nontraditional paths, work abroad, and start your own firm. When you finish reading this book, you may wonder, as I did, why something like this has not existed before now. Better late than never.

Architectural internship has long been a period fraught with frustration. Charles Dickens parodied it in his book *Martin Chuzzlewit,* which follows the exploits of Martin, a poor but aspiring architect, who works for the insufferable Mr. Pecksniff. Dickens exaggerates Martin's plight for dramatic effect, although I suspect some interns will recognize some of their own experiences in his story. But Dickens discerns in this, as well as in his other books, a situation that remains very much true today: The marketplace presents us with a new kind of wilderness, a place full of opportunity, yet also full of peril, in which we can easily get lost or even figuratively perish. That prospect underscores the need for the book you now have in your hands, a survival guide that you should take along with you and refer to often. You'll need it.

You might well ask why internship has to be so difficult. Actually, the profession and the schools have done a much better job over the past decade or so in clearing away some of the underbrush and in blazing some trails for recent graduates. An increasing number of schools provide career services to their students, and most architectural offices now take part in IDP. However, in a manner endemic in our profession, IDP and other internship aids have often been designed without enough input from their users. We know, for example, that as many as half of all architecture school graduates end up taking, at some point in their careers, nontraditional paths, a subject ably covered in this book. But IDP and most of the career services provided by the schools focus on traditional architectural practice in an office setting. It is as if the profession has blazed a few overcrowded trails through the wilderness of internship, paying almost no attention to the many other paths that people have had to forge mostly on their own.

Books like this, and Web sites like ArchVoices.org and InsideArch.org, are valuable because they look at these multiple paths from the point of view of their users: the interns themselves. As such, they represent a lesson in how to become an architect. A good book is like a good building: It comes from taking the time to understand and respond to current users and future generations. While entitled "Professional Practice," Chapter 5 is essentially about ethics, a subject that unfortunately gets a bad rap in both the schools and the profession because it is often written about as if it were simply a set of prohibitions. Ethics, at its core, is just the opposite. It demands of us just one thing: that we look at the world from the perspective of the other. Too much of what we design fails to do that, as does too much of what the profession has done for interns. So even after you survive your internship years, keep this book around and refer to it every so often, to remind yourself what we all owe to others.

Also, return to it occasionally to remember why you set off on this journey to begin with. Amidst all the anxiety of getting a job, learning how to practice, and constructing a satisfying career, you can find your way through internship and lose yourself in the process. A guide like this can tell you how to survive, but only you can answer the question of what you want to survive for. What ideals drive you? What passions excite you? What lifetime project do you want to pursue through the many paying projects you will work on as a professional? This book asks those questions, sometimes explicitly and sometimes implicitly, suggesting that surviving jobs or exams or career changes means little if your sense of purpose doesn't survive along with you.

The author herself offers a case in point. Grace Kim made her way through internship to become a registered architect, and then decided to take on the project of making it easier for others by writing this book. Professional ethics, for her, involved doing all she could to help future professionals. She also wrote the book while serving as a principal in a newly founded architectural practice; no small feat given the time-consuming character of architectural practice. It shows how much you can accomplish when motivated by a larger purpose. Finally, the book reveals a rarely traveled path for recent graduates: that of writing and advocating for interns. A few people have blazed that trail, and their work in books like this has demonstrated how much still needs to be done to keep clearing all the underbrush in the passage between architecture school and registration.

So after you read this book, consider doing more than just helping yourself. You might help others on the same path by becoming active in the AIA Associates Committee in your area, mentoring students or recent graduates from your alma mater, giving Archinect.com your feedback on some issue, or evaluating the firms in which you have worked on InsideArch.org. Or you might consider helping the many others in need of your skills, whether they be local K–12 students eager to learn more about design, your local community in need of help to deal with environmental or development issues, or your local Habitat for Humanity office looking for volunteers. You'll find these and many other ideas in this book, so I won't say more, other than to urge you to see your internship not just as something to survive, but as a time when you find the place and purpose within which you can thrive for the rest of your life. You owe it to yourself.

Thomas Fisher
Dean of the College of Architecture and
Landscape Architecture
University of Minnesota

ACKNOWLEDGMENTS

This book would not have been possible without the help of my best friend, husband, and fellow architect, Mike Mariano. More than 15 years of conversation and discussion with him has shaped much of what is written in this book. Thanks for giving me the support and "Grace time" needed to finish.

Thanks to:

My parents for all your encouragement and support in all that I have endeavored to do in my life. Special thanks to my mother, Young Kim—you are my life mentor.

The Mariano, Druzianich, and McFarland families for all your encouragement and patience over the past year as I've been absent from precious family gatherings to write this book. Your interest and support has been greatly appreciated.

The members of the Laddership Group, as well as the other interns who have sought advice and listened to my "war stories" over the years. Your questions have reminded me to listen and remember the difficulties and frustrations of being an intern.

My architect-friends Jill Lewis, Tricia Stuth, Ted Shelton, Kai Bergmann, and architect-brother Warren Kim—you have all been great mentors to me, and you've deeply informed my architectural values.

John McRae and Cecil Steward—who inspired me, while sitting in the Louisville airport, to continue carrying the torch for interns.

My former professor Paul Hirzel for reminding me that I've been invited to *the* party—and what a grand party it is!

My former bosses Jennie Sue Brown and Mark Simpson for teaching me all that I know about firm and project management.

My former coworker Donna Palicka for showing me that a professional woman can be feminine and still be respected.

My former supervisor Peter Freiberg for being a great architect and a tremendous mentor to me and many other young architects who have hallowed the halls of SOM Chicago.

All the contributors to this book. Your stories helped illuminate the text and provide insights into what interns might expect on their journey toward licensure.

The many friends who supported this endeavor through their patience, encouragement, and text edits.

Bethany Bright for assistance in graphics at the early stages of the book.

John Czarnecki, acquisitions editor at John Wiley & Sons, for inviting me to write on a topic of mutual interest and commitment, as well as the staff at Wiley for collaborating on the production of this book.

| # INTRODUCTION

This book is written for soon-to-be architectural graduates and architectural interns in their first few years of professional practice. It may also be helpful for those individuals who have not taken the Architectural Registration Exam (ARE) and find themselves in a perpetual state of "internship," as well as those seeking nontraditional careers. But first and foremost, it is a survival guide for interns pursuing architectural licensure.

In writing this book, I do not claim to have all the answers or the definitive solution to every internship situation. However, as a young practitioner and former IDP coordinator, as well as a mentor to many interns, I have seen what has been successful in terms of navigating internship and what could be better. In an effort to provide a viewpoint that is not myopic, I have solicited contributions from young architects and interns around the globe. Their essays are interspersed throughout the text and will hopefully provide you with additional insights. The contributors represent a variety of alternative viewpoints, not all of which I share. However, their contributions reflect the diversity of opinions and experiences that are present within our profession. If you find that a particular essay does not suit your needs, skip it and read another. It is for you to decide what is pertinent to you and your career.

Think of this as a book of questions that can prompt you to solve your own personal internship problems. As with any architectural problem, there is not just one right answer; the number of correct solutions is infinite. While some suggestions are provided in the pages that follow, they are intended as a guide to help in your decision making. What has worked for others may not be the correct approach for you. Read through the suggestions, talk to other interns to see what they have experienced, seek the counsel of your mentor, and make the decisions that feel right for you.

Chapter 2 begins with a series of questions that can help you develop a sense of your career intentions. Think of it as planning for a trip. Where is it that you want to go, and what do you want to do when you get there? Subsequent chapters provide a framework to help you prepare for various milestones in your development: finding a job, going through performance reviews, taking exams, and later becoming a leader in a firm or starting a firm of your own.

Acknowledging that we all have different ways of learning and synthesizing information, I have presented material in a variety of ways. In the early chapters, there are checklists and worksheets you can use when making decisions about where you want to live and work. Throughout the book, you will find "tips" embedded in the text. For some of you, these will be obvious statements; for others, they may highlight and bring attention to a common oversight or stumbling block.

There may be suggestions that will be entirely appropriate and helpful to you without much modification. But there may be others that simply don't fit with your personality or approach to your career. Pick and choose what you think will work for you. As you learn alternative methods that work better, make note of them in the margins or at the end of each chapter. A blank page has intentionally been left just for that purpose. That way, when you become a mentor to someone else, you can relay what was successful for you. You will likely find mentors along your career path who will augment what you read and offer their own experiences.

While you could read this book cover to cover, it is intended to help you as different circumstances present themselves throughout your career. Using this book as a departure point may help you think about how to approach a situation. The table of contents is intended to help you navigate the chapters and quickly find the pertinent sections. Where appropriate, resources are listed at the end of each chapter. A bibliography at the end of the book provides a suggested list of texts for further reading on particular topics that are referenced throughout.

Becoming an Architect: An Overview

While this could be the subject of a book in itself, if you have not yet begun your journey into architectural education, here are the basics. It is important to understand that one cannot legally call oneself an architect until one has satisfied the requirements of one's state registration board. Furthermore, licensure in one state does not immediately grant the title of architect to that person in any other state.

The Three-Legged Stool:
Education, Experience, and Examination

This metaphor is a commonly used by the National Council of Architectural Registration Boards (NCARB)[1]. Like a stool that needs three legs to support itself, an architectural candidate needs to obtain three "legs" to be considered an architect: education, experience, and examination. Please note that each state registration board has slightly different requirements for licensure, and many have Web sites; be sure to contact your state registration board for specific requirements. Most states have the following combination of education, experience, and examination requirements.

Education

A professional education in the United States is satisfied by a National Architectural Accrediting Board (NAAB)[2] accredited degree in architecture. Before starting your architectural education, you should verify that your program is NAAB-accredited, as this will affect your eligibility for licensure in some states. There are three types of NAAB-accredited degrees:

1. A five-year Bachelor of Architecture program intended for students who enter immediately after high school or who have no previous architecture training.
2. A two-year Master of Architecture program for students who hold pre-professional undergraduate degrees in architecture or a related area (engineering, landscape architecture, etc.).
3. A three- or four-year Master of Architecture programs for students with an undergraduate degree in another discipline.

    NAAB provides a list of accredited schools on its Web site. In addition, the Association of Collegiate Schools of Architecture (ACSA)[3] publishes annually a comprehensive list of programs offered by the various architectural schools in North America. This list includes a description of the degrees offered and the educational focus of the school. However, it should be noted that *not* all schools listed in the ACSA publication are NAAB-accredited programs.

---

[1] NCARB (www.ncarb.org) is a national body that develops model standards for licensure and for the regulation of architectural practice, which are in turn adopted by the individual state registration boards. NCARB is responsible for the administration of the Intern Development Program and the Architect Registration Examination.

[2] NAAB (www.naab.org) is the sole agency authorized to accredit U.S. professional degree programs in architecture.

[3] ACSA (www.acsa-arch.org) is a nonprofit, membership association founded in 1912 to advance the quality of architectural education. ACSA represents over 250 schools, including all accredited programs in the United States and government-sanctioned schools in Canada, as well as special programs offering two-year and international programs.

Candidates with degrees from schools outside the United States must obtain an Education Evaluation Services for Architects (EESA)[4] evaluation of their degree from NAAB.

Experience

The Intern Development Program (IDP)[5] is a national program administered by NCARB that, as of press time, has been adopted by 49 of the 50 states. To satisfy the requirements of this program, interns are required to obtain experience in 16 categories of architectural practice. The minimum amount of time it may take to satisfy those requirements is three years of full-time employment. Much like the residency period for a medical intern, IDP is intended to expose architectural interns to a broad range of experiences that they may encounter as a registered architect. Additional information, as well as tips for successfully completing this program, can be found in Chapter 3.

Examination

The Architect Registration Exam (ARE)[6] is the final step in the registration process, sometimes referred to as licensure. The ARE has nine sections — six multiple-choice and three graphic — that represent the various aspects of professional practice. Chapter 4 addresses the ARE in depth and provides some exam preparation tips.

If you have not already begun your journey toward licensure and you are interested in learning more about the process of becoming a registered architect, several books on the subject are listed in the bibliography. And if you have begun, I hope that the following chapters offer you guidance and support in these formative years of your career.

---

[4] EESA assists those individuals who wish to apply for NCARB certification or for registration by an NCARB member board and who do not have a professional degree in architecture from an NAAB-accredited school of architecture. EESA often works with internationally educated applicants and broadly experienced architects. Information can be found on the NAAB Web site (www.naab.org).

[5] Detailed information about IDP can be found on the NCARB Web site (www.ncarb.org) and by reading the IDP Guidelines, which are available upon request from the Web site.

[6] While architectural registration is granted by the individual state registration boards, the ARE is administered nationally by the overseeing body of NCARB. Detailed information about the examination can be found at www.ncarb.org.

CHAPTER 2 | FINDING THE RIGHT FIRM FOR YOU

Where to Start

As the end of the school year or graduation nears, the challenge of beginning a career in architecture looms in front of you like a freight train. Some of the questions that may be going through your mind are: "How do I find my first job? When do I have time to send out my résumé with my final crit quickly approaching?" For those of you graduating, you might also be considering, "Which city should I move to? What type of firm do I want to work for?"

Breathe . . .

Now think about the aspect of architecture school that you liked the most. Was it the studio project where you designed a glass museum? Or the 3-D studio where you completely modeled and rendered the interior of a house? Or the structural engineering class where you built a truss and stressed it to failure? Contemplate the projects that get you excited. Are they houses featured in your local newspaper, or skyscrapers in Shanghai pictured in the latest architectural journal? Start researching firms and compile a list of those you would like to contact.

Instead of sending out résumés to every firm in the Yellow Pages, conduct a targeted job search. Don't be discouraged by the low number of jobs advertised in the classified section. Most firms do not post job listings in the local newspapers. While you may be feeling the pressure to find a job—any job—resist this sense of desperation. Much as you would with a design problem, you need to analyze the context and develop a concept for how you would like to shape your career. Whether it is a summer internship or your first job after graduation, there are several ways to begin your job search.

Know Your Architectural Objectives

Before you start thinking about where to apply, you should consider the following questions: What do you want out of architecture? What are your career objectives? Do you want to become licensed? Are you interested in design for the sake of design, or do you want to design practical, purely functional buildings? Do want to have your own firm or be part of a larger entity? Do you want to work on high-profile, large-scale projects, or would you rather work on smaller projects with limited users? Are you intrigued by the profession for the end goal of construction itself or the service you will provide as an architect?

In addition, think about how you like to work. Do you find that your best work draws inspiration from within yourself or from perusing publications? Do you find that your best ideas are generated in a group environment where you bounce ideas off others? Which of your studio projects was most interesting, challenging, or rewarding, and why? What is your passion in architecture? Which firms do you admire for demonstrating this shared passion?

The answer to these questions can help you determine the type of firm that would best suit your personality and objectives.

If you want to work in a particular industry (e.g., healthcare or retail) or on a particular project type (e.g., commercial office buildings or multifamily housing), find out what publications or Web sites cater to those markets. Peruse Web and print publications to see which firms consistently have their work featured. Consider whether these are firms you would like to work for and whether they are located in cities where you would like to live.

Find the Right City

66% of respondents indicated that firm location was an important criterion in seeking their first job.

—2003 ARCHVOICES/AIA INTERNSHIP AND CAREER SURVEY

For some of you, your first job out of school will depend a lot on where you want to live when you graduate. If you want to move to a new city, do your homework. Consider the lifestyle you want—the types of amenities you would seek in your immediate neighborhood, and whether you prefer proximity to nature. Also consider the work opportunities. Is there a large architectural community to support internship positions? Take into account your resources. Are there alumni or friends in the area who can provide an introduction to get your foot in the door? Talk to them and learn about the market conditions for interns. Ask them how long it took them to find jobs.

A Look at Your Architectural Values

If you don't already know, the following steps may help you determine what you believe to be important in the architecture profession:

1. Think about recent magazines, books, travels, or studio projects — make a list of the projects that you liked the most.

2. Next to each project name, list the project type (e.g., public, private, museum, single family, etc.).

3. List the architect.

4. List the aspects of the project that stood out (materials, spirit of collaboration, location, etc.)

5. Review the list and see if there are common factors to the projects listed; create categories by circling or color coding.

6. If the categories define characteristics that are important to you in architecture, keep them in mind as you continue your job search. Come back to these characteristics as you decide which firms to apply to; check to see if firms satisfy these criteria. Refer to this list as a benchmark of requirements for the firm that extends you the first job offer.

name and location	project type	architect	special qualities
Inland Steel Building, Chicago	office building	SOM	design rigor, structural ingenuity, use of materials
Seattle Central Library	public library	OMA	innovative structural system, unique form
Federal Building, Chicago	office building	Murphy Jahn	Engages the public through open space, corten steel, artwork

In reviewing the sample chart, possible search criteria for firms to consider might be those that specialize in office buildings, are expressive of structure, and practice in metropolitan areas.

Ask about the architectural community, outdoor recreation, local politics, and the social scene. Make sure it is the city you think it is.

Given the uncertainty of our profession, most firms do not like to hire interns from out of town. (A recruiter for a large firm once told me that they interview prospective local applicants before out-of-towners for intern positions.) The individuals responsible for hiring generally do not want the burden of laying off an intern who has moved to town just for a job in their office, especially in a tough economy. (A former supervisor informed me a year into my employment that he had asked the chief operating officer of the firm two weeks before I was moving to town whether the workload indicated that my position would be secure or whether he anticipated another round of layoffs before the end of summer.) In a competitive market, if you really want to work in a particular city, you will likely have to move there before a job offer will be extended. However, in a booming economy, signing bonuses and other incentives may be offered to out-of-town applicants.

While the mid- and late 1990s were a great time to enter the profession, layoffs and tough economic times are cyclical. They are not, however, predictable. The unfortunate reality of our profession is that there have consistently been up and down cycles in our economy that are linked to the construction industry and real estate markets. It is important to bear this in mind as you contemplate moving to a new city, especially if you are moving to a city for a specific firm. You should consider whether there are other firms in the city where you would enjoy working if you were laid off. Does the city offer amenities that are attractive to you and might compensate for the job if it isn't as good as you imagined it would be? While these questions may seem pessimistic, there are many interns who become disenchanted with their jobs and realize they also hate the city in which they live, and there are others who move to a new city for a job, only to be laid off within the first year. While the job is important, so is the city in which the job is located.

Some people know the city where they want to work from the day they start architecture school, and they move there upon graduation with hopes a job will follow. Like many interns in New York, Adam knew he wanted to work in the Big Apple, but he lacked the professional contacts to secure a job prior to arrival. He shares his story of how he got by while he waited for his ideal job to materialize.

> The dream was always to move to New York City to begin my architecture career officially. Having grown up in Atlanta, a place where design is not highly revered, I wanted to go where there was appreciation for good architecture. New York had the firms, clients, and culture to support a career in architecture better than any other place in the country.

> I had previously worked in both large and small offices in Atlanta and Washington, D.C., but I always felt like these jobs were for practical experience and paying bills, not necessarily for the opportunities to work on great projects. The jobs were good, and I experienced working on projects of different scale, but the design always took a back seat to various other concerns. I felt that I had not yet worked at a firm where I was challenged from a design standpoint, and that my architectural interests were not fulfilled in the work being produced. I wanted my work experience after graduate school to be different.

> My job search began by figuring out whom I knew that knew someone else in New York. Hailing from the South and not really having any personal connections in the Northeast, I knew it would help to make the most of any connections I had

in order to get my foot in the door at a New York office. However, had I known when I started to what degree this was important, I would have been even more diligent in scouring my friends, colleagues, and professors for contacts. As it was, I had studied under a few professors who had worked in New York and knew people who might be able to help me. They all told me that it was a good idea when contacting the architects not to ask directly about hiring, especially given the economic climate in New York at the time; better to make contact, ask to visit the office, discuss my work, and perhaps ask whom they might know in the city who could have an opening. So, I developed a list of contacts and began making the phone calls, one by one. Sadly, with rare exceptions, I heard that "it was slow." The economic situation was pretty bleak overall, but I had hoped my previous work experience and school work would help me. I was wrong.

I sent many letters and résumés. However, I did not send graphic sheets or mini-portfolios as many other applicants did. I wanted to be able to present my work properly as well as to try to make a personal connection with the people for whom I wanted to work. My first round of contacts produced only one interview, though perhaps with the perfect firm. My favorite professor had worked with a few of the architects at this firm while he was in New York, and he admired them for their work and their architectural roots. The principal was from South Carolina, and one of the partners had gone to the University of Virgina, so I hoped they might have a soft spot for a fellow Southerner.

The first interview went very well. I had my résumé and portfolio and a couple of books we had put together at school showcasing our studio work. It was a brief interview, after office hours, with one of the partners. I knew that the design scene in New York, and this office in particular, was fairly casual, so I did not feel that a suit was necessary. I wanted to feel comfortable and demonstrate that I fit in, so I dressed appropriately. I had a great discussion with the partner about my school work, my professional experience, and the type of job I was looking for. My work was of interest to him, and he liked my attitude — professional but personable. That was the good news.

Unfortunately, the firm had gone through a tough spell, and they were waiting for a project to start before they could extend an offer. He told me that he would love to schedule an interview with the boss, but it was not something that needed to be done if he could not promise me a position, and he figured it would be at least a month until he could tell me anything. So I left and felt good about things and figured I'd have to wait a bit, but it would be worth it. This firm was exactly what I wanted — the work was exciting, the people were friendly and open, and the commitment to design was stronger than in any office I'd ever previously worked in or visited. The project that they were waiting for was in North Carolina, and nothing interested me more than working on a great building near my hometown.

So, I settled in for the wait. I had no other real leads, and I really wanted to give myself a shot at working for this office. In the meantime, I took a temporary position with the United Way, so I could pay my bills and the exorbitant New York rent. I spent my days doing data entry for very little pay, but it was enough to get by, and I had my eye on something larger. Diligently, I kept in close contact with the firm, and every week, the partner told me he couldn't tell me anything new. After almost two months, I was beginning to tire of my temporary job, the low pay, and the uncertainty of a permanent position. I had not yet put a deadline on this opportunity, but I had begun to look at other firms, researching the AIA Web site and other New York Web sites to find firms that did good work and satisfied my selection criteria. While I continued to send letters and résumés and call the people that I had already spoken with, I was anxious to hear from my first lead.

After another month, I finally received a call from the partner saying that he would like for me to meet the principal. The big project was about to start, and they were ready to consider applicants more seriously. I met with them both and presented my work, and they made me an offer on the spot. We discussed what my role would be within the firm and negotiated the salary, and I was told I would hear from them in the next couple of days, which I did. They were ready to bring me on, and after three months of scraping by on a meager hourly wage, I was more than ready to begin. Although the waiting had been difficult, I was offered a position at the perfect office for my skills, interests, and personality. The project got underway, and I took a central position on the design team, working closely with another young partner whom I liked a lot and who showed an appreciation for my work from the beginning.

The other architects in the office are young, energetic, and talented, and we never lack support from the partners to produce designs expressing a high level of creativity and innovation. It's a job that I love, with people I respect, in a place that will teach me how to be a better architect. The waiting paid off.

Adam Ruffin
Intern, Thomas Phifer and Partners
University of Virginia, Master of Architecture 2002

If you are not like Adam and don't know whether or not you'd like to live in a prospective city, use the Internet as a resource for learning about it. Conduct online research to find out what it might be like to live in a particular city. Look for the following Web sites:

Visitors bureau or tourism board—Find out about population (demographics), cultural events, opportunities for outdoor activities, what the city is known for.

Chamber of commerce—Check for business opportunities, growth potential for the region, leadership opportunities.

Health clubs or organized sports clubs—These can indicate the level of health and activity of the population.

Weekly events listings—Is there night life? Will there be something for you to do when you aren't working? Are there concert venues, art galleries, a variety of restaurants and watering holes?

Local newspaper—Read the headlines and editorial sections of recent issues to see if the topics relate to your interests/viewpoints.

Apartment rental listings—Are housing costs reasonable? Can you afford a place on your own, or will you have to look for a roommate to share costs?

Transportation schedules—Is public transportation available and convenient, or will you need to rely on a car to get around?

Finding the Right City

1. List the firms that interest you.

2. Next to each firm, list the city in which it is located.

3. Cross off the cities where you would absolutely not want to live.

4. Research the cities that remain and circle the ones where you would be most interested in living.

firm	city	activities and amenities

5. List the outdoor or cultural activities you enjoy (e.g., kayaking, movies, music, theater, Rollerblading, running, eating out).

6. Next to each activity, list the frequency (per week, month, or year) that you take part in it.

7. Does the city in Question 4 accommodate or support the frequency of these activities? If yes, congratulations! Send out those résumés. If no, consider how important these activities are to you. In a small town, you may need these familiar activities for continuity during this time of transition. But if you're moving to a major city, you may welcome the opportunity to find new interests.

Types of Firms

When thinking about your ideal employer, it's important to remember that there are many different types of architectural firms, not only in terms of the projects they take on or their designs, but also in terms of business practices and service delivery methods. While there is no industry-prescribed classification of firm types, several books attempt to distinguish the various business models firms use. For example, *The Architect's Handbook for Professional Practice,* 13th ed. (see Bibliography, page 249) describes six archetypes: Einsteins, Niche Experts, Market Partners, Community Leaders, Orchestrators, and Efficiency Experts. These archetypes have specific characteristics that provide direction for marketing and business decisions:

The Einsteins are innovators, generating new ideas and technologies. They produce high-profile designs and generally have a strong research focus, with firm leaders that teach and publish. They are distinctly known for their philosophies, which can transcend geopolitical borders.

The Niche Experts are specialists, with a focus on particular project types or services in a given market. They closely watch the developments of the Einstein firms and cater to specific market needs that are not being met.

The Market Partners lead in one or more major markets, such as health care or airports. They build their practice around these markets by sharing the values of their clients, attending industry trade events, and creating personal relationships with diverse members of the industry. Former client-side staff may hold marketing and project management positions in Market Partner firms.

The Community Leaders maintain leadership roles within their town or region that allow them to expedite political decision making and overcome obstacles more quickly than outsiders. Their commitment to and knowledge of the community make them invaluable team leaders to their clients. Their project base includes premier public buildings such as schools, recreation centers, and other municipal structures.

The Orchestrators focus on project management for complex projects, with an emphasis on speed, coordination, and control. As the client's advocate, they ensure that complex projects stay within budget and schedule. Of the six archetypes, the Orchestrator is most in tune with corporate businesses and is the most likely to have firm leaders holding MBAs.

The Efficiency Experts base their business on prototypes and site-specific applications of standardized designs. Their primary objective is to help their clients achieve financial success through fast and inexpensive volume rollouts. Efficiency Experts may provide expanded services that delve into the realm of real estate development and program management.

While it may be difficult to determine whether a particular firm is of one of these archetypes, it may be helpful to determine which archetype satisfies your architectural aspirations or simply to acknowledge that the differences exist. Knowing that you are interested in sports facilities may indicate that you should be looking for firms that are Niche Experts, such as Ellerbe Becket, HOK Sports, or NBBJ. Conversely, if you are not sure of the type of projects you want to work on, but you know that you are interested in working on local projects and becoming active in your community, you may seek out firms that are Community Leaders and that may not be nationally recognized but have outstanding reputations, such as OWP/P in Chicago and Pyatok Architects in Oakland.

The book *Architect's Essentials of Starting a Design Firm* (see Bibliography, page 249), provides another perspective by narrowing the types of firms to three major categories—Strong-Idea, Strong-Service, and Strong-Delivery—with two types of management styles: practice centered and business centered.

For the purpose of selecting the type of firm for which you would like to work, these categories may prove more helpful. At first glance, they may seem more general than the categories outlined in *The Architect's Handbook for Professional Practice*, but you will soon see the similarities:

Strong-Idea firms have a strong design focus, producing signature projects with a distinctive architectural style. Cutting-edge design and innovation are primary objectives of their practice. Design awards are a significant measure of their success. Einsteins and Niche Experts are the types of firms that have developed their practice around creating big ideas.

Strong-Service firms are customer service oriented, with client satisfaction being a primary concern. Repeat clients and client referrals are signs of their success. Awards generally come from industry associations and organizations. Market Partners, Community Leaders, and Orchestrators provide this client-focused approach.

Strong-Delivery firms focus on the business of architecture. The productivity of the firm and its employees is as important as its product; repetitive building prototypes are favored over single-application design solutions. Efficiency and profitability for both the client and the firm define success. Efficiency Experts are prime examples of this type of firm.

These categories are not black-and-white, and most firms will likely be a combination of types. It is mainly important to recognize that there are different types of firms, and that you should evaluate your values and interests to see if they align with the firms you are considering for employment.

Regardless of the type of firm you select, some generalizations can be made about the quality of your internship experience based on the size of the firm. While these are broad-brush statements about large corporate firms versus small to medium-sized firms, a quick survey of interns two to three years out of school suggests they generally hold true. To get a truly accurate picture of a firm you are considering, it would be best to talk with interns in similar positions at that office. If you are extended an offer for a position, you could request to speak with an intern currently employed at the firm to hear about his or her experiences.

Generally speaking, larger firms will provide you with more resources and a structured internship experience. Your first day at work will feel organized, with a formal orientation, forms to complete, and introductions to various people and departments within the firm. However, over the course of an internship, your role may become specialized, and you may have limited exposure to the diverse areas of the practice. In most cases, it is not likely that you will be able to satisfy all of your Intern Development Program (IDP) requirements at a large firm, particularly within the IDP's minimum three-year time period. On the other hand, the reputation of the firm, scale of projects, and design expectations from clients may provide exciting opportunities.

Conversely, smaller firms are less likely to be as organized for your first day, perhaps to the point of not yet having a desk or computer for you. However, during your internship, a smaller firm will generally provide you with a wide spectrum of experiences. And it is more likely that you will be able to satisfy all of your IDP requirements at a smaller firm within three years. However, unlike the larger firms, the projects may be more limited in scope or size, and design opportunities may be severely limited by budget or client expectations.

Finding the Right Firm

Once you've settled on a city, find out if the local AIA chapter produces a publication or Web site for their awards programs. Look through the entries and identify the companies that produce the type of work you are interested in. Organizations like the Good Design Museum in Chicago and the Van Alen Institute in New York City may also have exhibits of work by local architecture firms.

Whether you are looking for a summer internship or your first job out of school, there are a number of ways to learn about jobs and firms. While it might seem logical to check the classifieds in your local paper, not many architects choose to advertise their positions in this manner. It is more customary to post job listings at the local American Institute of Architects (AIA) chapter or online. But generally speaking, you will hear about jobs by word of mouth or by simply "cold calling" firms—actually sending résumés to firms without knowing whether there is a position available.

While the odds of a position being available when you call are not high, timing is everything—your call may be coming just after an intern submits his or her resignation letter or at the moment the firm lands a big job. In any event, most firms will keep résumés on file for a few months to a year.

One way to start your search for the right firm is by visiting the AIA Web site (www.aia.org). The AIA publishes a national list of firms, searchable by zip code and project type, called Architect Finder. By entering a zip code, you will obtain a list of firms within a 15-mile radius. From the brief entry, you can learn about the firms' project types, their contact information, and frequently their Web sites. You will also find a link to local AIA components (if they have a Web site), which often list member firms, with a link directly to the firm's home page. InsideArch.org, Archinect.com, and Entablature.com also provide nationwide lists of firms as well as links.

Once you develop a list of prospective firms, you should research them thoroughly. Some firms may have been written about in a monograph format or in magazine articles. View their Web sites to look at representative projects, company philosophy, and firm history. Just as with your own portfolio, you can learn a lot about a firm from the design of its Web site: the importance of design in the firm, the firm's mission, the office culture, the importance of its staff as individuals, and how others (e.g., peers, press, or clients) view the firm. A Web site that isn't well designed may indicate that the firm doesn't have resources to devote to it, or it may cast doubt on the thorough integration of design in the firm's overall philosophy. Try searching a firm or principal's name with a search engine to see what news articles or associated links come up. What other activities is the firm involved with? What organizations or causes does it support?

Most firms these days have a Web site, but don't be surprised if one does not or if it is not current. It takes a lot of money and time to develop a Web site, and small offices may not have the resources to devote to this. At the same time, if you can't find a Web site, make sure you are searching for the right name. If the company has a common name, its preferred domain may have already been taken, so the company had to be creative. Or perhaps the firm wanted a memorable domain. Regardless of the reason, searching for a Web site may require additional criteria. For example, the sustainable design firm Farr Associates in Chicago is www.farrside.com. Even one of our professional associations found its first choice for a domain name had been taken—ACSA is www.acsa-arch.org.

InsideArch.org: Rate Your Firm

After looking at a Web site, you might still be curious to know what the firm is really like. InsideArch.org is a great Web site where you can learn more about what your experience might be working as an intern in the firm. Its Firm Reports, compiled from actual intern surveys, provide insights into each firm's design philosophy, profitability, and office culture. Respondents provide candid comments and answer standard questions; the firms are then rated on a scale of 1 to 25. These reports allow job seekers to learn about the office culture without personally knowing someone working there.

InsideArch.org was started in 2002 by Scott Simon, a young architect in New York, in response to his own frustration at the difficulty of making good choices on job options. As many graduates will learn, beyond this Web site, there is little information available on which to base employment decisions. This excerpt from the Web site's Plan and Purpose page sums up the problem:

> When deciding where to send a résumé, how do we narrow the field of thousands of firms to those whose work will interest us, those who provide a valuable learning environment, and those where our contribution will be most respected? The majority of architecture firms are small firms. They don't receive a lot of press and may not have a Web site. Those few firms that do the "coolest" and most publicized work are inundated with unsolicited résumés, regardless of the quality of the experience they offer for the intern. Less well-known firms place "help wanted" ads that offer only cursory descriptions of the firm and its work and often don't even mention the firm's name.
>
> With a lack of reliable sources of information about the culture and quality of experience at many small and medium-sized architecture firms, we believe that this type of information is extremely valuable to interns and architects seeking new or better employment, answering the all-important question, "What is it like to work at this firm?"
>
> In this environment, firm-specific information from the people who know the firms best is invaluable. We believe that providing interns and architects at all levels with information about a firm's work and its culture will serve to improve the efficiency of the market for architectural talent, matching employers with better employees, and interns and architects with better opportunities.
>
> The primary goal of InsideArch is to gather quantitative and qualitative information about the work, culture, and employee experience at architecture firms, to synthesize and present that information in a meaningful, valuable format, to empower interns and architects to make career decisions more beneficial to themselves and the profession as a whole.
>
> Specific areas of inquiry include: Lifestyle or work-life balance, work atmosphere, access to top management, the flow of information and work at the firm, the decision-making processes at the firm, design input, perceived value of position, level of responsibility, how interesting/substantial is/was the employee role, criteria for promotions and advancements, corporate culture, education and skill level of architectural staff and management.

You can search reports by firm name, firm size, market, and geographic location. Future updates to the site will allow a visitor to input a series of search criteria, (e.g., 11 to 30 employees, a local clientele, specializing in medical office facilities, located in Phoenix) and obtain a list of firms that satisfy the criteria. The site will continue to become more useful as more interns log their experiences. At the time of this writing, more than 700 Firm Reports had been posted.

Checklist for Researching Firms

If you want a method for comparing firms, this checklist may be helpful for gathering data and keeping track of the firms you find interesting.

Name of firm: _____

Web address: _____

What aspects of the firm do you like?

☐ projects

☐ office culture

☐ firm philosophy

☐ location

Does the firm sound like a place that you'd want to work?

☐ yes

☐ no

Can you tell how the firm is structured?

☐ strong hierarchy

☐ all employees equal

☐ sole practitioner

☐ corporate

Where are the projects located?

☐ locally

☐ nationally

☐ internationally

Consider the body of work on the Web site. What types of projects are they? Are these projects of interest to you?

_____

_____

_____

_____

_____

Photo by Dan Schatter, 2004

Narrowing Your Choices

AECWorkforce published a book entitled *Finding the Right Job*. If you have developed a lengthy list and are having a hard time narrowing the choices, this book offers several matrices for quantitatively comparing firms.

If you are not familiar with the city's geography, make sure you understand where the firm is located and have a sense of whether you want to work in that location. For example, if you are moving to Chicago with the intent to live and work in the city center (known as the Loop), make sure you map the addresses of the firms that interest you. While you might think they are a Chicago firm based on published articles, their physical location may turn out to be near Midway Airport with poor access to the Loop or in a suburb like Naperville or Skokie.

Also, be familiar with the cost of living. If you are considering multiple cities, be prepared for interviews and prospective job offers by knowing the relative costs for housing, entertainment, transportation, and so on in the city and determining an appropriate salary package. If your first job is at a really great firm that pays okay, but you can barely afford to pay rent, you may soon become disenchanted with your job as well as with where you live.

The Power of Networking

Networking can be an effective tool in the job search process. Take advantage of your resources—professors, alumni, career centers, and career fairs are excellent sources for job leads.

Consider working for your professors who practice. Be sure to indicate your interest early so that they can keep you in mind for possible job openings. You can do this indirectly by asking them about the status of projects or more directly by asking if positions are available or to whom you should talk about employment opportunities. If your favorite professors don't currently practice, they can offer introductions or references to former colleagues and alumni.

At times, school alumni may ask professors to refer bright students to their firms. Alumni may also keep in touch with professors to let them know about changes in jobs or new ventures. As you start to look for a job, ask professors, staff, and administrators about possible alumni contacts. This is an easy way to obtain names of people with whom you immediately have something in common. Countless interns have told me what an invaluable resource alumni have been to the success of their job search, opening doors by way of introduction to a new city or a tough job market.

Attend career fairs at your school; talk with recruiters, and see what they are looking for in candidates. Practice interviewing and talking about your work. Make contacts. Even if you don't want to work for those firms, a good interview or phone conversation could lead to referrals for other firms that you are interested in. The following intern's account of her first job search demonstrates the power of networking.

In my fourth year of architecture school, I took part in my school's externship program over a winter break. The application process involved picking a city where I would like to spend a week and five firms within that city. I chose New York and the five firms I was interested in, and within a couple of weeks I received notice of my placement. If only the real job search would prove to be so easy.

During the week in New York, I realized that returning to New York after graduation would be incredibly exciting and yet intensely daunting. Friends who had been through the process of trying to find an architecture job in the post-9/11 economy told horror stories that shook the idealism that school had instilled in me. I realized that finding a job was going to be a lot of work.

I took advice from my sister, who was attending business school at the time: networking. In that sense, my job search started during that week I spent in New York—I made a lot of contacts. Finding a job meant entering the business world of architecture, and in business, deals were made by knowing people who knew other people. When I returned to school for my last semester, I talked to a lot of professors, who also turned out to be great resources. My classmates and I found that, throughout the school, there were professors who had either worked in the firms we were considering or had other contacts from their own professional careers. They could give us guidance as to which firms to apply to and give recommendations and serve as references. I also utilized the school's alumni directory to search for former graduates who now worked for or had their own firms in New York. Often, the commonality of our alma mater was enough to start a conversation or secure an interview. I accepted interviews with firms that came to the school to recruit, even if they weren't in New York, just to practice interviewing.

Despite all the research, the task felt overwhelming, so I scheduled an appointment with my studio professor to obtain additional advice. She gave me two very excellent tips: (1) just move somewhere, and (2) narrow the search criteria. The pace of the architecture industry was such that firms wanted someone who could start tomorrow, not in two months. If I knew I wanted to live in New York, I just had to go there and then find a job—which, of course, was much easier said than done. In addition, there were more than 1,800 architecture firms in Manhattan, and I was going to have to make a few decisions about what I was looking for— otherwise my search would never end.

I spent the next month wrapped up in making a portfolio and in graduation activities. Shortly after graduation, I returned to Manhattan with a stack of résumés and hopes of securing a job. I had taken my professor's advice and identified what I was looking for in an office. I had a few big priorities, the first of which was the company size. I knew that I did not want to work in a corporate environment, so I opted to apply to small to medium-sized firms—firms with fewer than 30 people. After talking to friends and professors, I felt that I would learn more and be exposed to more aspects of the profession in a smaller office. Also, I wanted to work at a firm that had a diverse portfolio of projects (commercial, residential, retail, institutional, etc.). My goal was to be exposed to as much as possible in the few years I planned to work before going back to graduate school. With these priorities in mind, I searched local job postings in places such as the New York Times and www.newyork-architects.com, which not only posted job listings but also provided profiles of firms, with links to their Web sites and contact information.

I started getting interviews, and I learned that I had unintentionally done something right. I found the chances of getting a job in Manhattan were exponentially increased if you had already worked in Manhattan, which was extremely discouraging for those trying to break onto the scene from outside. However, the one-week externship program in Manhattan six months earlier was enough to get my foot in the door at a lot of firms, and in many cases, it was the only reason people contacted me for an interview. I had participated in the extern program mainly to gain some experience; I didn't realize at the time that it would pay off so well.

Despite having better luck than I expected, I wasn't falling in love with any of the places I interviewed. Some were very technical and not very creative, and a creative environment was my second priority, after the company size. Some firms were very narrow in the work they took on, some were extremely traditional, and others seemed very stuffy. I came to agree with a friend of mine who once said that you could determine within the first five minutes of seeing an office whether you could spend a year there.

I had started feeling discouraged when my phone rang; my luck had just changed. It was a friend of mine who also graduated from UVa and was working in Manhattan. The office where he worked was looking to hire someone, and he encouraged me to drop off my résumé. When I brought it by the office, I ended up in an impromptu interview with one of the project managers and subsequently one of the principals. The networking had paid off; it turned out that my friend had told me about the position before it had been advertised publicly. It seemed like a great fit—the office had 20 employees, and the office portfolio showed a diversity of projects, ranging from commercial to retail, loft renovations to gallery space. The combination of personal connection and timing compelled them to offer me a position, which I accepted. I have now worked at the firm for eight months, and we continue to hire, almost exclusively, the friends of employees.

I realize now that if an office is looking for help, they are probably overworked and have very little time to actually recruit. They rely on the recommendations of people they trust and are looking for someone who can start immediately. Talking to all of my friends and professors turned out to be the best thing I could have done for myself. Everyone I knew in the field was aware that I was looking for a job, and whenever opportunities came across their desk, they passed along the information to me. The added advantage of networking with friends was that I heard about the office environment from those working within the firm and was better able to make an informed decision about whether it was a good fit for me.

My job has met the expectations I had at the outset of my search. I have been able to work on residential and commercial projects, a designer's studio as well as a television studio. Because of the size of the office, I have participated in the design and construction process from start to finish. I do a lot of drafting and drawing, but I also attend meetings with clients, contractors, and engineers. I have also participated in construction administration. I feel that compared to other classmates of mine, I have more responsibility at work and get to design more independently.

While in school, I was surrounded by the attitude that one's work should speak for itself, that the design portfolio alone should be enough to secure that dream job. In retrospect, I know that finding a job is about the business of design, and that by utilizing a network of friends, professors, and the university's career services programs, I had a competitive edge in my search. After a lot of work and a little luck, I feel extremely fortunate to be where I am. And as I write this essay now, looking out the window of my small East Village apartment, I know that I love this city and am happy about my decision to take the plunge.

Kate Thatcher
Designer/Intern, A+I Design Corp
University of Virginia, Bachelor of Science in Architecture 2004

Internships During School

In the 2003 ArchVoices/AIA Internship and Career Survey, almost half of the respondents indicated that their first job experience in an architecture firm occurred prior to graduation, during the school year or summer vacations. Internships during school can be invaluable in helping you decide which cities or types of firms to pursue. The search for an internship of this kind will be similar to the job search described in the upcoming chapters. If you haven't considered an internship, do. It is a great way to get your foot in the door at a firm prior to graduation. Internships can also give you exposure to different types of firms, which will help you determine the type of firm in which you would truly like to work upon graduation. Internships are generally paid positions, but without benefits, and they usually last for three to four months (the summer vacation) or are part-time positions structured around school schedules. Some schools, such as Rice University and the University of Cincinnati, require internships throughout the course of the program. Others will offer course credit for summer internships. While generally it is the responsibility of the student to locate an internship opportunity, many schools provide assistance in this process.

Another opportunity for internships is through the Federal Work-Study Program. If you qualify for this type of financial assistance, it is a great way to obtain work experience while in school. The school offering Work-Study will reimburse the employer a percentage of your hourly wage; so, for example, if your rate is $12 per hour, the firm employs you and receives the benefit of the work you provide, but may effectively pay only $6 per hour for your time. For small firms that would otherwise lack the resources to hire an intern, this is an attractive way to employ someone with little or no office experience.

 If you are interested in working for a small firm, it may help if you educate potential employers about the financial benefits of hiring a Work-Study student.

An externship is another way to gain exposure to an architectural office. The University of Virginia facilitates a one-week externship that allows students to be placed with sponsoring firms across the country. While students are responsible for all financial aspects of the externship, including housing and transportation, firms are responsible for providing oversight and direction while the students are in their offices. After being placed with a firm of their choice, students spend their externship participating in a variety of activities, such as drafting, building models, visiting construction sites, and attending client meetings. Unlike an actual internship, the program is more like a job shadow, and the quality of the individual's experience is solely dependent upon the initiative of the firm. The following statement from a past participant describes how an externship provided insight into the profession:

> *Most valuable was just getting into an office and seeing, feeling, and hearing how a medium-size firm operates. I was pleased and impressed with how workloads were shared, as well as ideas. I was excited to find out how much learning takes place after graduation. The experience put perspective on what my time in school can be about, as well as the freedom one has in school to push ideas.*

The following statement is from a student who learned that the firm he had selected was not, after all, a firm he would enjoy working for at a later date:

> *I sat in on a meeting with the architects, which was less than exciting, though it did expose me to the less interesting aspects of the job. The staff was very nice and helpful, but I was not really engaged by their projects or the way they ran their practice; it seemed like the senior partners ran it and the others had to follow them. Most valuable was that I finally really saw the daily life of an architect.*

The hierarchical team environment that exists at some firms can contrast starkly with the independence a student experiences in school. Being immersed in a firm exposes the student to the daily tasks, coordination, and document production that comprises projects everywhere. Students who attend schools that do not have a formal program can easily arrange a week-long externship on their own, obtaining contacts from professors and school alumni.

Regardless of when your first internship occurs, the first few days can be filled with anxiety as you figure out what is expected of you and how you fit in at the firm. The following firsthand account describes the diversity of tasks that an intern might encounter.

A Sampling of What Is to Come

I found my first architecture job through a classmate who had been working for an architect in the Warehouse District of New Orleans and was moving back home after graduation, leaving her position vacant. My interview with the architect hardly seemed like an interview, and I left feeling uncertain as to whether I had actually been hired. Nevertheless, I called a few days later and was informed when I could start.

My first day of work was eventful because the city of New Orleans had flooded the day before with water so high that cars were submerged. The office was on the ground floor of a historic walk-up, and floodwater had washed across the entire floor. So I spent my first day helping to clean up.

The office comprised the architect who owned the firm, one other intern, and myself. This meant I got to do a little of everything, thus building a great foundation for future jobs. The projects were mostly renovations—both historic and contemporary. During my time there, I worked on a nightclub, two houses, two restaurants, and a saddle factory that was being converted into apartments.

At the beginning, most of my work consisted of picking up redlines. Although CAD drafting was becoming mainstream, my first job predominantly called for hand-drafting. The drawings were set up so that the building was drawn on the front of the sheet in pencil. We would key all the notes on the reverse side so that any changes we made to the notes wouldn't erase the building itself.

Because the office was small, this first internship experience ran the gamut of the architecture profession. I completed as-builts and conducted site visits. I met with the city's building department and our consultant engineers, researched a historic building for a tax credit application, and studied the building code. I met with clients and went to construction meetings. Many of these things I did in the presence of the architect, but sometimes I would go with the other intern to measure a building or on my own to conduct research.

A project that exemplified the work I performed during my first internship was a remodel for a popular Cajun restaurant housed in a historic building on Julia Street in New Orleans. The firm had been hired to explore the feasibility of providing additional seating in a double-height space on the second floor of the building the restaurant currently occupied. The restaurant owner also wanted to expand into an adjacent space on the first floor to create a rentable banquet room.

This project afforded me numerous responsibilities. My first task was to measure the building to create the as-builts. These measured drawings documented all floor plans and exterior elevations. The building had originally been an icehouse, which made for fascinating explorations. The second story had numerous shutters that could be opened and closed to obtain the proper airflow for the ice. The building structure was heavy timber at the interior, with masonry exterior walls. On the second floor, I came across walls with heavy steel doors that were meant to be closed in case of a fire. Some of the upper floors had soft spots that made me nervous as I measured, since I could feel the sponginess of the floor and kept imagining falling through. Thankfully, that never happened.

After the as-builts were complete, I proceeded to the space planning and code research. The code research was an integral part of the space planning for the second floor. In order to determine how many tables we could fit, I had to determine how much space was needed between tables, how many people were allowed based on occupant load factors, and how to reroute egress for the building once we added the second story. My experience working on this project taught me early on that the building code represents the minimum requirements we must follow, which plays a key role in defining the parameters within which we design.

My first internship experience showed me that the architectural profession is filled with variety on a daily basis. With the inspiration this experience provided, I was able to continue through other internship experiences that were less fulfilling.

Terri Watson
Project Manager, Tonkin Hoyne Lokan
Tulane University, Bachelor of Architecture 1995

A Novice Again: Reflections from a Second-Career Intern

20% of the respondents entered architecture as a second career, bringing an average of 6.5 years of nonrelated work experience to the profession.

—2003 ArchVoices/AIA Internship and Career Survey

While many architectural graduates enter the profession in their early twenties with little to no work experience, an increasing number of interns have left other careers to join the ranks, bringing with them an extensive background of work and life experiences. Tamara is one such intern, and she explains how her previous career assisted her during her first internship:

I'm a nontraditional intern. I taught middle school math for 16 years, then went back to architecture school in my forties. My friends and colleagues thought I was very brave, but I just felt it was something I had to do. I knew if I didn't make the leap then, I'd never do it. So I closed my eyes, took a deep breath, and jumped.

After years of being the teacher in a classroom, the first year of architecture school was quite humbling as I found myself in the position of a lowly student. Along with my peers who had bachelor degrees, I was taking classes with junior undergraduates.

However, the school experience was nothing compared to my internship. I began my first job during my last semester of school. Including myself, there were 2 interns in an office of 15 architects. I was the newer intern and quickly discovered just how little I knew. After I had emerged from a successful teaching career as a leader among my colleagues, it was quite disheartening to be the "newbie" — the one who didn't even know how to draw a door detail.

I quickly realized that I had a lot to learn, and found that the best way to learn was to ask lots of questions and study previous project sets prepared by the firm. I peppered everyone around me with questions, to the point that they would often groan as I approached with yet another problem. I recorded all that I learned in a notebook, so I would only have to ask once. When unsure about a detail, I would draw and print out a bare sketch of the area in question and ask for help filling in the specifics. Because I never asked the same question twice, learned from my mistakes, and tried to figure out the answer before I asked anyone, my colleagues began to offer help even before I asked.

So that I didn't always feel like the inexperienced intern, I made it known that I had some skills that were unique in the office. I know Photoshop quite well, so when I worked on a window replacement project, I digitally altered photos of the existing building to depict "before" and "after" shots of the proposed changes. The architect I was working with used the images to help the client make decisions on colors and mullion placement. Because no one else in the office had Photoshop skills, my knowledge helped me to stand out. However, I did not want to be pigeonholed into doing only Photoshop at the expense of drawing. Fortunately, that has not happened, and even though I've taught a few other employees some basic Photoshop skills, the architects and executive director still come to me when they have a special project.

I also use my unique background as a teacher to my advantage. My firm focuses on designing K–12 schools, so I have been able to leverage my past experience into the role of "faculty liaison" and have gained expertise in communicating between architects and educators. I've participated in interviews with potential clients interested in hiring the firm. I've also met with school principals and teachers to discuss their facility needs. This is not what a "typical" intern would be doing two years out of school, but because I had a previous career and some unique experiences, I brought a depth of knowledge to the team.

My advice to all interns would be to admit when you don't know something, ask lots of questions, keep good notes, and find some way to make yourself stand out. Those interns who have made a career change should realize that a good firm will value your perspective and your maturity. Your previous life and work experiences are invaluable; don't be reticent about letting your firm know that.

There's a quote by Kobi Yamada that I found the summer before I began architecture school, which I posted first at my studio desk and now keep at my work station. It reads: "Sometimes you just have to take the leap, and build your wings on the way down." I think that says it all.

Tamara Redburn, Assoc. AIA
Intern Architect, Fanning/Howey Associates, Inc.
University of Michigan, Master of Architecture 2003

CHAPTER 3 | THE JOB SEARCH

Getting Your Stuff Together

Your résumé and cover letter will give potential employers their first impression of you. So carefully consider what impression you would like to make. With final projects and exams weighing heavily on your mind, it is too easy to fall into the trap of picking up a ready-made résumé and substituting your information. While this works for students in almost any other major, it does not work for architectural students (or, for that matter, any fine arts, graphic arts, or design students). If you are going to do this, be sure you use a model geared toward design professions.

Because your profession requires clear graphic communication, your presentation is very important. Clarity and brevity are concepts to keep in mind; you should strive for a balance of graphics, text, and informative content. Flashy graphics can detract from your architectural concepts or, conversely, become an obvious foil for poor content. While you may find some resources online, take time to go to the library and review graphic design publications for examples of résumés and work samples. *Communication Arts, Print,* and *How* are just a few of the publications that offer creative examples of résumés and self-promotion packets. You don't have to go all out and spend a fortune producing your résumé, but you should make sure that what you send out represents your personality and design aesthetic.

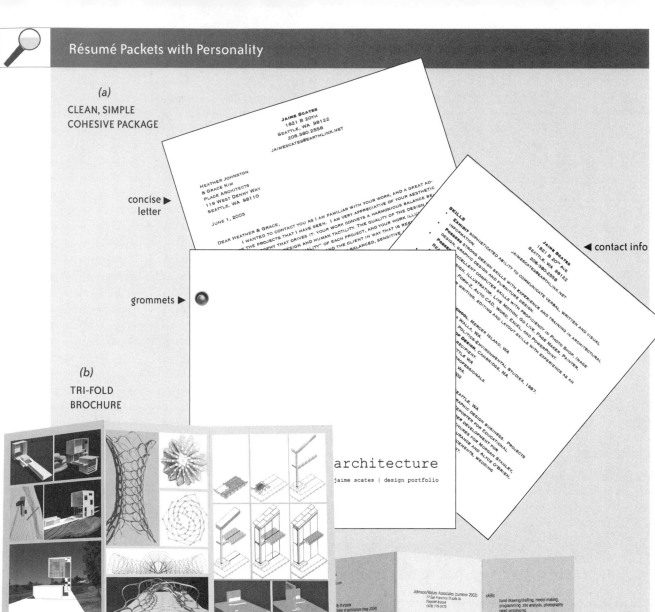

(a)

CLEAN, SIMPLE COHESIVE PACKAGE

concise ▶ letter

◀ contact info

grommets ▶

(b)

TRI-FOLD BROCHURE

▲ efficient use of a single sheet

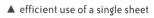

▲ variety of experiences and skills

◀ contact info

(a) Courtesy of Jaime Scates Schmitz
(b) Courtesy of Eric Nebel

Cover Letter

While many interns send generic cover letters, you should not. The cover letter is the most critical component of your application package. This is your opportunity to demonstrate writing ability and knowledge of the firm, and to highlight any special talents that might set you apart from the crowd. Depending on the office size, the person reviewing the letter may be receiving one résumé a week or ten a day. Make sure yours stands out.

If you don't already have a contact name, check online or call the office and ask to whom you should send your résumé.

 Speaking to a live person is the best way to verify names and addresses; speaking directly with the senior architect responsible for hiring is even better. Online Yellow Pages or even Web sites may not have the most up-to-date information if a firm has recently moved or if the contact person has changed. I've personally experienced a situation when time-critical project information needed to reach a renowned architect my firm was collaborating with and it was returned to us because of an incorrect address. When I called to follow up, the firm explained that they had moved the year before but didn't have the resources to update their Web site.

The appropriate contact may be a firm principal or the human resources director. *Never* address your letter "To whom it may concern" or "Dear Sir." An impersonal salutation will make it look like a form letter from a person not really interested in that specific office. By knowing whom to address the letter to, you demonstrate your knowledge of the firm and imply that you believe you have qualities that would really fit with that firm. For example, if the only two principals in a firm are women, the prospective intern who addresses a letter "Dear Sir" is indicating that he knows nothing about the firm's leadership.

If you have a personal contact currently working at the firm who is willing to offer you support, send this individual your letter and résumé so that they can be hand-delivered to the appropriate person with a verbal recommendation of your abilities. Any personal contact with someone currently in the office can go a long way toward securing an interview.

> When asked to indicate how strong or weak they considered teaching of writing skills at their school, 66% of administrators, 65% of faculty, 42% of students, and 59% of alumni said "weak."
>
> —Ernest Boyer and Lee Mitgang, *Building Community*

Remember that your letter and résumé demonstrate your communication skills— spelling and grammar count. Be sure to utilize word processing tools like spell-checker.

Have friends or family members proofread your letter and résumé before you mail them. If you are not confident about your writing skills, refer to these two books for further guidance on how to prepare a professional cover letter: *Writing for Design Professionals,* by Stephen Kliment, and the *AEC WorkForce Guide to Finding the Right Job in the Design and Construction Industry,* by Christopher J. Klein (see Bibliography, page 249). Many schools have writing labs; schedule some time for a tutor to provide constructive criticism for your letter.

What Should You Include in Your Letter?

Your cover letter should answer the questions "Why do I want this job?" and "Why should you select me?" The first paragraph should clearly state the position you are seeking and provide a brief description of your qualifications for this position — be careful not to restate your entire résumé. Think about the talents or skills that set you apart. Your letter should demonstrate to readers that you have done your homework and are specifically interested in them. Briefly refer to a specific project that you particularly admire and state the reasons. Keep the letter to one page and conclude it with a word about your next actions: "I will contact you within the next two weeks to discuss any employment possibilities" or "I will be in Atlanta the week of June 18 and will contact you to see if you might be available to conduct an informational interview during that time." After reading the letter, readers should be absolutely convinced that they need to talk to you. The letter should be concise and include the date and your return address.

While the next piece of advice may seem obvious, many people do not follow it: Keep hard copies of the letters you send, perhaps in a binder or file folder for easy reference and note-taking when you follow up.

Checklist for Preparing Your Cover Letter

- ☐ Verify your return address, e-mail, and phone number
- ☐ Verify the spelling of the addressee's name and that he or she is still actively employed
- ☐ Verify the spelling of the firm's full name and address
- ☐ State where you learned about the position (company Web site, newspaper ad, referred by) or explain why you are interested in the firm
- ☐ Briefly describe any special skills or experiences — demonstrate how can you bring value to the firm's team right away
- ☐ Tell how and when you will follow up
- ☐ Spell-check the document
- ☐ Keep a copy for your records

A Good Example of a Cover Letter

Sally Archit
1234 Ballet Shoe Drive
Seattle, WA 98111

November 30, 2004

Kim Shapiro
Calson Architecture, Inc.
2607 Western Avenue, Suite 1100
Seattle, WA 98121

Dear Ms. Shapiro:

I graduated from Kent State University this May with a Bachelor of Architecture. I recently moved to Seattle and am very excited to experience the Pacific Northwest both personally and professionally. I have reviewed the work of your firm via your Web site and am very interested in the internship position at Calson Architecture.

I believe I could offer valuable services to your firm while gaining vital experience in my personal pursuits of becoming a licensed architect. I have worked in various small architectural firms over the last three years and have had experience in master planning, schematic design, design development, architectural renderings, presentations, working drawings on AutoCAD 2000, site visits, client meetings, and working on teams. I also have skills in computer-generated 3-D modeling and physical model making.

I would like to set up an interview at your convenience to discuss any available opportunities. I can be reached by mobile phone at 419.550.5551 or by e-mail at sallyarch@lycos.net. I look forward to meeting you.

Sincerely,

Sally Archit

A Poor Example of a Cover Letter

19 July 2005

Schemata Workshop
Attn: Human Resources
159 Western Avenue West, #483
Seattle, WA 98119

The salutation is generic and it implies a form letter ▶

This information may deter the employer

Dear Sir/Madam:

I obtained your contact information by visiting your website. I write to you today to briefly introduce myself and my qualifications. Hopefully in reviewing my qualifications, you might consider my application for any immediate or future positions with your firm.

I graduated from Western Kentucky University with an Associates of Science degree in Architecture in December 2001, followed by a BS in Architectural Design and Construction in May 2002. I have already completed the IDP requirements and hope to become a licensed architect within the next year as I am preparing myself to take the A.R.E. I also hope to pursue and earn my masters degree in architecture or business in the near future.

I currently work as an architectural designer and project manager at ABC Designers Inc in Louisville, KY. Our firm manages projects in thirty states specializing in many commercial projects such as hotels, motels, restaurants, retail and department stores. My duties include designing the project based on client expectations and code provisions. The work is completed under the supervision of a senior architect. The goal is to work within the allocated budget and meet the deadlines with proper design work. Other duties include coordination of the project's work in various stages between the different disciplines. I also meet with clients and update them with the progress of the work from start to finish. When necessary, I travel to the project's site for either meetings or supervision of the work done based on our specifications.

The content restates the résumé. The typography is very dense ▶

During summer 2001 while I was still in school, I completed an internship for Tegnestuen Bolig, an architecture firm in Denmark. My duties included making modifications to floor plans based on the given specifications. I also drew and rendered elevations for client presentations. As a student member of the team, I was encouraged to participate in the firm's design team. This opportunity enabled me to learn more about the design procedures from concept to finish, as well as the process involved in presenting the ideas. I have become familiar with many building products as well as some of the latest construction methods and materials used in the region.

My communication and cooperation capabilities have been increased due to my past jobs and my work experiences have had a positive impact on expanding my leadership skills.

Please find enclosed my resume as well as a summary of all the projects in which I have been involved during my years of employment here at ABC Designers Inc. In general I believe that my extensive work experience, work ethics, and familiarity with different cultures makes me a suitable candidate for any challenging opportunity at a firm like yours.

My hobbies include traveling, meeting people from different places and making friends. Other areas of interest include outdoor activities, sports, various types of music. I can read, write and speak Arabic, English, Danish and some German and Turkish.

Should you need any work related references, you may call Dave Sax, Senior Architect – NCARB registered at 502.555.1515 or Eliza Fekety, Structural Engineer at 502.555.6212. Additional or other references may be available upon your request.

I certainly appreciate your time for reviewing this letter and I look forward to hearing from you soon!

No indication there will be a follow-up action from the applicant

Sincerely,

Shimon Moeller

The Title of the Position You Seek

As you indicate the position you seek in your letter, remember that the title *architect* is legally reserved for those who have satisfied the registration requirements of their state board. In some states, derivations of the word *architect* — for example, *architectural intern* or *intern architect* — are also restricted. You can learn about such restrictions by reading the laws regulating architectural practice, generally accessible from the Web site of the state registration board.

While many employers will look past this, some may be quite dogmatic about the application of those terms. Be aware of this as you look for job postings; you may quickly realize that there are no intern architect positions listed, but lots for designers and job captains. Similarly, be careful not to misrepresent your experience level or professional status by stating in your cover letter that you are a "young architect looking for a challenging employment opportunity."

E-Mailing Your Cover Letter and Résumé

Many firms don't mind receiving e-mailed copies of cover letters and résumés. You can either paste the text into the body of your e-mail or attach a PDF or Word document. These two file formats are nearly universal and don't rely on costly software to view. Be wary of sending large files that might clog the recipient's inbox or cause difficulty when opening on a slow computer. Also recognize that some fonts that are not included in the basic Microsoft font package will likely translate to a courier font on the receiver's end. By saving everything to a PDF, you can be assured that firms will receive the graphic design layout you intended.

Résumé

Keep it simple; keep it short. As an intern, your résumé should not exceed one page. It's common to want to list every single activity, honor, and experience you can think of. If you have a string of publications or really great experiences that you feel are relevant or add value, incorporate them into your cover letter. The résumé shouldn't be a comprehensive list of your accomplishments; it should contain the information about you that is most pertinent to the particular job or firm. If you want to keep track of all that, keep a running curriculum vitae[1] (CV) to record everything you've done to date and keep it current throughout your career.

---

[1] A curriculum vitae, also known as a CV or vita, is like a résumé but tends to be focused more on academic and research positions. CVs do not have a prescribed format, are not held to a page limit, and can therefore provide great detail about academic, research, or project experience.

Education

The résumé should include the schools you attended and the degrees you have earned. Unless you are an honors student graduating magna cum laude, leave off your grade point average. Architecture is more about critical thinking and real-life situations, and employers are more interested in your work experience and your communication skills—both graphic and written.

Work Experience

Generally speaking, list only architecturally related work experience (construction or arts-related jobs count). Provide the name of the business at which you were employed, the dates of employment, and the types of responsibilities. Be specific about your duties and the projects that you worked on, but don't over-inflate your experience.

 Don't burn any bridges. The architectural community is extremely small. While prospective employers won't contact a current employer, they may know someone at the firms on your résumé whom they may call to verify your work experience and inquire about your performance, even if you don't provide them as a reference.

There are instances in which nonarchitectural work experience should also be included. For example, if the firm does a lot of recreation centers, your previous job as a lifeguard or summer activity program director may be helpful for the planning and design of its projects. Similarly, if you worked retail jobs during high school or college, a firm specializing in retail stores and shopping malls might find your firsthand knowledge of the industry useful. These types of related work experiences would be appropriate to list on your résumé for those specific firms.

If you don't have any architectural work experience, then you should try to list three previous jobs. Although not related, any prior work experience will indicate that you have been able to maintain a job and understand the responsibilities of being on time and fulfilling duties. If you don't have any work experience at all, emphasize studio projects that are similar to the types of projects the firm performs. Similarly, list involvement with student or community organizations, especially calling attention to leadership opportunities you have taken and group projects you may have completed. This will reflect upon your personal initiative and ability to work in teams.

Technical Skills

Both manual and electronic technical skills should be indicated. Firms both large and small will be looking for prospective employees with a wide range of skills. CAD drafting is required for most entry-level positions; some firms require proficiency in the particular CAD software they use. In addition, basic skills in Microsoft Word and Excel will be required for daily correspondence within the team and with consultants. Proficiency with Adobe products such as Photoshop and InDesign will come in handy in the preparation of presentations and marketing materials.

While computers play a large role in architectural work, most firms will still want to see the hand-sketching and hand-lettering skills that are integral to daily work. Physical model building skills should be identified as well. When describing skills, indicate your level of proficiency, but do not overstate your skills in any area, as this may quickly be noticed if you are hired. Listing these skills will help prospective employers understand how you might be able to contribute to the work from the first day.

Other Skills

While you won't be put into a management position as an intern, organizational and leadership skills should be indicated to demonstrate your ability to work independently, prioritize tasks, and work in a team environment.

Objective

The résumé does not need to include an objective. If you are "seeking an entry-level position as an architectural intern," then you are limiting yourself to one kind of position and may miss the hidden jobs that a firm may have—for example, design library assistant, marketing and graphic design assistant, or project manager (for those of you who have previous careers).

Achievements or Awards

Leave your high school achievements off your résumé. It's time to leave high school behind. However, if there are awards and honors from your university experience, especially if they are related to a specialty or area of focus, you should include those.

Fraternities and Sororities

For those affiliated with the Greek system, be sure to consider the stereotypes associated with fraternities and sororities and describe your experiences in ways that reflect leadership (e.g., acting as "rush chair" might be better phrased as being "responsible for membership recruitment").

Personal Interests

If there is room at the end of the résumé, include some personal interest areas. This is an opportunity to provide insight into your personality and can help break the ice during an interview. Interests that frequently appear in this category are travel, sports, and music. As with all items on your résumé, if you list personal interests, be ready to speak knowledgeably or enthusiastically about them. Failure to do so may imply that you are not passionate about your interests or that you "padded" your résumé by fabricating or overstating information. Both good and poor examples of an architectural intern's résumé are provided here.

A Poor Example of a Résumé

Amanda Architect
615 Maple Street, Apt. B
Pullman, WA 99163
(509) 332-5111

Objective   A career opportunity in architecture to acquire the necessary experience in preparation for the Architectural Registration Exam.

GPA   3.83

Profile   Experienced with CAD and rendering applications
Excellent analytical, organizational, and problem solving skills
Personable and productive; functions well as a team member or on an independent basis
Can speak and write conversational Korean

Education   Washington State University – Pullman, WA
Bachelor of Architecture with Honors, May 2004
Minor in Business Administration, May 2004
Bachelor of Science in Architectural Studies, May 2003

Bellevue Community College
AutoCAD courses – Summer 2003

Activities   American Institute of Architecture Students – Offices held include Chapter President, FORUM Chairperson, CEACC Representative. Attended Grassroots '01, FORUM '02 & '03. Served on NAAB accreditation team to Cornell University.

Sigma Tau Chapter of Kappa Delta Sorority – Offices held include Treasurer, Assistant Treasurer, Delegate to National Leadership Conference

Member of Tau Beta Pi National Engineering Honor Society

Member of Golden Key National Honor Society

Member of the Presidents Honor Roll

YMCA Big Sister Program

Experience   Washington State University - School of Architecture
Teaching Assistant–August 1999 to present
Provide mentoring and assistance to student in the design studio during class and evening help sessions. Collect and grade assignments.   Was recommended for this position by a department instructor.

Seattle School District – Capital Levy Projects
4141 4th Avenue South, Seattle, WA 98134
Construction Observer – Summer 2002
Observed and recorded progress of the General Contractor. Attended weekly site meetings.
Worked on an in-house remodel, which included space planning, scheduling, and project management
of the Human Resources department of the Administration and Services Center.

Whitty Jackman Architects
1218 3rd Avenue South, Seattle, WA 98101
Intern–Summer 2001
Responsibilities included drafting structural details, preparing and assembling project manuals and
bid proposals, and miscellaneous CAD work.

China Passage Restaurant
22006 66th Avenue, Mountlake Terrace, WA 98043
Waitress–Summers 1999-2001
Received, organized, and delivered food and beverage orders in a friendly and timely manner.

References   Kim Sighrs, Associate Professor, WSU School of Architecture; Adjunct Associate Professor, WSU
School of Electrical Engineering and Computer Science. (509) 553-7315.

David M. Scott, Professor, WSU School of Architecture. (509) 553-7393.

Douglas McCudden, Project Manager, Seattle School District. (206) 298-5111.

A Good Example of a Résumé

amanda architect

615 Maple Street, Apt. B
Pullman, WA 99163
(509) 332-5111

education	Washington State University – Pullman, WA Bachelor of Architecture with Honors, May 2004 Minor in Business Administration, May 2004 Bachelor of Science in Architectural Studies, May 2003
experience	Washington State University - School of Architecture Teaching Assistant – August 1999 to present Provide mentoring and student assistance in the design studio. Collect and grade assignments. Recommended for this position by a department instructor. Seattle School District – Capital Levy Projects 4141 Fourth Avenue South, Seattle, WA 98134 Construction Observer – Summer 2002 Observed and recorded progress of the General Contractor. Attended weekly site meetings. Worked on an in-house remodel which included space planning, scheduling, and project management of the Human Resources department of the Administration and Services Center. Whitty Jackman Architects 1218 Third Avenue South, Seattle, WA 98101 Intern – Summer 2001 Responsibilities included CAD drafting as well as preparing and assembling project manuals and bid proposals.
activities	American Institute of Architecture Students – Offices held include Chapter President. Served on NAAB accreditation team to Cornell University. Sigma Tau Chapter of Kappa Delta Sorority – Offices held include Treasurer, Assistant Treasurer, Delegate to National Leadership Conference. Member of Tau Beta Pi National Engineering Honor Society Member of Golden Key National Honor Society Member of the President's Honor Roll YMCA Big Sister Program
skills	Proficient in AutoCAD, 3d Studio, Photoshop, InDesign, and Dreamweaver Conversant in Korean (written and verbal)

References

While you do not need to include them on your résumé or waste valuable space on your résumé by stating "references are available upon request," make sure you have at least three references (name, employer, e-mail, and preferred telephone number) that you can provide to prospective employers who request them. It's important that you maintain good references from previous employers and professors—individuals who are in a position to speak to your leadership, design, communication, or organizational abilities.

References should not be solicited from people you've never met (such a request is awkward for the person from whom you are seeking the reference, since he or she has no basis on which to speak of your skills) or from friends or family members (unless they have served supervisory roles and can speak to your architectural or leadership abilities). Furthermore, it is important to ask individuals for permission to list them as a reference, as well as to ask if they would provide a positive reference—that they agree to offer their opinion doesn't necessarily mean that they will say nice things about you or your past performance.

If a job offer has been extended, you should always notify your references and thank them for their assistance (even if they were not contacted). If an offer is not extended, you should never question someone about what they said to jeopardize your job opportunity. Cultivating a solid list of references is an art in and of itself. If you are successful in keeping your references abreast of your achievements and life changes, these relationships can be maintained over the course of your career.

Recommendation Letters

If you would like to include letters of recommendation with your résumé packet, be sure to consider the following. The letters should come from professors or previous employers who can speak directly to your abilities for the position that you seek. In obtaining letters, be sure to specify certain skills or abilities that you would like them to address.

A recommendation letter should be concise yet descriptive of your specific qualifications. To illustrate, a letter from a supervisor that indicates that you are a nice person and a hard worker but does not provide specifics about your performance or how you contributed to the firm does little to help readers understand why you would be an asset to their firm. In fact, the omission of performance-related information may cause the reader to question whether there were performance issues that the writer is trying to avoid. Conversely, a letter from a professor describing your role as a teaching assistant, citing your ability to help students understand concepts, and commending the timeliness with which you graded papers or completed tasks can be very informative to the reader about your performance as well as your ability to mentor others.

Example of a Bad Work Sample

A large firm recruiter shared this story about an intern who submitted a résumé and work samples in the form of a matchbook. Admittedly, it was a clever idea, and it probably took a lot of time for the applicant to reproduce and prepare the images in such a small format. But at the firm it was seen as an unfortunate waste of effort and money, since the images were too small and difficult to read and impossible to reproduce for routing to various studio heads.

The lesson here: Know your audience. The matchbook format would probably have been fine for a smaller, design-focused studio, where the novelty and hand-crafted quality of the matchbook would have been appreciated. But to a large firm, the small format was annoying, and the work was trivialized.

Photo by Grace Kim, AIA, 2005

Work Samples

According to one large firm recruiter, only 20 to 25 percent of all applicants send samples of work; sending work samples is an easy way to set yourself apart. Representative work should show a diversity of skills, including sketching or drawing, the production of construction documents, computer and physical model building, and other artistic work.

Work samples can range from mini-portfolios (which can be really expensive to produce if you are sending them to more than a couple of firms) to a single page tri-fold attached to the résumé. What you provide as a work sample is up to you and your budget. But here are some things to keep in mind.

Cost

Tailor the scope of your samples to the number you intend to send out. If you are sending out only two packets, you may decide it is worth it to invest considerable time and money. However, recognize that if your preliminary efforts are fruitless, you may want to simplify your approach.

Do not send a mini-portfolio unless you've been asked to. Such an investment can be costly and will not guarantee you an interview. Firms may not have the file space to keep more than the letter and résumé. So if you'd rather not see your hard work and limited funds end up in the trash, simplify the work sample you send to a couple of pages.

Format

If your intent is to send out numerous résumé packets, simplify what is sent out so that the samples are (1) integral to your résumé, or (2) a single sheet that can be attached to your résumé and letter. If thoughtfully prepared and well executed, an effective method to integrate photos is to incorporate them into your résumé. However, this can be difficult to carry out successfully. Illustrated here are two résumé packets: one a timeline with related photos, the other a folio that holds the résumé and letter, with images interspersed.

Résumé Example — Timeline

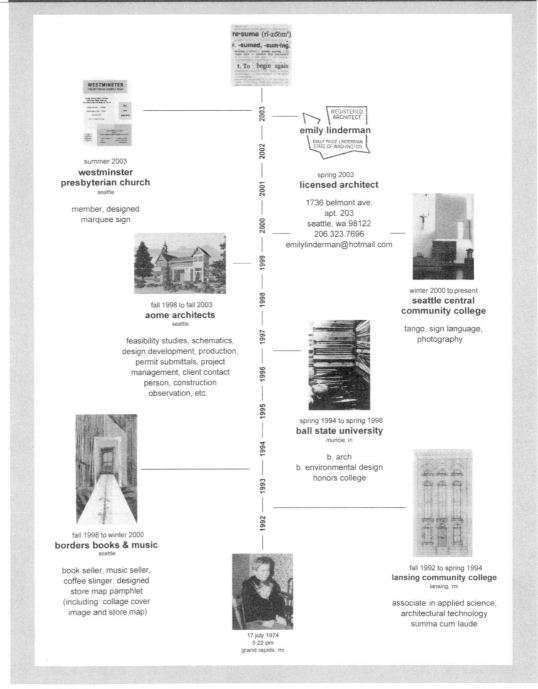

re·sume (rĭ-zōōm')
v. -sumed, -sum·ing.
1. To begin again

WESTMINSTER
PRESBYTERIAN CHURCH DOOR

summer 2003
**westminster
presbyterian church**
seattle

member, designed
marquee sign

fall 1998 to fall 2003
aome architects
seattle

feasibility studies, schematics,
design development, production,
permit submittals, project
management, client contact
person, construction
observation, etc.

fall 1998 to winter 2000
borders books & music
seattle

book seller, music seller,
coffee slinger, designed
store map pamphlet
(including collage cover
image and store map)

REGISTERED
ARCHITECT
emily linderman
EMILY PAIGE LINDERMAN
STATE OF WASHINGTON

spring 2003
licensed architect

1736 belmont ave.
apt. 203
seattle, wa 98122
206.323.7696
emilylinderman@hotmail.com

winter 2000 to present
**seattle central
community college**

tango, sign language,
photography

spring 1994 to spring 1998
ball state university
muncie, in

b. arch
b. environmental design
honors college

fall 1992 to spring 1994
lansing community college
lansing, mi

associate in applied science,
architectural technology
summa cum laude

17 july 1974
5:22 pm
grand rapids, mi

2003
2002
2001
2000
1999
1998
1997
1996
1995
1994
1993
1992

Source: Emily Linderman

1   cohesive graphic layout utilizing standard letter size for easy filing
2   concise letter
3   contact information
4   strong résumé
5   other skills and personal interests
6   concise project descriptions

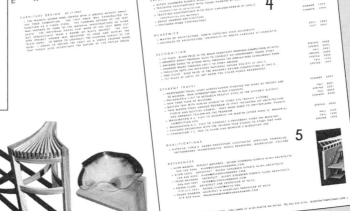

Source: Jon Gentry

Show a wide range of work. Rather than sending five renderings of the same project, be sure to include a variety of images to demonstrate broad skills. Presented together, computer-generated renderings, CAD-drafted working drawings, hand-sketched process drawings, and travel sketches demonstrate the variety of skills that you possess and give the viewer a sense of how you think and what catches your eye. They also indicate to the employer how you might contribute to the firm.

Paper

Try to select a paper size that is easy to reproduce. The following examples are based on an 8½ × 11 sheet. Use interesting papers that have visual or tactile qualities. For general legibility, be careful not to select a paper that competes with the text.

Ease of Viewing

Stick to one or two fonts. And note that fonts that are too small, too light in color, or difficult to read can also detract from the content. The following examples help illustrate the importance of selecting the right font type and size.

Urban High Rise: Dallas, TX
This is an example of a font that is really distracting or difficult to read. Using such a font can detract from the content or cast an unprofessional tone on the work you are presenting.

```
Urban High Rise: Dallas, TX
This is an example of a font that is really
distracting or difficult to read. Using such a font can
detract from the content or cast an unprofessional
tone on the work you are presenting.
```

Urban High Rise: Dallas, TX
This is an example of a font that is really distracting or difficult to read. Using such a font can detract from the content or cast an unprofessional tone on the work you are presenting.

Urban High Rise: Dallas, TX
This is an example of a font that is really distracting or difficult to read. Using such a font can detract from the content or cast an unprofessional tone on the work you are presenting.

Also, make sure no extra effort is required to view your work samples. For example, a PowerPoint presentation submitted on CD-ROM may be a comprehensive and visually powerful way to present your work, but requiring employers to wait for the file to open up on a computer (or worse, sending the file to an employer who does not have PowerPoint and cannot open it) might have the same effect as not having sent a work sample at all. Keep it simple. Reduce the number of steps it takes to view your work.

Quality of Reprographics

A pixilated, low-resolution scan or a dark photo can detract from the content of your work. Make sure that the quality of the images is high and presents your work in a positive light. It may be better to show a good "texture" image showing the context of your project than a poor-quality, uninteresting construction shot of the concrete form work on your studio design/build project. Don't assume that employers will look past a bad photo. While some will, others will move on to the next résumé with well-photographed or well-composed images that show greater attention to presentation.

Simplicity

As with design, restraint can be your most significant challenge in presenting work. You may recall your high school English teacher jokingly referring to the K.I.S.S. rule — "Keep it simple, stupid." This applies to your work samples as well. Your work should speak for itself, and you should not need to rely on eye candy to cover up poor content. Demonstrate your presentation skills, but don't get carried away. Make sure the graphics are not too busy and are not competing for attention.

Applying to Large Firms

If you are applying to a large corporate firm like Ellerbe Becket or CUH2A, you will find that they have recruiters on staff who post job listings and sort through the high volume of résumés. Some firms, such as RTKL or NBBJ, generally prefer to have you apply online so they can track your résumé and match it to the positions available. Their Web site will have a dedicated section for employment opportunities where you can review current job openings as well as post your résumé and update it over time. They may still accept or request copies of résumés or letters, but the electronic versions allow them to easily share the files with studio heads and project managers who will conduct the actual interviews. The recruiters are generally not architects, but individuals with backgrounds in human resources or business management. They will generally screen the initial applicants and conduct the first round of interviews. They will be looking for content, not just good graphics.

Note that larger firms may route copies of your letter, résumé, and work samples to several studio heads at once. If your work samples are over- or undersized, or difficult to print or copy, they will not be included in the routing. If the images turn black or wash out when photocopied, this will detract from the overall first impression. When applying to larger firms, try photocopying the items you are sending to see what happens to them when they are run through a copier on the basic settings. If your work samples rely on color, ask in advance how many copies you should submit with your résumé.

Following Up

Now that you've sent your letter, résumé, and work samples, what next? In the cover letter, you should indicate that you will be contacting the company within a certain amount of time; generally, a week is adequate. So when that time comes, pull out your letters and start calling.

Consider the day and time you place your call. Think about time zones and whom you are calling. If you are following up with the HR director, most times will be convenient, since hiring is one of the HR director's primary duties. However, if you are calling a principal or senior associate, remember that reviewing résumés is for them a minor responsibility. While it may be convenient to you, first thing Monday morning or late on a Friday afternoon may not be a good time to reach a potential employer. Right before or after lunch may also be bad times to call. But late in the day or even after 5 PM may be a good time to reach a principal. In smaller firms, the principal may even be the one to answer the phone after regular business hours.

Leave a message — but not too many. While finding a job is of the utmost importance to you, interviewing prospective employees may not be the highest priority for the principal. So when leaving a message, remember that there is a fine line between persistence and pestering.

When following up, don't call to "see if you received my résumé." This causes recipients to stop what they are doing, access their files, and find out if it was, indeed, received. If they are in the middle of something urgent, your call will register as a nuisance. The point of your call is to express your interest in a position, provide a callback number, and indicate dates available for an interview. With this information, the person you are calling can log your call and refer to it later when he or she has time to respond.

The Interview

As you prepare for your interview, remember that you are interviewing the firms as much as they are interviewing you. So be prepared and do your homework.

Much as you did when considering which firms to send résumés to, surf the Web. Look for information on the firm, its projects, and their locations. Learn the names of the partners or principals. Find out if the firm is a leader in its industry or if it has won awards—not only design awards, but also industry-specific awards granted by the institutions it works for. For example, if the firm specializes in health care, find out if the health care industry has acknowledged its innovative design solutions. Or if the firm's specialty is housing, has it received acknowledgement from the National Association of Home Builders that would indicate its success or leadership in the industry?

When you first meet the interviewer, firmly shake his or her hand and introduce yourself by clearly stating your name. A firm handshake is an important indicator of self-confidence.

As silly as it may sound, practice your handshake with friends or family. A wimpy handshake implies a lack of self-confidence. A knuckle-cracking handshake can be too rough or aggressive. Try to perfect a comfortable yet firm handshake, not just for interviewing purposes but for the business world in general.

The interview will likely have three components: an introduction to the firm and its work, a review of your portfolio, and questions. While the first portion will be up to the interviewer, the latter two require preparation from your side. Much like a résumé, your portfolio speaks to your skills and your personality, so spend some time in designing the layout. The same rules of thumb that were discussed for the résumé packet should be considered in preparing your portfolio.

Before the interview ends, establish the next steps. If the interviewer is going to take the next step—forwarding your résumé to the studio head or setting up another meeting with a partner—determine a timeline so that you can get in touch. If no positions are available at the time of your interview, let the interviewer know you will contact him or her in a month to follow up. If a referral is to be made to another firm, make sure you get the contact information. At the conclusion of your interview, be sure to firmly shake hands and thank the interviewer for his or time.

Obtain business cards from all those who participate in the interview so that you can follow up with a thank-you note acknowledging each of them by name.

A personalized, hand-written or typed thank-you letter will go a long way toward making a lasting impression.

Your Portfolio

When potential employers are flipping through your portfolio, they are looking for three things: (1) the quality of your work, (2) the visual clarity of your work, and, perhaps most important, (3) your verbal presentation of the work.

Diversity of Work
As with your work sample, be sure to include a wide variety of projects to demonstrate your full range of abilities as an architect. Show physical models as well as computer-

generated renderings or photomontage. Include conceptual design sketches as well as working drawings. Mention any construction or office experience, even if it's not directly related to architecture. At the same time, don't include every single project you have ever worked on—just show the best work in each category. It's better to show three to four good projects thoroughly than rush through ten okay projects that demonstrate similar skills. You might also specifically compose the order of the projects or the actual projects shown for each interview.

Be Concise

The written description could be limited to the project name and location. Don't include a verbose description in the actual portfolio unless you are not interviewing in person and plan to send the portfolio ahead for review prior to a phone interview. And even then, it should not be too lengthy. If you provide too much information in writing, you risk losing the interviewer between reading and listening. If you must, write a few bullet points to help prompt you during the interview. For a portfolio you will not present in person, limit the text to a few sentences that briefly describe the scope of the project (or in the case of student work, the program or project type), your concept or design approach, and a sentence about what you learned from the experience.

The ability to write a good project description is a valuable skill. As an intern in a small to mid-sized firm, you may be called upon to produce or supplement marketing materials, writing project descriptions for projects you may not have worked on. The concise project descriptions in your portfolio demonstrate your communication skills and a clear understanding of the project.

Presenting Your Work

After the initial introduction, mentally decide if you will flip pages or let the employer flip. Whoever flips the pages determines the speed at which the projects are presented. Regardless of who turns the pages, remember to read your audience and take visual cues from the interviewer. As you describe each project, if the interviewer quickly flips past the project before you can finish the description, you are probably talking too much. Recognize that your reviewer may have limited time, and pace yourself so that you can cover all the projects in your portfolio. It would be unfortunate to miss talking about your best project because you talked too long about another and the reviewer was called away for a client meeting. Practice presenting the portfolio to a professor or fellow student to determine how much you should explain and where you should elaborate.

Your presentation skills will be evaluated during the interview. Prospective employers are considering your effectiveness in communicating with clients, consultants, and the public. Depending on the size of the firm, you might not have these opportunities right away. However, in smaller firms, it is likely that you will be interacting with clients and consultants relatively soon, and employers want to be assured that you will be able to positively represent the firm and clearly communicate your ideas.

Describing Your Role

If you have professional experience and are showing projects from previous firms, clearly describe your role on the project team and which drawings or models you produced. Be honest and don't overstate your role. You don't want to set up false expectations that will come back to haunt you should you end up with a job for which you are not qualified.

Everything Counts

It is highly unlikely that you will be hired as an intern primarily to do design work. Demonstrating that you know about the other aspects of architectural practice and office functions will make you more attractive to a potential employer. Recognize that smaller firms will be more interested in this diversity—they will want agile interns conversant in many areas. Larger firms may not be as interested in nondesign skills since they will have more experienced staff to coordinate those areas of work.

The Wrapper

While the work itself must be strong and well organized, the notebook or case in which it is presented also makes a statement of some sort. It is easy to get carried away designing and fabricating an elaborate book or finely crafted case. There are many available for purchase in a variety of materials (plastic, leather, wood, Lexan, metal, rubber, or paper) in an equally varied price range. I personally do not think it is necessary to purchase something costly or precious. Like a museum containing fine art, the portfolio cover should quietly complement the work, not compete as a piece of art in and of itself. However, the choice is entirely personal. Whether it's a simple three-ring notebook or a custom leather sleeve, select something that reflects your sensibilities.

Prepare for Questions

For most, the portfolio review will be a minor part of the interview; the remaining time will be spent talking. The interviewer will likely tell you a little about the firm and some of its current projects. But the majority of the time will be devoted to finding out whether you possess the skills to perform the job and whether your career objectives fit with the long-term needs of the firm. So you should be prepared to answer a variety of questions about yourself, your architectural values, and your career goals. These are some of the most commonly asked questions:

- What inspired you to study architecture?
- What excites you about the profession?
- What types of projects are you interested in working on? (Do your homework. If you are most interested in airports and the firm doesn't do airports, you are either indicating that you don't know much about the firm or that you don't want to work there.)
- What do you hope to get out of this job?

- What skills and talents do you bring to this office? (The answer to this may vary with each firm.)
- Where do you see yourself in five years?

Illegal Questions

Title VII of the Civil Rights Act of 1964 prohibits employment discrimination based on age, race, color, religion, sex, or national origin. So there are some questions that are illegal for employers to ask, such as, "How old are you?", "Do you have any disabilities?", or "Are you married?" These questions would be construed by Title VII as unfair measures for job consideration. However, there are subtle differences when the questions pertain to your ability to perform the work or their ability to legally employ you. For example, potential employers can't ask you if you are a U.S. citizen. But they can ask you if you are authorized to work in the United States.

If you are asked a question that you feel is illegal, you could (a) answer, knowing that you are not obligated to do so, or (b) refuse and risk being considered uncooperative. So your best bet is to try to understand the nature of the question and answer it indirectly.

The AEC Workforce Guide to Finding the Right Job provides some good examples of how to deal with such questions. For example, if an employer asks if you have children, he or she may be trying to determine how often you are likely to miss work. If you feel that having children (or not having children) has no relevance to your position, you could answer that you will not have a problem meeting the attendance requirements for the position.

Two Frequently Asked Questions

The following are two different questions that are frequently asked and difficult to answer on the spot. So consider them in advance and have an answer prepared that puts your best foot forward.

What Are Your Strengths and Weaknesses?

Hopefully, talking about your strengths will be easy. But if not, ask someone who knows you well (parent, classmate, professor) what he or she considers to be your strengths and discuss how they may relate to your work.

Remember to consider the tasks that you will likely be asked to perform. Organizational skills will be extremely helpful to employers who need help filing client invoices, maintaining product binders in the reference library, and archiving drawings and documents from completed projects. Adeptness at learning new computer programs may be useful. Physical model making and Photoshop skills may be extremely helpful for the presentation of the firm's work. Desktop publishing may be helpful in preparing marketing materials for the firm. As an intern, your ability to conduct research on new materials or products may be extremely helpful to project teams.

Tips for Interviewing at a Large Firm

Greta Gillisse, a recruiter for Callison Architecture, a Seattle firm with more than 400 employees, provided the following tips. While her comments are specific to Callison, her views are likely similar to other recruiters for large firms.

During the interview we are looking for communication skills. Candidates should be able to articulately describe one to two projects. We are looking to see what skills were learned at previous jobs and how they might immediately contribute to a team.

The recruiters conduct the first round of interviews, which is the second level of screening. Being invited to interview was the first level. When I interview intern-level candidates, they are being evaluated about 60 percent on content and 40 percent on communication and verbal skills.

Questions that might be asked during an interview:

- What was your favorite studio and why?
- What spaces inspire you?
- What misgivings, if any, do you have about big firms?
- Who are the other firms you are interviewing with? Why did you select us?
- What do you want to do in five years? (If the candidate says he or she wants to be a sole proprietor designing single-family residences, then maybe Callison is not a good fit.)
- How would you self-rate your skills (beginning, intermediate, or advanced) for computer/CAD programs?

These questions help the recruiters learn about a candidate's design interests and also help guide studio placement and career development needs.

When describing your strengths to a prospective employer, be succinct and make sure the strengths are related to the work you will be expected to perform. If you have identified numerous strengths in preparation for an interview, pick the top three and mentally list them in bullet form with a brief example to illustrate. Note that there is a fine line between self-awareness and boasting.

Be sure to think seriously about your weaknesses. Be able to state at least one and what you are doing to improve upon it. If your area of weakness is the inability to complete projects because you can't stop designing, consider how you can structure your design process to make decisions and move forward in order to meet your deadlines. Remember to phrase your weaknesses in a positive way and describe what you are doing to improve upon them. For example, if time management is not your strength, don't say that you are always late for meetings and appointments. Instead, indicate that you are sometimes overly ambitious about what you can achieve in a short amount of time and need to learn to prioritize tasks and budget your time appropriately.

Conversely, there may be weaknesses to avoid highlighting, such as the inability to work on teams. This may not be one to bring up unless you have a clearly defined plan for change. Teamwork is essential to any architectural practice, and if you are not a team player, that is not a weakness that you will want to draw attention to. Acknowledging this weakness to yourself may help you to be sensitive and adapt to the collaborative nature of the architectural profession.

Avoid mentioning a weakness that you have not taken measures to change. However, be aware that ignoring a weakness doesn't make it go away. It can exacerbate the problem for everyone who interacts with you. Self-awareness is the first step; action is the next. Find a way to improve upon all known weaknesses.

Tell Me a Little Bit about Yourself

Stories are a great way to tie your outside interests into a discussion while describing how you handle situations. Think of three real-life situations in which you demonstrated a quality you think your employers would like to see in their employees. These may revolve around the following: integrity, dedication, responsibility, following through, going the extra mile, flexibility, adaptability to unexpected situations, or conflict resolution. Practice telling these stories aloud so that you can relay them succinctly and effectively. If asked a tough question that you are not sure how to answer, try to use one of these stories to demonstrate your talents. For example, you may not have had a chance to demonstrate leadership within school or an architectural context. However, you may have had these opportunities as an Eagle Scout or as a volunteer at a hospital. Stories can be effectively used, but only if it feels natural and genuine. Practicing the way you tell these stories is a good idea, but during the interview remember to be conversational so that the story doesn't come across as being rehearsed.

The more you interview, the more familiar you will become with the types of questions you will be asked. It's okay, and actually might impress the interviewer, if you take notes during the interview so that you can ask intelligent follow-up questions. After each interview, write down the questions that you felt were tough so that if you think they might be asked again in the future, you can prepare a thoughtful answer. If you feel like you answered a question poorly, you could also send a follow-up response to your interviewer by e-mail or in your thank-you letter.

Questions to Ask the Employer

Asking questions of a potential employer does two things: It indicates your interest in the firm, and it helps you evaluate what it might be like to work there. Here are just a few questions that you may consider asking:

- What types of tasks will be expected of the position I am applying for?
- What are other interns with my experience level currently working on?
- What is the average work week? How many hours a week do most people actually work?

- How does the firm support interns enrolled in IDP?
- For purposes of IDP, will my daily supervisor be a registered architect? If not, who will be signing my IDP forms?
- How easy, or difficult, is it to move from one project team or studio to another?

The following questions might be asked at a second interview or after an offer has been extended:

- Are the hours above 40 per week compensated as overtime pay, or is there a compensation time policy?
- What benefits are provided with my compensation package? And when am I eligible?
- May I talk to someone in a similar position to the one I am considering? (This gives you a chance to see how others like working there and what their experiences have been to date.)
- How does the firm foster the office culture? Are there staff retreats? If so, do they occur during the week or over a weekend? Is it just employees, or do families come along? How frequently are there office-wide staff meetings? Are there separate office-wide design crits? If not, how do employees know what is going on in other parts of the firm?

What to Wear

Regardless of your personal style, dress professionally and know your audience. A firm's Web site may have pictures of the office and staff to inform you of their dress code. It can be just as damaging to arrive for a corporate interview dressed in jeans and a T-shirt as it would be to show up in a navy suit and tie at an office that is known for its casual and creative environment and clientele. Ask yourself how the employer would answer this question: "Can I take this intern to a client meeting with me?" Making a good impression is as much about grooming and personal hygiene as it is about talents and abilities. It comes down to professionalism—and depending on your office and their clients, that may or may not mean a suit.

How Much Should I Ask For?

If things are going well, many employers will ask during the interview what you are expecting for a salary. Be prepared for this question by doing your homework beforehand. Try to find out what other interns in the area are making. Your best resource will be the AIA Compensation Survey, which is published every few years. The Emerging Professionals page on the AIA Web site posts the results of the intern salary survey as a free PDF download (see the table on page 53). This is the best gauge of what you can expect.

Average Starting Salaries				
Average (Mean)	Entry Level	Second Year	Third Year	Architect Design
national	30.3	34	39.2	41.6
firms with fewer than 5 employees	28.4	29.3	36.6	37.2
firms with 5 to 9 employees	28.5	32.4	36.7	37.9
firms with 10 to 19 employees	30	34	37.3	39.9
firms with 20 to 49 employees	31.7	34.5	39.5	40.7
firms with 50 to 99 employees	31.3	33.2	39.3	45.4
firms with 100 to 249 employees	30.7	35.4	38.7	41.6
firms with 250 or more employees	27.7	36.5	45.2	43.8
New England (ME, NH, VT, MA, CT, RI)	33.2	38.2	42.3	41.5
Mid-Atlantic (NY, PA, NJ)	29.9	31.7	39.4	44.5
East North Central (OH, TN, MI, IL, WI)	30.2	33.7	38	39.5
West North Central (MN, IA, MO, NE, KS, SD, ND)	28.2	35	37.9	41.9
South Atlantic (WV, MD, DE, DC, VA, NC, SC, GA, FL)	31	33.6	38.3	39.9
East South Central (KY, TN, MS, AL)	30.6	33.6	36.9	37.7
West South Central (OK, TX, AR, LA)	30.4	34.8	41.3	40.6
Pacific Northwest (MO, WY, ID, WA, OR, AK)	29.5	34.2	38.1	39.7
Pacific Southwest (CA, HI, NV, UT, AZ, NM, CO)	30.2	34.4	38.6	42.6

Note: Compensation figures are noted in thousands of dollars and include salary, bonuses, profit sharing, and other incentive compensation.

Definitions

Entry level:	Intern in first year of internship
Second year:	Intern in second year of internship
Third year:	Unlicensed architecture-school graduate in third year of internship; develops design or technical solutions under supervision of an architect
Architect/design:	Recently licensed architect or nonregistered graduate with three to five years' experience; responsible for particular parts of a project within a firm.

Source: 2002 AIA Compensation Survey

Photo by Michael Mariano, AIA, 2003

Comparing Apples to Apples

Make sure both you and the prospective employer understand whether you are talking about an hourly or annual salary. Graduating from architecture school in 1993, a classmate shared his excitement over accepting a salary of "18" with a highly regarded local design firm. When I told him I thought that was low, he asked what I had been offered. After I told him I was offered "25," we discussed what we individually thought that meant. We realized that he had assumed the offer he had been given was $18 per hour, whereas I understood it as $18,000 per year. Much to his chagrin, a quick phone call confirmed that the yearly salary was what the firm intended as well.

Quick math: There are 2,088 hours in a year for a 40-hour workweek. Therefore, a rule of thumb is that the hourly rate is about half of the first two numbers in a yearly salary. (i.e., $18,000 per year is about $9 per hour. Conversely, $18 per hour roughly translates to $36,000 per year.)

Photo by Grace Kim, AIA, 2005

If you want something else to compare the AIA figures against, you can look online for some general guidelines at Salary.com and the Bureau of Labor Statistics (www.bls.gov — search under "Occupation"). Note that these general sources do not provide a breakdown of intern versus registered architect salaries.

While this should go without saying, I'm always surprised to hear about interns agreeing to work for free. Don't do it! Working for free to "gain some experience" undermines the profession and undervalues your skills. If they are offering you an unpaid position, this may be a symptom of other employee inequities and overall poor business management practices.

If you do accept an unpaid position, it will make it that much harder for you to command a higher salary in the future. If a prospective employer calls references and learns that you weren't paid wages for a previous internship, it will be hard for you to justify requesting any salary higher than entry level.

Similarly, don't take a job that offers you low pay and expect to get a huge raise after you "demonstrate your value to the firm." If they value your work to begin with, they will compensate you fairly from the outset. Many interns fall into this trap. Remember, if you start low, you are likely to stay low.

If you really want the job, but the employer wants to see you demonstrate your abilities before compensating you with the salary you seek, be sure to request a review of your performance and compensation at a predetermined date. Request in writing the time at which the review will take place, and if possible, what performance criteria will be used to determine whether a salary increase is appropriate — generally three months provides ample time for the office to evaluate your skills and contribution.

Questions to Ask Yourself

After you leave the interview, ask yourself, "How did it feel?" Consider the people that you met, the physical environment, and the work of the firm. Was the office a place you would look forward to coming to every day? Your gut reaction is a good one to note in writing, as you may wish to refer to it later if multiple job offers are extended to you. Your first impression may provide insights that will help you decide.

Prepare for the Unexpected

While this chapter has tried to anticipate what you might need to know for most interview situations, recognize that you will come across firms that don't interview in a typical manner. The intern-issues Web site Archinect.org may be a good source of information on what to expect in an interview. In response to a recent query about interview experiences, several interns described a typical interview scenarios: two that did not involve a portfolio review, one that required a ten-minute lettering sample, and another that included a battery of unprofessional and seemingly irrelevant questions. While it is difficult to prepare for every interview, hopefully you can prepare for the majority of situations and adapt your responses on the off chance the interview takes an odd direction. The key is to be professional regardless of the setting. Demonstrate to your potential employer that you can think on your feet and react appropriately in any situation.

Accepting an Offer

While it doesn't occur often, you may be offered a job at the conclusion of an interview. An offer is more likely to be made in a subsequent phone conversation or follow-up interview. Regardless of the timing, it is important to get in writing the terms of your offer before giving notice at your current job or even canceling a previously scheduled interview. At a minimum, this letter should include the title of the job being offered, the exact details of the salary (exempt or nonexempt status, overtime, etc.), your eligibility for benefits, the office location and exact hours, and the anticipated start date. Without such a letter, you are not guaranteed a job if you show up. (It should be acknowledged that there are no job guarantees in our profession, especially for those of us in "right-to-work" states, but that is a topic for discussion in and of itself.) This letter should indicate a deadline by which you must respond to accept the offer.

Negotiating Your Offer

There may be times when you will want to negotiate your offer. While it might not be advantageous to try negotiating a higher salary when few jobs are available during boom times when there are more jobs than qualified people, it would be foolish not to. But do not be cavalier about it. You must first do your homework to know what other firms are offering and what other interns are accepting. You must also provide reasons why you believe you deserve more than is being offered—point out strengths or special skills that set you apart and will bring value to the firm.

If you have multiple offers, point out differences in the compensation and benefits packages and what you would like to see amended. Recognize that they may not be able to match one for one, but establish a baseline for your expectations. Also consider what benefits are important to you. While a firm may not be able to provide a higher salary, they may be able to allow for more vacation or personal time. While some firms might offer a lower salary, they may pay for all of your medical benefits and have a 401(k) matching program. Perhaps they will pay for your AIA dues, Architect Registration Exam (ARE) or IDP fees, or license renewals. Perhaps they will pay for professional development seminar fees and time. Perhaps they will allow you the flexibility to work 32 hours for the same salary, enabling you a free day to work on art or study for the ARE.

Be prepared to walk away from a job offer. If a "design firm" tells you they can't pay you the going intern salary because they are just starting up and don't have the resources to pay you what you are asking, you should consider whether they actually have the workload to sustain your position for any substantial length of time. If you are trying to negotiate for overtime pay or medical benefits and the firm is annoyed by your questions and tells you indignantly that "there are plenty of interns who would jump at this opportunity," then you might ask yourself whether you really want this job or whether it should be offered to one of those "other interns" instead. Firms that take this cavalier, take-it-or-leave-it, "we're a designer firm" attitude may not be interested in intern development or your long-term growth. Firms that don't manage their human resources well may also have poor business management practices, lacking the skills to negotiate good fees for their projects or collect on their outstanding accounts.

Benefits

Once interviewers ask about salaries, they have given an indication of their interest to hire, and it is fair to discuss compensation and benefits without seeming greedy or self-serving. While you don't have to know the finite details at the time of initial interview, if you are offered a job, you should know what benefits are included before accepting the position. At this point, you should not be worried about losing the opportunity for a job by asking the employer to provide in writing the compensation and benefits package that is being offered.

Firms may elect to pay for benefits outside of your salary figure or to deduct them from your paycheck. You should be aware of what your employer intends. Employer-paid benefits can add $1,000 or more to your annual salary (see page 122 for more specific information). According to the AIA Large Firm Roundtable, all large firms (defined as having more than 100 employees) provide medical insurance, holidays, paid vacation, and sick and personal days. While many small to medium-sized architecture firms may not provide many benefits, those firms that are interested in attracting and retaining the best employees will try to provide some of the benefits described in the following pages.

Medical Insurance

Whether you pay or the employer does, make sure you understand your coverage. While a medical insurance program may be offered, dental and vision are frequently not. Each insurer will have its own coverage requirements, so check with your employer. The firm will have brochures from its insurance provider. Find out when you will become eligible for medical coverage. The start date can range from the first day of employment to the start of the following month or later. Some firms don't offer it until after a probationary period has passed.

Holidays

According to a recent article posted on www.howstuffworks.com entitled "How Employee Compensation Works," by Lee Ann Obringer, the national average for paid holidays (for all types of companies) is 10½ days. While all of the large architecture firms offer paid holidays, the number of days may vary from firm to firm. Many smaller and medium-sized firms do not offer paid holidays but may allow employees to take holidays off without pay.

The firms that do offer paid holidays generally offer these six days off: New Year's Day, Memorial Day, Fourth of July, Labor Day, Thanksgiving, and Christmas. Some firms may offer two additional days, either as floating religious holidays or designated national holidays such as Presidents' Day or Martin Luther King Day.

Paid Vacation

In the firms that provide paid vacation, the standard is 10 days (or 80 hours) annually. Those hours are usually accrued incrementally per pay period. Some firms may allow you to "go negative," or borrow against your future vacation time, while others may not allow you paid vacation time within the first few months of employment. If you have a vacation planned for early in your employment, be sure to discuss this during your negotiations.

Depending on the firm, you may be offered additional vacation days with increased tenure. For example, five years with an office may entitle you to three weeks of paid vacation time.

Sick and Personal Days

As with paid holidays and vacation days, most large firms offer paid sick leave; small and medium-sized firms will have varying policies. If provided as a benefit by the employer, sick and personal days are also generally accrued per pay period. The firms that provide this benefit generally provide five days per year, but the policy will vary from firm to firm. Some call these "sick days" and stipulate that you must truly be sick in order to use them. In some offices, doctor appointments can be logged against those hours. Other firms simply call them "personal days" and allow you to use them when you aren't feeling 100 percent, when your dog or child is sick, or when you just need a mental health day. In either case, the unused days generally do not roll over from year to year.

Retirement Savings: 401(k), IRA, Simple IRA

Some companies give you the opportunity to make self-elected, pretax contributions toward a retirement savings plan. If this benefit is offered by your company, take advantage of it. While it may seem hard to deduct money for retirement from your annual pay, the contribution reduces your taxable income, so the net effect on your paycheck may be negligible. In addition, some companies provide matching funds for a certain percentage of your contributions, often doubling the amount that goes into your retirement plan. Inquire about your eligibility for these programs. Some firms allow contributions from the first day; others only accept contributions during election periods or upon a one-year employment anniversary. Make sure to ask when you are vested in the company-matched funds; some firms expect you to stay a minimum number of years before the matched funds really become "yours." Each retirement savings program is slightly different, so ask your employer to explain it carefully.

Professional Development

Some firms may pay for all or part of your AIA dues, registration fees to attend seminars and conferences, application fees for IDP, or examination fees for taking the ARE. Other firms may not pay for these direct expenses, but they may pay for your time by providing an office overhead job number. This overhead job number might also be used for seminars and workshops both inhouse and outside the office without having to "make up" those hours. Some firms fund professional development on a case-by-case basis, and others provide each employee with an individual professional development budget. The latter is generally preferable for the employee in that it is equitable and can generally be applied toward any combination of workshops, exams, or conferences desired by the employee. This would be a good question to ask during the interview or the first few days at work.

Bonuses

Your salary and benefits package may also include bonuses. These can occur quarter-ly, annually, or perhaps in association with a project milestone. Some firms only pro-vide senior-level staff with bonuses. Others can tell you a percentage they anticipate providing as year-end bonuses based on previous years. Remember that these are just estimates, and the actual dollar amount really depends on the current financial health of the firm. Bonuses can range from a few hundred to several thousand dollars. While it may sound attractive when a potential employer estimates a bonus of a certain per-centage, it's important to ask when the firm last distributed bonuses. A firm with good intentions may not have the cash flow to follow through. Firms that "intend to pay out 15 percent in bonuses," may not have been able to for the past ten years.

Profit Sharing

Some firms may share profits at the year end (providing a benefit similar to bonuses). If your firm does, ask how much these benefits have been in the past and how they are distributed. Ask about the vesting schedule—is there a minimum time that you must stay to receive all of the funds in your name?

Travel Programs

Some firms provide funding for senior staff trips. Frequently, such trips are group vis-its to architectural sites that provide an opportunity for staff bonding. Senior-staff trips are becoming more common in large firms. Less frequently, smaller, design-oriented firms may sponsor a weekend trip after five years and a weeklong sabbatical after ten years of service to encourage staff retention, boost morale, and foster staff cohesion.

A Word of Caution

Be aware that some architectural firms may offer few, if any, of these benefits. Architects often view themselves as artists, with little regard for or training in business, and they have taken shelter in that fact for years. Practices that are common in the business world, such as providing benefits, are sometimes viewed as extravagant or exorbitant, both by employers and employees. If employees continue to accept the poor standards our industry has set, they will only aid the perpetuation of poor human resource management practices. A firm's benefit package can be a clear indicator of how you will be treated as an employee. Firms that provide benefits show that they value their employees as their greatest resource and hope to retain them. Firms that do not provide benefits may lack financial resources, implying poor business manage-ment practices, or have other reasons for opting out, but they should understand that they are sending a poor message to their employees. Obviously, it is up to you to decide how desperately you want the job and whether you are willing to compromise on this issue.

Stories from the "Front Lines"

At this point, you may be overwhelmed with the tasks ahead of you and uncertain how your job search will turn out. Remember that your job search is likely to be a difficult process, requiring diligence and perseverance. Keep in mind that while it may seem daunting, there are many others experiencing the same anxieties and frustrations as you. This chapter concludes with firsthand accounts from interns hitting the job market. While they are not necessarily indicative of what you will encounter, I hope they will provide you with insight as you embark upon your own job search.

Finding My First Internship

My first architectural internship took place after my freshman year at Southern Illinois University, with an outstanding 150-person office in central Illinois. I worked primarily with the criminal justice studio of the firm and was exposed to a wide range of tasks, from ADA assessments to assisting with the punch list for a large facility. In fact, it was while I was working on the design for a new police station that my interest in planning and design emerged as a career focus. Certainly, every day wasn't a picnic, and I had to complete some tasks that I didn't necessarily enjoy. However, I was challenged, and what I learned during that formative time still influences the way I think and process information today.

Getting the position proved to be most challenging. At the time I was looking for that first internship, the industry was in a down cycle, so I knew that landing a job would be difficult. After carefully crafting cover letters, sending résumés to firms I respected, and placing countless follow-up calls, I was able to arrange for three interviews—including one with a local firm that was my overall first choice. Although many firms declined to interview, going through the process enabled me to hone my communication skills.

To prepare for my interviews, I carefully compiled my studio work, along with sample CAD drawings from a previous summer job at a city planning office. AutoCAD 7.0 was new to the market at that time, and I knew that my CAD experience would help differentiate me from other applicants. Each interviewer reviewed my portfolio and qualifications, but to my surprise, they spent even more time discussing my personal goals. Similarly, I expected to speak about each of my project concepts, but the employers were more interested in how I communicated or how I fit with the firm's culture.

Following the three interviews, my first-choice firm offered me the position that launched my architectural career. What made the firm special was the connection I felt with the interviewers—for whom, to this day, I hold a great deal of appreci-

ation. They both served as great mentors, and one actually allowed me to board in his house for the summer because of the great distance from my home to the office. In many ways, I owe much of who I am as an architect to their stewardship during my first internship.

Shannon Kraus, AIA
Associate, HKS Dallas
University of Illinois at Urbana-Champaign, Master of Architecture and MBA 1998

While Shannon was fortunate enough to land his first internships without too much difficulty, this is not necessarily the situation for most interns. Depending on the economy, it's possible for bright and talented graduates to spend several months searching for a job, and moving to a new city could exacerbate an already difficult job search. The following account was written by an intern who took a huge step by moving across the country to a new city during a time when available positions were scarce nationwide.

Jobless in Seattle

Finding my first job after graduate school took hard work, perseverance, and a dose of good luck. I moved to Seattle from the East Coast in December 2002, thinking, "If I don't move out there now, I never will." I wanted to try a new place and see new things. I also thought that since a friend had easily found a good job in Portland, perhaps there were more job opportunities on the West Coast. I was wrong. The long months that followed were incredibly frustrating.

When I first arrived in Seattle I knew exactly three people, and not one of them was in architecture. I had one thing to get me started: A professor back in Virginia had given me the name of a former student teaching in Seattle. I found her e-mail address and wrote to her, unsure what to expect. Despite her busy schedule she was very understanding and quick to respond to my queries. She suggested that I contact a former coworker of hers, who was a project manager in one of the city's prominent firms. Hence, I started my journey.

I hadn't realized how difficult my job search would be. I had an MArch from a good school and a well-prepared portfolio of work. But I also had almost no work experience and had gone to school on the opposite coast.

I called the project manager and explained that his friend and former coworker had suggested I contact him. I told him of my situation and asked if he might have some time to speak with me about architecture in Seattle, "even if your firm is not hiring at the moment." That became a key phrase in all of my subsequent contacts. During the course of our conversation, he gave me the names of four more people to contact. I had the opportunity to speak with two of these contacts, and they in turn gave me more names. This process went on for several months. Some called me back, many didn't. None knew of any openings. I was at my wit's end.

I did what I could to get my name out and look for jobs outside of my tiny network: I went to a local architectural publication's quarterly open house. I sent out "cold-call" letters and résumés. I volunteered for a local nonprofit architectural organization. I checked the online classifieds of every local paper. I went down to the local AIA office to look at their job book and research firms to approach.

In the meantime, one architect I met suggested that I talk to a principal in a small, woman-owned design firm. In May, after a few weeks of trying to schedule an appointment, we finally met. Her firm wasn't hiring, but she said she'd keep her eyes open and let me know about job prospects. She also advised me to join the local Young Architects Forum LISTSERV to find out about possible job leads.

For eight months, my job search was a series of ups and downs, with lots of open ends, and about one week's worth of hourly work in architecture. I was waiting to hear back from my latest interview when I received a call from the helpful principal at the woman-owned design firm. This was July, two months after my initial informational meeting. Her firm was being interviewed for a design/build tenant improvement project that would last three or four weeks, and they were so busy with other projects that they didn't have anyone on staff to work on it. Unfortunately, they didn't know if there would be any work after the project was over, so it was really a temporary position. After her partner at the firm did a quick review of my portfolio, I was hired for the project and was asked to attend the second interview with the client later that day. The project ended up lasting nearly two months, during which time I began working on a second project. In October, I was made a full-time salaried employee, and I've been with the company ever since.

Here's what I've learned from the process:

Network: A recognizable name can be an invaluable key to establishing contact.

Persevere: Don't give up with a couple of dead ends; you never know what's around the corner.

Presentation: Always put your best foot forward, even if you know the person with whom you're speaking doesn't have a job to offer at the moment.

Confidence: Believe in yourself and what you have to offer, especially if you have little experience on paper.

Don't be afraid to take risks: That up-and-coming young firm might see something in you that you didn't know you had.

Samantha Beadel
Intern Architect, Place Architects
University of Virginia, Master of Architecture 2002

The following intern writes about his frustrations during his first job search in a small architectural community. Unlike Samantha, he didn't have a network to draw upon or access to the appropriate resources when seeking his first job. This story may be familiar to many interns in smaller cities across North America.

What's an Intern to Do in Alaska?

I was born and raised in Anchorage, Alaska. The universities in Alaska do not offer architecture or design-related programs, so interested individuals have to leave the state to receive their formal education. I attended Montana State University in Bozeman and returned to Alaska in the summers to compete for jobs.

In my fourth year of school, architecture "clicked" for me, and I wanted to understand the profession at a different level. I was tired of working odd summer jobs—bank teller, bookseller, retail salesperson for outdoor gear. I was running out of choices! I was ready to become more proactive about my profession and wanted relevant work experience. My friends in Bozeman had gotten summer architecture jobs at firms around town with ease. They were getting valuable experience and, in some cases, were assured of a job right after graduation. But finding a job in Alaska turned out to be much more difficult than I had anticipated. Anchorage is not an especially "design-sensitive" city. At the time there were only about 15 local architecture firms, and only about 3 of these focused on high-quality design work.

The local AIA office did not have a job board or a network for interns. Distraught at this discovery, I wondered how I would find a job. The Yellow Pages were my only reference. Armed with résumés and a mini-portfolio, I dropped by every firm in the city, including one that was located on the fourth floor of the local mall. I even applied at a firm in Fairbanks, which is about 300 miles north of Anchorage. I thought I had a good chance of landing a job, because few Alaskans go to architecture school, and the competition was sparse.

But even in the absence of competition, I wasn't getting any responses. Trying to gain entrance to the local architecture scene was like trying to get into an exclusive club. When I called firms to follow up, I asked if they were looking for an intern or if they would have time for an informational interview. Their typical responses were, "We don't do that kind of thing," or "We don't really hire interns." These weren't exactly words of encouragement. Feeling angry and bitter, I began to question my abilities and experienced lingering self-doubt and fear. I had spent so much time and energy working hard at school. Would I find I had no job opportunities after graduation?

Luckily, a professor of mine had worked for a firm in Anchorage, and he put me in contact with the principal, who was well respected in the architectural community and whose firm was committed to doing quality work in Alaska. This con-

tact led to my first interview, which went well. I had researched the firm's projects, which I had seen around town, and I got the firm tour. Even with the interview jitters and the portfolio perusing, I felt that the interview was going in the right direction.

"Great work, but we aren't looking for anyone right now." The interview was a good experience, but it didn't end with the job offer I had hoped for.

Discouraged because that had been my only "professional" connection, I was afraid I was destined to work another retail job for yet another summer. After the interview, I actually picked up an application for a cashier position at the local big-box hardware store. In fact, I was headed to a group interview for that position the next day when I made one final stop at a firm to which I had forgotten to send a résumé. At that point, I wasn't really hoping for anything, but to my surprise, the firm called and asked me to come in for an interview that afternoon.

This was a ten-person firm specializing in commercial and educational work, with an emphasis on sensitivity to Alaska's special environmental conditions. The firm had an Alaskan quirkiness, with model floatplanes hanging from the ceiling. My interview with the principal went great, and I felt at ease. The firm offered me a position, which I accepted. Even with my lack of AutoCAD skills, I was put to work right away on a small highway weigh station for the State of Alaska Department of Transportation. The project, located outside Anchorage, was built that summer. In addition to the drafting assignments, there was plenty of office work, such as filing product literature, and a project for a new terminal at the Anchorage International Airport afforded plenty of model-making opportunities. Not all the projects that I worked on were glamorous or high-profile, but that was fine with me. As far as office culture goes, I was the only individual under 30. Everyone else was late thirties or older, married and with kids. It was hard for me to relate to them sometimes, and this reaffirmed my perception that Anchorage was a place for people who wanted to settle down, not for young and single "mover-and-shaker" types.

It took me about a month to find that first job. It was difficult trying to get a job in a place where there were few resources for young design professionals and where architecture was not highly regarded. Looking back, I wish that I had built more of a network, either through my university or through a local organization, because the local AIA wasn't as helpful as I had hoped it would be. I gained plenty of confidence by dealing with rejection, and I am thankful that I was offered a job, but the search made me realize that it can be hard to thrive in a place where few opportunities exist.

I returned to Anchorage to work the summer after graduation and then decided to move to the Lower 48, where, despite the added competition for jobs, more opportunities were available.

As a result of my experiences, I realize that being persistent and having confidence are critical in looking for an internship position—or any job, for that matter. It also helps if you understand your lifestyle and what you want out of your job. The resources are available, but it takes some time and effort to locate them.

Mark V. Mappala
Intern, Callison Architecture
Montana State University, Master of Architecture 1999

While many interns have described their job search experience in a targeted city, the following intern shares his job search tale that sent him traveling the far corners of the country.

A Tale of Four Cities

On a blazing hot day in June, I left the university and boarded a plane for San Francisco. I had done my homework and had several interviews scheduled for the following week, half a dozen leads, and a nice thick portfolio. Life was good. I asked the flight attendant for extra peanuts to compensate for my lack of income.

I took the Metro downtown, schlepping my bags to my hotel, a building of dubious safety in a low-rent location. The next morning, I headed down to BART and rode out to Berkeley for my first interview. After walking a mile through industrial South Berkeley, I came upon a likely building: high windows fitted to old garage-door frames, nice door hardware. I knocked on the door. After waiting several minutes and peering in the windows over piled geraniums, I pushed the door open and called out, "Hello?" I walked in, threading my way between stacked boxes of concrete and colorant. Perhaps I had the wrong building. I called again, and a young woman came in. She asked who I was. I told her my name, and added that I had an interview scheduled for ten minutes earlier. She looked puzzled and left the room without a word. I waited. When I finally had the interview, I thought it went well; I admired the firm's details and toured their woodshop. I never heard back from them.

After lunch, I called my next interview—just down the street—from a payphone. She canceled, with apologies. I rode back into town and spent the evening and the next day exploring the city.

Several days later, I was back in Berkeley, walking unfamiliar streets, on my way to my next interview. The principal showed me around the office, and we sat down in the middle of the open space. We talked about my portfolio and then about the projects currently in the office. He warmed up, speaking excitedly about a school on the boards: a courtyard scheme. I heard from the firm a week later: a tentative offer. A week after that, it was still tentative. Two weeks later: still tentative. Hunting interviews, I went up to Seattle, making lists and calling friends. I called back to the firm in Berkeley and asked for a final answer. The answer was no.

Seattle, in the midst of its dot-com crash, was a rainy, exceedingly gray city. After three weeks and one interview, my sister's couch developed lumps. I began to reply to newspaper ads, and one firm called me in for an interview. The interviewer was fascinating, like an ambassador. A bit wiser to the interview process, I asked to see the office and the projects they were working on. A representative project was an immense house whose design showed scant attention to quality and aesthetics. The next day, I drove to Montana.

I tried the paper there, and soon I had an interview with a big A&E firm. Did I know CAD? I did. And I got my first real job offer! I thought long and hard. What about my ideal of working in a small firm, doing a bit of everything? What about learning how to detail? I called the big firm back and said no, thanks. Montana is a dry place, lovely, honest, and mostly empty. I bought a one-way ticket to Washington, D.C.

By this time, I knew the drill. I began to put together a list. I sent out letters to good firms. I asked friends for recommendations and contacts. I followed up. The interviews came rolling in. In two weeks, I had five interviews.

Interview One: I walked down an unmarked hallway and entered a ribbon-windowed office under low-hanging fluorescents. I couldn't envision practicing architecture in that setting.

Interview Two: I met with a bespectacled man in a brick carriage house who wasn't sure what I could do for him.

Interview Three: I went through two layers of security and met with a very suave interviewer. As I left I noticed that the next interviewee looked similarly polished. My sleep grew troubled.

I went to dinner with my girlfriend and spent the weekend among palms in the National Conservatory. Renewed, I continued with the interviews.

Interview Four: I got off the Metro at Dupont Circle and met with a professor who ran an architecture practice on the side. We talked about the theory of detailing, the psychology of materials, and the weather in France. Seven hours after the interview began, I caught the late-night Metro home. The professor said she'd get back to me.

Interview Five: The next day I met with a small "green" firm in a shoebox office. The firm was less than a year old. The architects were young and hungry. They showed me their projects: residential remodels, restaurant refits. We didn't discuss running a firm or the practice of architecture; instead, we talked about design and modern architecture. They were proud of each cable rail, each aluminum angle, every bit of modern carved out of the slough of D.C. vernacular. I was impressed with their fervor. We went out for a drink after the interview. They asked me about my life, where I was from, why I was in D.C.

A few days later they called to make an offer. The professor had not yet gotten back to me. Should I wait for a second offer? Barter for a better package? It was August. I was tired of peanut butter and crackers. I took the job.

In three years I've come full circle and am currently working for a superb mid-size firm in Missoula, Montana, and looking foward to a summer of swinging a hammer as my own house takes shape. When I look back to that first job in D.C., I remember the chaos of a new architectural office coming into being. I learned valuable things about running a business, negotiating the trajectory of a startup, and rather less about the modern. Like many architects, I grew to detest CAD (and learned that it's okay to say it). I had known in advance that big firms can fall prey to false economies. I found from experience that small firms can do the same.

I did my best to stay active: I volunteered, threw pottery at a local studio, and worked on a book of poetry. My outside interests helped me come to terms with an internship process that was sometimes frustrating and dispiriting, in an environment that was often less than fully challenging. I know now that there are real differences in firms, that the fit of firm to intern is never guaranteed, and that nothing in the internship process is truly necessary. Although I followed a trajectory I couldn't have planned, after two times around the country and many moments of doubt, I wound up somewhere good.

Luke Phinney
Landscape Architect/Architect in Training, OZ Architects, Missoula, MT
University of Virginia, Master of Architecture 2001

Resources

Job Search Web Sites

AECJobBank.com	Architectural job posting
AECWorkForce.com	Job search, résumé tips, career advice
AEJob.com	Job postings
architects.org	The Boston Society of Architects — classifieds, competitions, fellowships
ArchVoices.org	Intern issues, job postings, career advice
arcspace.com	General design/architect profiles
designguide.com	Clearinghouse for A/E job postings
Entablature.com	Nationwide list of firms
e-architect.com	Job postings
InsideArch.com	Firm reports, insider accounts
web.mit.edu/career	Job listings, résumé posting, job search resources

Department of Labor Web Site

dol.gov	Fair Labor Standards Act, exempt status, overtime

CHAPTER 4 | INTERN
DEVELOPMENT
PROGRAM

In the past, architects learned their practice through a process of apprenticeship. However, as our education system evolved and buildings became more complex, this model no longer seemed sustainable. It eventually became the norm for architects to attend universities and then toil in offices for a number of years (three in most states), drafting toilet room details and building models before they became "eligible" to take the registration exam. Yet when architects compared the experience of an intern at a large office to an intern at a small office, it soon became clear the range of experiences was quite disparate. It was determined that "seat time" was not a proper indicator of whether or not an individual knew enough about the profession to be granted licensure. In response, the National Council of Architectural Registration Boards (NCARB) established a program loosely modeled on the idea of a medical intern's rotations in a hospital, intended to expose architectural interns to a broad range of the experiences they may encounter as a registered architect.

What Is IDP?

The Intern Development Program (IDP) is a national program intended to provide interns with a well-rounded base of practical knowledge. In a minimum of three years, interns are required to obtain experience in 16 Training Areas of architectural practice that range from site analysis to contract negotiation. IDP can be a difficult process; it has its own jargon and lots of forms. So it is the intent of this chapter to demystify it and break it down into "bite-sized" pieces of information. But remember, IDP is your responsibility. Each intern must be proactive to ensure timely completion of the program. This chapter will help prepare you.

IDP Training Requirements

IDP Training Requirement

You must acquire 700 training units to satisfy the IDP training requirement. One training unit equals eight hours of acceptable activity in a given training area. The following chart lists the IDP training categories and areas and the required training units for each.

Category A: Design and Construction Documents   **Minimum Training Units Required**

1. Programming 10
2. Site and Environmental Analysis 10
3. Schematic Design 15
4. Engineering Systems Coordination 15
5. Building Cost Analysis 10
6. Code Research..15
7. Design Development 40
8. Construction Documents 135
9. Specifications and Materials Research 15
10. Document Checking and Coordination 10

Total Training Units Required 350*
This total includes the 275 minimum training units required, plus 75 additional training units that must be earned in any of the training areas 1–10.

Category B: Construction Contract Administration

11. Bidding and Contract Negotiation 10
12. Construction Phase—Office 15
13. Construction Phase—Observation 15

Total Training Units Required 70*
This total includes the 40 minimum training units required, plus 30 additional training units that must be earned in any of the training areas 11–13.

Category C: Management

14. Project Management 15
15. Office Management 10

Total Training Units Required 35*
This total includes the 25 minimum training units required, plus 10 additional training units that must be earned in either training area 14 or 15.

Category D: Related Activities

16. Professional and Community Service 10
    Other Related Activities 0

Total Training Units Required 10
TOTAL IDP TRAINING UNITS REQUIRED 700*

The required minimum in Categories A, B, C, and D totals 465 training units. The additional 235 training units may be acquired in any of the listed categories.

Source: www.ncarb.org

The Lingo

Training categories—Areas of architectural practice. There are four categories, A through D.

Training areas—The specific areas of work encountered in architectural practice. There are 16 areas, some quite easy to obtain, others requiring creativity and conscious effort.

Training unit—A measure of experience equivalent to eight hours of work. Each training area is assigned a minimum number of training units, as is each category. The sum of the training units for each training area does not equal the number of required training units for each category. This is to allow some latitude in how all the requirements are met. For example, while 70 training units are required for Category B, the sum of the requirements for the three training area under Category B is 40 training units. The remaining 30 training units may be obtained in any of the three training areas under Category B.

Training unit report—Every three to six months, you will need to submit a report of your work activity to NCARB. Copies of the IDP Training Unit Report form will be mailed to you after your initial application, but they can also be downloaded off NCARB's Web site. A report should also be filed when changing employers. (See the figure on pages 72–73.)

IDP Periodic Assessment Report—After logging the training units submitted on the Training Unit Report, NCARB will send you a summary of your progress called the IDP Periodic Assessment Report. It will include the number of training units that you have obtained and the balance you need to satisfy the requirements. This is a great tool for a performance review (see Chapter 7). However, the form will always be out of date as soon as you receive it due to the lag time between when you submit the report and when NCARB responds. (See the figure on page 74.)

Council Record—Your IDP number and file are called a council record. Your council record is established by submitting your application and fee. Your council record may also aid in obtaining an NCARB certificate after your initial registration. An NCARB certificate facilitates reciprocity, or subsequent registration, in other states.

Registration or licensure—Two words with essentially the same meaning in the context of IDP: the satisfactory completion of all licensing requirements (set forth by each individual state board) that protect the health, safety, and welfare of the public.

IDP Training Unit Report

EMPLOYMENT VERIFICATION   *Please use a separate form for each period of full-time or part-time employment.*

Please complete ALL numbered items. The release authorization (item 9 and 10) must be signed and dated BEFORE sending the form to your daily supervisor to complete items A–I. IDP applicants must complete the IDP Training Unit Report on the next page. ARCHITECT APPLICANTS NOT WISHING TO RECEIVE IDP TRAINING UNIT CREDIT MUST COMPLETE ITEM VI ON THE NEXT PAGE.

1. NCARB File No.: _____   2. Your name: _____

3. Your current address: _____ City _____ State/Prov. _____ ZIP/PC _____

4. Name of organization where previously or currently employed: _____

5. Organization's address during reporting period: _____

   City _____ State/Province/Foreign Country [   ] ZIP/PC _____

6. Reporting period: From ___/___/___ to ___/___/___ Hours per week (including overtime): _____
   Month Day Year   Month Day Year

   Please use a separate form for each period of full-time or part-time employment.

APPLICANT

7. Your status in organization: ☐ Partner/Corporate Director ☐ Employee ☐ Other _____

8. Check one employment description:

		Maximum IDP Training Units (TUs) allowed— See item V for IDP Training Categories
☐ A	■ Organization encompasses the comprehensive practice of architecture (*all* areas in item V on next page) ■ Direct supervision by a registered architect	No limit in Categories A, B, C, and D
☐ B	■ Organization *does not* encompass the comprehensive practice of architecture ■ Direct supervision by a registered architect	465 TUs in Categories A, B, C, and D
☐ C	■ Organization *outside of U.S. or Canada* engaged in the practice of architecture ■ Direct supervision by a foreign architect (not registered in U.S. or Canada)	235 TUs in Categories A, B, C, and D
☐ D	■ Organization provides services directly related to architecture ■ Direct supervision by a registered engineer or registered landscape architect	235 TUs in Categories B, C, and D only
☐ E	■ Organization provides services that involve the design and construction of the built environment ☐ Construction ☐ Interior Design ☐ Planning ☐ Other_____ ■ Direct supervision by a person experienced in the discipline checked above	117 TUs in Categories C and D only
☐ F	■ Full-time teaching or research in a NAAB-accredited or CACB-accredited professional degree program	245 TUs in Category D only
☐ FF	■ Performing professional and community (volunteer) service when *not* employed in A-F above	10 TUs in Prof. & Comm. Service

I hereby authorize NCARB to make inquiries of the person listed below with respect to my background and character. I invite full and complete response to all inquiries. I release said person from any and all claims, including claims for libel and slander, which may arise out of the communication of any information to NCARB. I hereby certify that all information I furnish herein or attached hereto is correct.

9. Your signature: _____   10. Date: _____

SUPERVISOR

This portion of the form must be completed by your DAILY SUPERVISOR at the referenced organization. Daily supervisor: Please complete ALL lettered items. Use separate sheet if required.

A. Is all information shown above correct? ☐ YES ☐ NO If no, make corrections above or clarify below:
_____

B. Are the experiences correct as shown in item V on the IDP Training Unit Report OR in item VI on the next page? ☐ YES ☐ NO If no, please make corrections where appropriate.

C. Your title: ☐ Architect ☐ Engineer ☐ Landscape Architect ☐ Other_____

   Your position in (or relationship to) the organization in item 4 above: _____

D. If employment description A, B, C, or D has been checked in item 8 above, please verify that you hold a license in the state/province or foreign country identified in item 5 above:

   Lic. #: _____ or N/A State/Province/Foreign Country: [   ] Date initially granted: ___/___ or N/A
                                                                              month year

E. Your name: _____

F. Name and address of your current organization: _____

   Phone number: _____ E-mail: _____

I hereby certify that all information furnished herein or attached hereto is correct.

H. Your signature: _____   I. Date: _____

G. To the best of your knowledge, rate the following:

Technical Competence
☐ Excellent
☐ Satisfactory
☐ Marginal
☐ Unsatisfactory*
☐ Not qualified to answer

Professional Conduct
☐ Excellent
☐ Satisfactory
☐ Marginal
☐ Unsatisfactory*
☐ Not qualified to answer

*written explanation required

Form 123-1   9/03

IDP Training Unit Report

IDP TRAINING UNIT REPORT AND ARCHITECT EXPERIENCE % REPORT

IDP applicants must complete items I-V below in addition to items 1-10 on the Employment Verification form. Accurate start and end dates in item IV are mandatory. Report period dates may not overlap with other report periods. Do not project any training activities beyond the reporting period. Your daily supervisor must verify all activities.
ARCHITECT APPLICANTS NOT WISHING TO RECEIVE IDP TRAINING UNIT CREDIT MUST COMPLETE ITEM VI.

I. NCARB File No.: _____   II. Name: _____

III. Is/Was employed by: _____

IV. Reporting period: From ___/___/___ to ___/___/___ Hours per week (including overtime): _____
                        Month Day Year   Month Day Year

Is this your first Training Unit Report for this employment? ☐ YES ☐ NO

V. Indicate the IDP Training Units earned in each Category during the above period. One Training Unit equals eight hours of acceptable experience. Twenty (20) Training Units per month are typical for full-time employment (35 hours/week minimum). Please limit decimal notation to two places.

Refer to item 8 on the Employment Verification form for recording IDP Training Units.

Employment Descriptions A, B, C
Employment Description D
Employment Description E
Employ. Des. F or FF

	IDP Experience	Supplementary Education[2]
Category A: Design and Construction Documents[1]		
1. Programming		
2. Site and Environmental Analysis		
3. Schematic Design		
4. Engineering Systems Coordination		
5. Building Cost Analysis		
6. Code Research		
7. Design Development		
8. Construction Documents		
9. Specifications and Materials Research		
10. Document Checking and Coordination		
SUBTOTAL	0.00	0.00
Category B: Construction Contract Administration[1]		
11. Bidding and Contract Negotiation		
12. Construction Phase—Office		
13. Construction Phase—Observation		
SUBTOTAL	0.00	0.00
Category C: Management		
14. Project Management		
15. Office Management		
SUBTOTAL	0.00	0.00
Category D: Related Activities *(Please describe each activity listed in 17-20 in Diary.)*		
16. Professional and Community Service		
17. _____ ▾		
18. _____ ▾		
19. _____ ▾		
20. _____ ▾		
SUBTOTAL	0.00	0.00
TOTAL	0.00	0.00

Your AIA transcript or list of AIA Supplementary Education Handbook activities must be attached.

VI. ARCHITECTS
Indicate % of total experience in each area

Must be completed by architects NOT wishing to receive IDP Training Units.

TOTAL 0.00%

DIARY
Please list any changes of employment status, supplementary education activities, etc.
_____
_____
_____
_____
_____
_____

MENTOR
For all employment after July 1, 2000, the IDP Mentor MUST sign and date this form where indicated to acknowledge that he or she has met with you to review training progress. The IDP Mentor does not verify IDP Training Units. Your daily supervisor may serve as your Mentor.

VII. IDP Mentor signature (for interns only):
_____

VIII. Date: _____

Note 1: If employed in Experience Description D (item 8), Training Units for any activity in Category A must be recorded in Category D. If employed in Experience Description E (item 8), Training Units for any activity in Categories A and B must be recorded in Category D.
Note 2: List any supplementary education in Diary. To receive credit for programs other than AIA Supplementary Education Handbook activities, an official AIA/CES transcript must accompany this report. Refer to most current IDP Guidelines for information regarding acceptable supplementary education activities.

Form 123-2   9/03

IDP Periodic Assessment Report

Yong Sun Lee/ 100376   ***Last Reporting Period: 2/14/2004 to 5/30/2004**

This IDP Periodic Assessment Report displays your activity as of the latest Employment Verification/IDP Training Unit Report that has been evaluated by NCARB. If you notice an error in this report, please notify Customer Service at customerservice@ncarb.org or by calling 202/879-0520.

Click here **for information regarding the schedule for submitting future Employment Verification/IDP Training Unit Reports, tips for documenting training on a daily basis, and documenting changes of employment.** Click here **to download Employment Verification/IDP Training Unit Report forms.**

Training Categories & Areas	Training Units Earned This Period*		Training Units Earned to Date		Min TU's Required	Add'l Training Units Required
A. Design & Construction Documents	Sup. Ed.	Experience	Sup. Ed.	Experience	Experience	Experience
1. Programming	0	0.93	0	0.93	10.00	9.07
2. Site & Environmental Analysis	0	2.5	0	12.08	10.00	0.00
3. Schematic Design	0	4.31	0	9.59	15.00	5.41
4. Engineering Systems Coordination	0	0	0	0	15.00	15.00
5. Building Cost Analysis	0	0	0	0	10.00	10.00
6. Code Research	0	0	0	1.19	15.00	13.81
7. Design Development	0	3.6	0	7.6	40.00	32.40
8. Construction Documents	0	0	0	34.51	135.00	100.49
9. Specifications and Materials Research	0	0	0	28	15.00	0.00
10. Document Checking & Coordination	0	1	0	1	10.00	9.00
TOTAL CATEGORY A		12.34		94.90	****350**	255.10

**This total includes the 275 minimum TU's required, plus 75 additional TU's that must be earned in any of the training areas 1-10.

B. Construction Administration	Sup. Ed.	Experience	Sup. Ed.	Experience	Experience	Experience
11. Bidding & Contract Negotiation	0	0	0	0	10.00	10.00
12. Construction Phase - Office	0	0	0	1	15.00	14.00
13. Construction Phase - Observation	0	0	0	0.5	15.00	14.50
TOTAL CATEGORY B		0.00		1.50	****70**	38.50

**This total includes the 40 minimum TU's required, plus 30 additional TU's that must be earned in any of the training areas 11-13.

C. Management	Sup. Ed.	Experience	Sup. Ed.	Experience	Experience	Experience
14. Project Management	0	0	0	0	15.00	15.00
15. Office Management	0	29.6	0	491.21	10.00	0.00
TOTAL CATEGORY C		29.60		491.21	****35**	15.00

**This total includes the 25 minimum TU's required, plus 10 additional TU's that must be earned in either of the training areas 14 or 15.

D. Related Activities	Sup. Ed.	Experience	Sup. Ed.	Experience	Experience	Experience
16. Prof. and Community Service	0	0	0	10	10.00	0.00
TOTAL CATEGORY D		0.00		10.00	**10**	0.00
GRAND TOTAL		41.94		597.61	***700**	

**This total includes the 465 minimum TU's required in training categories A, B, C, and D. The additional 235 TU's must be earned in any of the listed categories. For detailed descriptions of the IDP training categories and recognized supplementary education activities, see IDP Guidelines.

TU = IDP Training Unit
Sup.Ed. = Supplementary Education

Courtesy of Yong Lee

Where to Get Info

As the administrator of IDP, NCARB provides information on its Web site at ncarb.org. Along with general information about IDP, you can request an IDP Information Package and download worksheets for logging hours as well as standard forms for reporting work experience and transmitting educational transcripts. You will also find answers to frequently asked questions and a timeline for the IDP process.

The IDP Guidelines booklet comes with the IDP Information Package. An hour-long read of this informative booklet will provide you with a comprehensive overview of IDP, answering most questions you may initially have. A small percentage of the questions specific to an individual's unique situations (i.e., foreign study or work experience, deceased employers, construction experiences, etc.) can be answered by your state IDP coordinator. The state coordinator is a volunteer appointed by a state AIA component to be an advocate for interns during the IDP process; state coordinators can offer insight and help to demystify the IDP Guidelines. (More information about IDP coordinators can be found later in this chapter under the section "Who Is involved?") While they can also help you become familiar with your state registration requirements, remember that they are *not* representatives of the state board and, therefore, should not be your sole resource as you prepare for licensure. If you have specific questions regarding conformance to your state requirements or if you have a unique situation (i.e., foreign education or work experience), you should contact your state registration board. A list of state registrations boards is available at ncarb.org/stateboards.

Who Is Affected?

As of press time, Arizona, Guam, Virgin Islands, and the Northern Mariana Islands are the only U.S. jurisdictions that have not adopted IDP as a requirement for licensure. Therefore, nearly all future graduates of architectural programs will need to satisfy the IDP training requirements.

When to Sign Up

Wait until graduation or the start of your first architectural internship to register, since the application fee covers the first three years of participation. (Note: You may want to consider tracking the hours you worked prior to graduation. See comments under the Documentation section on pages 77–79.)

As a rule, the IDP Guidelines indicate that no training units may be earned prior to satisfactory completion of:

- Three years in an NAAB- or CACB-accredited professional degree program
- The third year of a four-year preprofessional degree program in architecture accepted for direct entry to an NAAB- or CACB-accredited professional degree program
- One year in an NAAB- or CACB-accredited Master of Architecture degree program for interns with undergraduate degrees in another discipline
- Ninety-six semester credit hours as evaluated by the NAAB in accordance with NCARB's education requirement, of which no more than 60 hours can be in the general education subject area

However, not all states have adopted NCARB's education and training standards, so it is possible in some states to begin recording IDP hours prior to these educational milestones. Check with your state registration board for your specific education requirements and talk with your state IDP coordinator about how to document your state's provisions on your application form (otherwise NCARB may inform you that you are not eligible to start IDP).

If you have graduated and begun your professional career, you should sign up immediately in order to initiate the process and begin tracking your time. As a former state IDP coordinator, I often heard interns proclaim, "I'll send in my application when I've compiled all my previous time cards." My response was always, "Don't wait until you have everything in order. Send in your application right away." The initial application is straightforward and does not require a tally of training units. After your application is processed, NCARB will send you several forms so you can obtain detailed work history information from your former employers. The time delay between sending in application and receipt of forms can be several weeks, which should provide ample time to collect the necessary time sheets and personal employment files. Getting the ball rolling by sending in the actual application seems to be the largest mental hurdle for the interns I have advised.

Costs

The dollar amounts in this section are correct as of press time. They are provided for illustrative purposes only. Current fees can be found at the NCARB Web site.

The initial IDP application fee is $285 and covers three years. (After the initial three years, you will have to pay an annual maintenance fee of $50.) Students and recent graduates (within six months of graduation) have the option of paying $100 up front and deferring the remainder of the application fee until their records are ready to be transmitted. However, those individuals run the risk of an application fee increase with the balance due and, thus, higher costs than paying the total up front. You should also ask your employers if they will help pay for IDP application fees.

If you've procrastinated signing up for IDP (as many do) and decide to record all of your training units at once, you will need to pay an additional fee of $400. If your record is completed within a year of application, the application will be viewed as late and will be assessed the fee in addition to the $285 application fee.

Documentation

How to Record Hours

While there are many ways to log your hours, take it from someone who did it the most laborious, time-consuming way possible and *log your time as you go.*

A workbook can be downloaded from the NCARB Web site that functions as a daily IDP time sheet. It allows interns to track their daily progress against the overall requirements.

Tallying IDP Hours

As an intern, I assumed that my weekly office time cards would suffice to re-create my work history for IDP documentation. *Wrong!* After two years of working full time, I decided to apply for IDP and compile my records for five years' worth of summer internships and professional experience. I quickly realized that the five standard phases of architectural service listed on typical office time sheets could not be adequately translated into the 16 IDP training areas. Since I didn't have a computer at home, I hand-tallied my old time sheets, laying them out on the floor in a semicircle around me. After hours of sorting and tallying, I found that I had 90 training units in Construction Observation and Office Management (thanks to two different summer jobs), over 330 training units under Related Activities (teaching CAD and other software programs), and over 400 training units in Programming, Site Analysis, Schematic Design (SD), and Design Development (DD). There were scattered training units in the remaining areas, but I needed a lot of hours in many categories. While I knew that I had spent time coordinating with in-house engineers and researching materials and codes, I had no way of documenting those hours, since my time sheets simply indicated the project phase. Fortunately, I had kept my past desk calendars, where I had recorded some of my daily tasks. Another laborious effort involved the reallocation of some SD and DD training units to other categories. I wasted an entire weekend doing work that would have taken minimal effort had I worked on it daily. Now that I know there are tools available, my advice is to begin using them at the start of your first internship and save yourself a lot of wasted time in the future.

Photo by Grace Kim, AIA, 2005

IDP Training Unit Workbook

Name: Amanda Architect
Employer: Studio X Architects

Training Unit Log

Week Seven 10/24/04–10/30/04

DESIGN & CONSTRUCTION DOCUMENTS	Sun	Mon	Tues	Wed	Thurs	Fri	Sat	Total Hours for Week	Units for Week	Total Units in Workbook
Programming		5.00	1.00					6.00	0.75	2.00
Site and Environmental Analysis		3.00	5.00	1.00				9.00	1.13	2.38
Schematic Design				5.50	7.50	5.00		18.00	2.25	4.63
Engineering Systems Coordination								0.00	0.00	2.25
Building Cost Analysis								0.00	0.00	1.25
Code Research			2.50	1.00		1.00		4.50	0.56	1.95
Design Development								0.00	0.00	1.25
Construction Documents								0.00	0.00	1.28
Specifications and Materials Research								0.00	0.00	1.25
Document Checking and Coordination								0.00	0.00	1.25
								37.50	**4.69**	**19.48**
CONSTRUCTION ADMINISTRATION										
Bidding and Contract Negotiation								0.00	0.00	0.00
Construction Phase—Office								0.00	0.00	0.00
Construction Phase—Observation								0.00	0.00	0.00
								0.00	**0.00**	**0.00**
MANAGEMENT										
Project Management								0.00	0.00	0.00
Office Management		0.50						0.50	0.06	0.06
								0.50	**0.06**	**0.06**
RELATED ACTIVITIES										
Professional and Community Service							3.00	3.00	0.38	0.38
Select								0.00	0.00	0.00
Select								0.00	0.00	0.00
Select								0.00	0.00	0.00
Other/Please Specify								0.00	0.00	0.00
								3.00	**0.38**	**0.38**
Hours Logged Per Day	0.00	8.50	8.50	7.50	7.50	6.00	3.00	**41.00**	**5.13**	**19.92**

Week Eight 10/31/04–11/06/04

DESIGN & CONSTRUCTION DOCUMENTS	Sun	Mon	Tues	Wed	Thurs	Fri	Sat	Total Hours for Week	Units for Week	Total Units in Workbook
Programming								0.00	0.00	2.00
Site and Environmental Analysis			1.00					1.00	0.13	2.50
Schematic Design		7.00	10.00	11.75	4.50			33.25	4.16	8.78
Engineering Systems Coordination			2.00					2.00	0.25	2.50
Building Cost Analysis								0.00	0.00	1.25
Code Research								0.00	0.00	1.95
Design Development								0.00	0.00	1.25
Construction Documents								0.00	0.00	1.28
Specifications and Materials Research						8.00		8.00	1.00	2.25
Document Checking and Coordination								0.00	0.00	1.25
								44.25	**5.53**	**25.02**
CONSTRUCTION ADMINISTRATION										
Bidding and Contract Negotiation								0.00	0.00	0.00
Construction Phase—Office								0.00	0.00	0.00
Construction Phase—Observation								0.00	0.00	0.00
								0.00	**0.00**	**0.00**
MANAGEMENT										
Project Management								0.00	0.00	0.00
Office Management		0.50			0.50			1.00	0.13	0.19
								1.00	**0.13**	**0.19**
RELATED ACTIVITIES										
Professional and Community Service								0.00	0.00	0.38
Select								0.00	0.00	0.00
Select								0.00	0.00	0.00
Select								0.00	0.00	0.00
Other/Please Specify								0.00	0.00	0.00
								0.00	**0.00**	**0.38**
Hours Logged Per Day	0.00	7.50	13.00	11.75	5.00	8.00	0.00	**45.25**	**5.66**	**25.58**

IDP Training Unit Workbook Summary

IDP Training Unit Workbook Summary

For the Report Period Beginning: 9/12/04   **Ending**
Name: Amanda Architect
Employer Name: Studio X Architects

	TOTALS				
	Units to Be Reported	Previous Unit Total	Current Unit Balance	Required Minimum	Add'l Units Required
A. DESIGN & CONSTRUCTION DOCUMENTS					
Programming	2.00		2.00	**10.00**	8.00
Site and Environmental Analysis	2.50		2.50	**10.00**	7.50
Schematic Design	8.78		8.78	**15.00**	6.22
Engineering Systems Coordination	2.50		2.50	**15.00**	12.50
Building Cost Analysis	1.25		1.25	**10.00**	8.75
Code Research	1.95		1.95	**15.00**	13.05
Design Development	1.25	57.10	58.35	**40.00**	-18.35
Construction Documents	1.28	89.30	90.58	**135.00**	44.42
Specifications and Materials Research	2.25		2.25	**15.00**	12.75
Document Checking and Coordination	1.25		1.25	**10.00**	8.75
Total Category A	**25.02**	**146.40**	**171.42**	**350.00***	**178.58**
B. CONSTRUCTION ADMINISTRATION					
Bidding and Contract Negotiation	0.00		0.00	**10.00**	10.00
Construction Phase—Office	0.00		0.00	**15.00**	15.00
Construction Phase—Observation	0.00		0.00	**15.00**	15.00
Total Category B	**0.00**	**0.00**	**0.00**	**70.00***	**70.00**
C. MANAGEMENT					
Project Management	0.00		0.00	**15.00**	15.00
Office Management	0.19	1.28	1.47	**10.00**	8.53
Total Category C	**0.19**	**1.28**	**1.47**	**35.00***	**33.53**
D. RELATED ACTIVITIES					
Professional and Community Service	0.38		0.38	**10.00**	9.63
Select	0.00		0.00	**0.00**	
Select	0.00		0.00	**0.00**	
Select	0.00		0.00	**0.00**	
Other/Please Specify	0.00		0.00	**0.00**	
Total Category D	**0.38**	**0.00**	**0.38**	**10.00**	**9.63**
Total Units Earned	**25.58**	**147.68**	**173.26**	**700.00****	**526.74**

* These totals include the minimum training units required, plus additional training units that must be earned in any of the training areas in this category.

**This total includes the 465 minimum training units required in training Categories A, B, C, and D. The additional 235 training units must be earned in any of the listed categories.

Instructions and Notes

1) Enter the ending date for this report period from the last weekly Training Unit Log completed. Beginning date is from Week One of your Training Unit Log.
2) To include previously reported training units in your Current Unit Balance, enter them in the Previous Unit Total column in Workbook 1. For workbooks 2–10, these units will automatically be included in your cumulative totals.
3) Write this report period's training units from the yellow Units to Be Reported column onto your NCARB IDP Training Unit Report (form 123-2).
4) Complete the Employment Verification portion of the NCARB Form 123 and forward it to your supervisor for verification and signature.

NCARB'S DURATION REQUIREMENT: To receive training credit, you must work at least 35 hours per week for a minimum period of 10 consecutive weeks, or at least 20 hours per week for a minimum period of 6 consecutive months.

Do not submit this form to NCARB.
Send only the NCARB Employment Verification/IDP Training Unit Report.
Do not submit reports for overlapping time periods.

Making Your Categories Count

Before you start recording your IDP hours (or worse, tallying your time sheets), review the descriptions of the 16 training categories in the appendix of the IDP Guidelines. Carefully consider the types of activities that could count toward fulfilling the training areas. While most tasks can easily fall under the general headings of Schematic Design, Design Development, or Construction Documents, take care to distinguish specific tasks. The time spent coordinating structural drawings during Design Development or meetings with your mechanical engineer during Construction Documents can be logged under Engineering Coordination. A few hours here and there can add up when tallied individually, but the training units can be difficult to obtain all at once. Similarly, the two hours you spent reviewing exiting requirements for the permit drawings would be best logged under Code Research rather than Design Development. You can see how quickly we lump hours into the "obvious" training areas at the expense of contributing to the categories that may be more difficult to complete.

Making the Most of Your Experience

For those of you who work in small firms, hours spent performing "administrative" tasks such as filing or archiving projects shouldn't be discounted as "nonarchitectural," because they actually count toward Office Management. The time spent organizing a product library (a rite of passage for many interns) can count toward Specifications and Materials Research. Don't view organizing the product library as a mundane or menial task; take this opportunity to learn the Construction Specifications Institute (CSI) specification divisions.

When to Start Documenting Hours

I can't stress this enough: *log your time as you go.* If you are working a summer internship and have not yet signed up for IDP, download the training report, complete it, and ask your employer to sign it at the end of the summer. This will simplify your application process in the future. You can return a copy of it to your employer with NCARB's Employment Verification Form when the appropriate time comes to apply for IDP. It is very difficult for firms to confirm employment records more than a couple of years old if they archive their accounting records each year. In addition, your supervisor may no longer be with the firm, or in the worst case, you may not be able to locate your supervisor at all. A signed training report will go a long way toward establishing your IDP record.

The following intern contribution reflects the tendency toward procrastination that most interns can relate to when it comes to starting a council record for IDP.

Even if you are in your first professional job after school, you may have decided to delay applying for IDP. Despite the delay, you will want to track your hours and complete training reports as you switch jobs. It will be much easier to establish an IDP record if you have maintained accurate files. It will also be simpler to have former employers verify employment history if you provide them with a summary of hours that they previously signed.

Like most new interns, I planned to start my NCARB record immediately upon graduation and stay current in logging my hours. In the office, my coworkers inundated me with comments like "Don't do what I did—don't procrastinate." Three months passed; six months came and went; and suddenly I realized that I had been out of school a year and had yet to submit my transcript. When I finally sat down to look over the IDP categories, I was surprised to see I had banked many hours in nearly every category.

I believe that small firms have a decided advantage in producing well-rounded interns. When my classmates and I were searching for employment after graduation, we discovered a sad truth: There are architecture job positions that define a specific task to be performed every day with no opportunity for change. In those firms, it seemed that completing IDP would be impossible. At my firm, intern involvement ranges from collaboration on larger projects to greater roles, with supervision by a principal, in smaller projects. Shortly after I started, I was told that one of the ways my firm encourages growth is by giving you more than you think you are ready for. I believe that this "baptism by fire" ideology works as long as interns are surrounded by people willing and ready to serve as resources.

My biggest challenge in IDP was simply getting started. I was intimidated by IDP for many of the same reasons I'm intimidated and procrastinate with rebates. Both contain fine print necessary to complete the process. IDP seems to have its own vernacular made up of acronyms and terms like training units. Time sheets used in my office have to be translated, since the training categories of IDP don't correlate with the phase and task designations used at my firm. And hours have to be converted into training units.

Once the process is set into motion, certain areas are easier to obtain credit in than others. Construction Documents seems to be the easiest category in which to log hours, even though it has the largest requirement. The category in which I have the most difficulty obtaining is Specifications and Materials Research. Because of the structure of my office, it is difficult to log hours working with

> specifications, but my solution is simple: More of my time will be devoted to the materials research portion of that category, which can be more easily fulfilled working with the product library and researching window sizes or flooring.

Nicole Hoppenworth
Intern, InVision
Iowa State University, Bachelor of Architecture 2004

Transmitting Your Records to Your State Board

Many interns make the mistake of sending in the last training report and waiting. They do not realize that they must notify NCARB in writing to transmit their records to the state board. A standard letter can be downloaded from the NCARB Web site. You can submit that at any time (i.e., immediately upon establishing your IDP record) to ensure that you don't forget. However, note that this letter informs NCARB of the state to which you would like your records sent. If you plan to move around during your internship period, you should wait until you are nearly done with your training units before sending this letter. This will ensure that your records are transmitted to the proper jurisdiction. After the first transmittal to a state registration board, transmittals to additional states will cost $270 each.

Who Is Involved?

While IDP is ultimately the responsibility of the intern, successful completion requires the participation of three additional parties: the firm, a supervisor, and a mentor.

The Firm

While the level of the firm's involvement can vary, many employers realize that interns are likely to be more committed to their work and willing to stay longer if a firm supports IDP than if it doesn't. Some firms support their staff by helping pay IDP costs; others offer special lunchtime programs to help interns obtain exposure to areas that may be difficult to fulfill. Offices may offer firm-wide mentoring programs or individual mentor matching for IDP. Given the resources available, larger firms generally offer a greater level of support. Whether large or small, firms that do not support interns in the IDP process will likely realize higher turnover as interns reach a "ceiling" of attainable experience and go elsewhere to complete their training.

In 2004, two competing Iowa firms, InVision and FEH, were named IDP Firm of the Year. They took unprecedented measures to help their interns navigate through difficult IDP training areas by opening their doors and sharing resources with each other, thereby offering high-quality IDP experiences to interns in both firms. The following account was written by an intern who helped coordinate cooperation between the firms.

I was fortunate to have mentors within my firm who valued my growth in the profession and looked at nontraditional ways to guide me through the process. InVision Architecture encourages interns to do more than the minimum required to get their IDP units and helps us realize our potential as future leaders in the community by encouraging us to sit on local boards, as well as financially sponsoring our involvement in local leadership programs. Our community involvement helps educate the public about the roles of architects and the impact their designs may have on the community. It also gives interns an opportunity to learn about the "politics" of architecture and, most important, teaches interns to voice their opinions on the future of their community.

One very successful InVision initiative encourages the entire staff to act as mentors to one another. The entire firm is educated about IDP and the process an intern must complete before sitting for the ARE. From principals to receptionists, everyone can help interns look for ways to obtain their required units. Because most interns seem to have trouble completing their site observation requirements, InVision distributes site visit schedules and punch lists to the interns so that they can talk with the principals and be included in the scheduled site visits. Interns do not simply join the architect on the visit but are expected to take notes and photographs and help write the field report. Interns have daily contact with the principals, which makes it easy to ask questions and to learn by observing how principals handle everyday situations. Principals know each intern's personal goals for completing IDP and the timelines they have set for themselves as they work toward becoming licensed. Everyone works together to help interns fulfill their requirements, because they value the benefits the process creates for the entire firm.

InVision has also made IDP an integral part of the employment package. When they fill out W-4 and insurance forms, interns receive an NCARB spreadsheet to help them record their hours. At each of the four office locations, a designated employee sits with interns, explains the IDP process, and helps them register with NCARB to establish a record. I have been fortunate enough to learn what goes on "behind the scenes" in an architectural office by being asked to sit on the human resources (HR) committee. InVision asks one intern to sit on the HR committee to help give interns a voice in the firm and help them better understand the decisions that are made. The intern on the committee can let the firm know what measures are working to help interns obtain the required units, as well suggest areas for improvement.

Although InVision has provided many opportunities to accumulate the required IDP units, it has been helpful to talk with interns in other firms to learn about ways to satisfy requirements more quickly. Working in a small firm and being the only intern architect in our Sioux City office, I sought out an intern in a competing firm to discuss our internship experiences and progress with IDP. Our discussions quickly evolved into researching ways to improve and accelerate our IDP experience.

Reading the IDP Guidelines, she realized it was possible to obtain 149.5 training units by completing exercises in the AIA Supplementary Education Handbook (now called the Emerging Professionals Companion). We showed this information to our principals and, with their encouragement, began contacting other local firms to invite their interns to join us as we worked through the book. Interns at two other firms were interested, creating a four-firm collaboration. The four firms varied in size and structure and provided us with a broader range of shared experiences and knowledge. This expanded the lines of communication between interns and principals in each office, as well as introduced new lines of communication between the firms.

Each week we worked through the handbook and gave "reports" back to our principals, spurring each firm to continue the process and try to exceed the assistance offered by a competing firm. This healthy competition proved most beneficial to the interns, because principals and interns were jointly proactive in their efforts to integrate the IDP into the firm structure.

Competing requires recognizing where you fall short. Each firm had to take a hard look at what it was doing for its interns. Employers talked to interns to see what wasn't working and how training could be improved. Interns learned not to be afraid of failure but to instead embrace the challenge to try new things. I think it is important for every firm to regularly revisit its internship program, determine what isn't working, examine what opportunities other firms are offering their interns, and decide how the firm can be competitive in that market. All of the interns involved in the four-firm collaboration found that the ability to access the resources and mentors of all firms made their IDP experience more complete.

The principals' commitment to intern development was evident in their willingness to spend time with the interns on a weekly basis. They demonstrated their trust in us by sharing information they knew we would discuss with the interns of competing firms. It was the nontraditional mentoring and the ability of the firms to collectively act as mentors to many interns in the community that provided me with the most valuable lessons. This dedication to IDP demonstrated that competing firms could set aside self-interest and invest in the greater good of the profession.

Lisa Burkholder, Assoc. AIA
Intern Architect, InVision Architecture
Iowa State University, Bachelor of Architecture 2002

IDP Firm of the Year

The IDP Outstanding Firm Award is awarded annually to an architecture firm that demonstrates exemplary commitment to the professional development of architectural interns. Since 1991, this national award has recognized firms that provide comprehensive training opportunities, continuing education programs, and a strong commitment to IDP.

2004
- InVision, Waterloo, IA
- FEH Associates, Des Moines, IA

2003
- James, Harwick + Partners, Dallas, TX

2002
- Payette Associates, Boston, MA

2001
- Gorman Richardson Architects, Inc., Hopkinton, MA

2000
- No awards were presented.

1999
- NBBJ, Columbus, OH

1998
- Everton Oglesby Askew, Nashville, TN
- Loebl Schlossman & Hackl/Hague Richards, Chicago, IL

1997
- Giattina Fisher Aycock Architects, Birmingham, AL

1996
- Collins Rimer & Gordon, Cleveland, OH
- Schmidt Associates, Inc., Indianapolis, IN
- Watkins Hamilton Ross Architects, Bellaire, TX

1995
- BSW International, Tulsa, OK
- Einhorn Yaffee Prescott, Washington, DC
- Naval Facilities Engineering Command, Alexandria, VA

1994
- Albert Kahn Associates, Detroit, MI
- Cynthia Easton, Sacramento, CA
- Johnson, Laffen, Meland, Grand Forks, ND
- Klipp Colussy Jenks DuBois, Denver, CO

1993
- Jeffrey S. Conrad, Architect, Oxnard, CA
- Earl Swensson Associates, Nashville, TN
- Western Michigan University, Kalamazoo, MI

1992
- HKS Architects, Dallas, TX
- Luey Architects, Tigard, OR

1991
- Askew Nixon Ferguson, Memphis, TN
- Clark Nexsen Owen Barberi Gibson, Norfolk, VA
- Gilley-Hinkel Architects, Bristol, CT
- Kekst Architecture, Cleveland, OH
- RTKL, Baltimore, MD

Photo by Bethany Bright, 2004

Your Supervisor

Your supervisor is the person who oversees your day-to-day activities.

 Your supervisor must be a licensed architect in the state in which you are working.

Difficulties may arise if you work for an out-of-town firm that opens a local office for a specific project. Be wary if your office is mostly younger, nonlicensed staff, with a principal that comes in once a week from the "head office" in another state. If this principal is not licensed in the local jurisdiction and there are no other registered architects in the local office to verify the hours, you may not be able to receive credit for your experience.

In large firms, it is common to have a supervisor who is not a licensed professional. However, there should be a licensed principal in the office overseeing your supervisor. If your supervisor periodically communicates to the principal your roles and responsibilities on a project, it is acceptable to have the principal sign as your supervisor.

 If licensure is ultimately your goal, you should ask during your interview whether your supervisor will be a licensed architect.

If you are told "someone will take care" of your forms and sign off when needed, you should proceed with caution—this firm may not be interested in your career development, but rather getting around the bureaucracy of the IDP paperwork.

If you change projects within the office prior to your quarterly training report, you should document that period of time on one training report and start a new one for the next project. This approach will make it simplest for you and your supervisors to verify the training units you report for a given period.

Your Mentor

While your supervisor is assigned to you based on your in-office project assignment, your mentor is someone you select. Your mentor will provide professional guidance throughout your career. Ideally, your mentor will serve in that capacity long after you've completed IDP and will be able to advise you on a variety of professional issues.

While you may have numerous supervisors throughout your IDP period, hopefully you will have just one "official" mentor. Your IDP mentor can be someone within your office or even the same individual as your supervisor. However, there are many reasons to select a mentor outside your firm.

A mentor outside the firm can provide advice without the constraints of office politics. He or she can provide a fresh perspective and additional suggestions for obtaining experience in training areas that have been difficult for you to achieve. The following account illustrates how one intern used his mentor as a sounding board before requesting experience in a category that is often considered difficult to fulfill.

> *I found that both my mentor and my supervisor were good allies in my effort to gain necessary experience. I met with my mentor regularly to discuss the projects I was working on, and he always asked insightful questions to verify that I was learning. On one occasion, I told him that I had redlined plans to integrate the code notes. He suggested that I learn how to do the code review, instead of just producing redlines.*
>
> *Armed with this challenge, I was able to talk to my supervisor and point out that my IDP requirements included time spent conducting code research. She immediately recognized an opportunity for me to perform the code review for an upcoming project. I was able to work closely with my supervisor and the project manager on this task. Given the project's schedule, allowing the additional time it took me to complete the review (compared to someone with experience) would not have been feasible if we had not planned for it well in advance. Had my mentor not suggested it, my supervisor would not have thought to set aside the time. I was very fortunate to have good mentors both inside and outside the office to continually assist me in this way.*
>
> *Although it took me longer to complete the task, the project fee was not affected because of my lower billing rate. I believe that my further understanding of how the building code affected the project made me more effective later in the project, when I was made responsible for construction administration.*
>
> **Geoff Anderson, AIA, LEED® AP**
> Associate Principal, The ORB Organization
> University of Washington, Master of Architecture 1998

Supervisors are generally willing to support an intern's development; however, interns can be proactive by clearly defining how experience might be obtained. If you rely on the supervisor or your firm to look out for your interests, you are waiting for someone else to solve your problems. By taking the initiative and suggesting to your supervisor specific tasks in which you might assist, you can help your supervisor be part of the solution. The following illustration demonstrates the conflict that could occur if your mentor is also your supervisor.

Imagine that you are an intern at a large firm that primarily works with corporate clients overseas. After two years, you realize that you have only worked on competitions and schematic design packages. In considering the work of your studio, you do not see any future opportunities to produce construction documents, manage projects, or participate in contract bidding. You indicate to your mentor concerns about whether you will satisfy your IDP requirements within the team and ask to be reassigned to another project team that is entering into the Construction Documents phase. Your mentor happens to be your supervisor and is understanding and empathizes with your situation. However, knowing your team has a deadline coming up, he tells you that he will talk to the other project manager after this deadline. When you inquire with the mentor/supervisor several weeks after the deadline, it is clear that he has not made any inquiries. You are extremely frustrated by your mentor and do not understand why he is not helping you with this situation.

Consider the situation from the supervisor's perspective. As your supervisor, he values your skills and is concerned about the performance of his project. If you are competent and a hard worker, it is not in the supervisor's interest to recommend that you be transferred off his team. Additionally, your request to move to another team might signal to others that his team is not a desirable one.

Even working on different teams within the same firm as your mentor can be a disadvantage. Here is an example illustrating why.

You are preparing a permit set, and the principal responsible for signing the drawings is unexpectedly sick that day. As the drawings are being printed and collated, your project manager is getting ready to leave for a meeting. When she sees that the drawings are not ready, she asks you to forge the principal's name over the stamp before sending them out for prints. The permit intake is first thing in the morning, and she will not be back before the end of the day.

You feel that this is very unethical and ask your mentor within the office what you should do. He assures you that "this is okay" and that "the principal never reviews the drawings anyway—she just signs them." Obviously, this unethical practice is accepted within the firm and is even "standard practice." He urges you to just sign them and make sure the prints are sent out because the permit review time is extremely long and the client is eager to start construction as soon as possible.

If you had a mentor outside the firm, a quick call would have told you that your uncertainty was well grounded, as this defies state regulations about who can stamp drawings. An outside mentor could have provided you with an objective suggestion as to how you should address the situation.

While these may be extreme examples, they illustrate the point that business practices, both good and bad, can become entrenched in the culture of a firm and difficult to see from within. A mentor outside the firm is free from the institutional and political cloud that might impair the perception of someone working within the firm.

While you will find many mentors to guide you in various aspects of your career development, having the same mentor throughout the IDP process will ensure that you get consistent feedback that acknowledges previous concerns. For suggestions on how to select a mentor, refer to Chapter 9.

IDP Coordinators

Each state is supposed to have at least one IDP state coordinator, and likewise each school of architecture is supposed to have one IDP educator coordinator. In theory, these AIA-appointed volunteers are intended to be liaisons between the IDP and interns. The educator coordinator is responsible for making sure that students are aware of IDP and know how it impacts their path toward licensure. They also assist student interns with questions they may have about IDP. State coordinators assist interns who have graduated and have begun their professional careers.

In reality, a few of these positions are occasionally vacant or filled by appointees who are not interested in or knowledgeable about IDP. Fortunately, in many cases, the individuals assigned to the position are outstanding advocates for interns and have a firm understanding of IDP and the issues facing interns. For example, interns in Alabama benefit from several state coordinators and educator coordinators working in concert to ensure an informed transition from academia to practice. Upon graduation in Alabama, interns receive a letter from a state coordinator welcoming them to the profession and informing them how to enroll in IDP.

State coordinators may hold informational sessions, answer questions about how to complete the forms, and help interns locate mentors outside their firms. While they can advise an individual on their unique circumstances, state coordinators do not have authority to make any decisions or interpretations on the behalf of the state registration board. However, they may have helped other interns who have had experiences similar to yours and can offer their knowledge of precedents. A state coordinator is an invaluable resource for interns as they initiate and conclude the IDP process. It is interesting to note that while IDP is an NCARB-administered program, the state coodinators and educator coordinators are appointed and supported by the AIA. A current list of state and educator coordinators can be found on the AIA Web site at www.aia.org/idp_coordroster.

It is important to remember that the state coordinators are all volunteers. Most of them have day jobs as architects and educators, and they have agreed to serve as coordinators with no compensation from the AIA or NCARB. They are generally compassionate individuals with a firm commitment to intern development, and you should always remember to be respectful of their time and the requests that you make of them.

Keep Others Informed of Your IDP Activity

If your project managers and supervisors don't know you are enrolled in IDP, it is impossible for them to help you gain the experiences necessary to fulfill all of the training areas.

Inform the person responsible for staffing projects of the training areas in which you are deficient. Do this on a monthly or quarterly basis to ensure you are considered for new projects as they arise and your time is available.

Your firm and its leaders are not mind readers—they can't help you if they don't know you need help.

If you lack experience in Specifications and Materials Research and another team is ready to compile a project manual, the informed project manager can have you temporarily assigned to that project in order to help out the team and your training. Similarly, if you need to obtain training units for the in-field portion of construction observation, an informed project architect could suggest that you attend the weekly construction meetings and take minutes while she leads the meetings. If they do not know that you have a need or desire to obtain experience, they will likely assign it to someone already on the team.

Difficult Training Categories

While it may be quite easy to obtain training units in Schematic Design, Design Development, and Construction Documents, depending on the size of your firm, it may be difficult to get experience in any of the other categories.

So how is a second-year intern supposed to get experience managing a project or writing a specification? The appendix of the IDP Guidelines provides suggestions for activities that would provide you exposure to various training areas. For example, some of the suggested activities for Documents Checking and Coordination are to develop a list of all project drawings and other documents including a brief description of their contents; assist in cross-checking products and materials called for in the specifications for consistency with corresponding terminology and descriptions in the construction documents; coordinate drawings prepared by others for accuracy of dimensions, notes, and indicator abbreviations; and compare consultants' drawings against architectural drawings for possible conflicts of plumbing lines, ductwork, structure, electrical fixtures, and so on. This list should be reviewed with your supervisor to see if there is a way to engage in similar activities for your project. Remember that if you offer suggestions, it is easier for a supervisor to agree or think of more-appropriate activities than if you were simply to ask them to come up with something for you to do to satisfy the category requirements.

For example, if you work at a large firm, it is not likely that you will be allowed to sit in on a client meeting in which fees are being negotiated, not even just to take notes. However, you could read the signed contract and discuss with the project manager how the fee relates to the project deliverables and schedule. (This can be a great way to learn about negotiating project fees and a way to gain the IDP experience.)

Talk with Other Interns

If you are having difficulty obtaining specific experiences in your firm, chances are others are too. Talk to them to see what they have found successful; you can all benefit from this shared knowledge. Their supervisors and mentors may have offered suggestions different from yours.

Trading Places

One of the interns I mentored bemoaned working in a large firm. "How will I ever get any experience working in CDs?" she asked, "I've become so proficient and productive doing SD drawings in the past two years, my supervisors won't give me a chance to work on CDs or CA." This is a common problem for many interns who find themselves hitting the ceiling for IDP credits after three or four years.

So if that is your situation in one studio, chances are there is another intern in another studio who has fulfilled her CD experience and would love to get a chance to design or work on SD drawings. Ask around, and find out who that person is. Go to lunch together for the next few weeks and learn the details of what the other does. Get your supervisors onboard, show them that you understand each other's roles and ask them to give you the opportunity to trade places for a project. Throughout the project, you will not only have your supervisor as a mentor, but the other intern, who can tell you the most efficient way to sketch five options in two hours for the supervisor's review, or how to cross-reference CAD files to minimize redundant drawings.

Look around and take advantage of your resources and those around you. A large firm offers many resources, but sometimes you have to be creative if you want to satisfy all your IDP requirements there.

Photo courtesy of Schemata Workshop, 2005

If, after talking to other interns, you find that there are some common holes in experience, bring these training areas to the attention of your supervisors or human resources department. Work together with them to define opportunities for interns within the office to gain exposure to these areas. Some firms have arranged for periodic job site visits during lunch to help interns obtain construction administration field experience. Some firms conduct in-house workshops on subjects such as how to process shop drawings or encourage attendance at AIA seminars on project management.

Emerging Professionals Companion

The Emerging Professionals Companion (EPC, www.epcompanion.org) is an online resource that became available in late 2004 to replace the Supplementary Education Handbook as a means for interns to obtain IDP credit. The depth and variety of exercises provided offer great opportunities to apply knowledge and learn new skills. There are 16 chapters, corresponding to the IDP training areas. Self-study exercises and reality-based scenarios are presented to accommodate a diversity of learning styles and experience levels.

Chapters 1 through 15 of the EPC are each organized into ten sections. The first section provides an overview of the chapter topic. Sections 2 through 6 are exercises and scenarios organized by experience level — beginner, intermediate, and advanced, to be completed for credit toward IDP. Sections 7 through 10 provide references for those looking for more information or additional opportunities. Chapter 16 is a comprehensive resource for emerging architects looking for opportunities in professional and community service. However, no exercises are provided and no credit can be obtained for this online chapter.

The EPC reflects current practice models and recognizes the varied paths that an architect may encounter during his or her career, and the various ways different people assimilate information. The broad range of information accessible on this Web site can be used by interns firsthand to obtain IDP credits, but it can also be a resource for in-office educators developing IDP programs as well as academic instructors teaching professional practice courses. It should be noted that IDP will only accept a total of 235 training units obtained through supplementary education activities such as the EPC exercises.

Using IDP to Your Professional Advantage

Interns listed the following as the most valuable aspects of IDP: exposure to practice (83%); professional development (70%); passing the ARE (60%); and advancing one's career (47%).

— 1999 AIA Survey on Internship

While many interns bemoan IDP as a costly bureaucratic process, it can be a highly effective performance review tool. After receiving your training report, NCARB provides a summary of your progress called the IDP Periodic Assessment Report (see the figure on page 74). This summary can be a credible validation of your request for experience in an area of practice to which you've had little exposure. For example, if you have exceeded the requirements for Construction Documents, but need Code Research or construction administration experience, it is easy to request assistance in obtaining the experience by showing your IDP Periodic Assessment Report. By providing a physical document that logs your progress against the requirements for licensure, IDP gives your employers the opportunity to help you attain your licensure goals.

At the same time, be prepared with suggestions on how you might obtain the experience you need. If you have only six months of experience, it is unlikely the firm will send you into the field alone for construction observation. However, the appendix of the IDP Guidelines offers suggestions on how your employer may help you gain this experience. It may be that you can process the shop drawings and submittals, conducting the first level of in-office review, and then review questions and concerns together with your supervisor. You might also attend the weekly construction meetings, recording and distributing the meeting minutes. Supervisors are often willing to provide the experience if they see how you can be involved without added effort or expense.

If your supervisor isn't interested in helping you satisfy the IDP requirements, you may consider discussing this with another senior member of the firm. And if your supervisor is the most senior or there is no support for completing your IDP requirements, it may be time to reconsider whether your licensure goals align with those of the firm.

Community and Professional Service

Having been taught the idea of community service and philanthropy throughout high school and college, I never thought twice about volunteering my time as I embarked upon my professional career. Thus the IDP requirement for 80 hours was not a daunting task; in fact, it was probably the first IDP category that I completed.

As a former IDP state coordinator, I was always surprised and perplexed by the frequency of questions I received related to professional and community service. "How do I satisfy these ten training units?" and "I've fulfilled all my IDP requirements except for Professional and Community Service—is there a way I can get these credits over the weekend?" were questions that I repeatedly heard. Since ten training units translates into 80 hours, it is quite impossible to complete it in a 48-hour weekend.

NCARB established this IDP category for the pure and simple reason that our communities need the contributions of architects, not only as citizens but also as stewards of our profession.

Hopefully, this introduction to community service through IDP will encourage all interns to serve as mentors to future interns, participate in architecture programs at a local grade school, or run for government office. These activities raise awareness of the value architects bring to the community, enriching the profession and our society. What better time to instill this principle than during the internship experience?

The training units needed to satisfy the Professional and Community Service requirement are not limited to architecture-related activities. Community service can include:

- Planting trees with a neighborhood group
- Reading to the blind
- Helping a senior citizen with errands or chores
- Being a Big Sister or Big Brother to a disadvantaged child
- Serving on a homeowners' association board
- Volunteering at an event raising awareness for cancer research
- Serving meals to the homeless

Architecture-related service could include:

- Being a docent for a local historical society
- Organizing an AIA committee event
- Serving on the facilities committee of a local church or arts group
- Working at a Habitat for Humanity construction site
- Designing a playground or park for a homeless shelter
- Conducting an architecture awareness program at a local school
- Serving on a Red Cross emergency disaster response team

As you might guess from the nature of the activities listed above, these tasks cannot be accomplished overnight. They should be scattered throughout the internship period so that you get into the habit of volunteering your time as you advance your career.

Does My Past Work Experience Count?

Many interns wait until they have worked a couple of years before starting to think about licensure and only then realize they must satisfy the IDP requirements. Questions inevitably arise as to whether previous work experience is eligible for retroactive credit toward the training unit requirements. The answer is generally yes (with some caveats).

All recent work experience performed under the supervision of an architect registered in your jurisdiction will count toward your training requirements. At one time, an NCARB employee suggested that "recent" meant "within the past seven years," but that determination will likely be evaluated on a case-by-case basis. Beyond that, there are numerous stipulations on the maximum number of training units you can count in the four categories. For more information on the various work settings under which you can obtain IDP training units, refer to Appendix E in the IDP Guidelines or contact your IDP state coordinator.

Foreign Experience

If you are employed with an American or Canadian firm and receive supervision from an architect registered in the United States or Canada, all of your work experience will count. This experience falls under "Training Setting A" as defined in Appendix E of the IDP Guidelines. However, if you are employed with a registered architect of another country, you are working within "Training Setting C" and can only document credit for one year of experience (or 235 training units).

Working for Contractors, Engineers, and Others

Some interns have the opportunity to work for registered engineers or landscape architects, which NCARB describes as "Training Setting D." Experience in this capacity is limited to 235 training units in categories B, C, and D.

Work experience may be obtained in other related fields, such as construction, interior design, historic preservation, and product sales. While these can be highly valuable experiences, only 117 training units can count toward the IDP requirements, and only in the areas of management and related activities (Categories C and D).

As previously stated, detailed information on the various scenarios in which you can obtain IDP training units can be found in Appendix E of the IDP Guidelines or by contacting your IDP state coordinator.

Bumps in the Road (Frequently Asked Questions about IDP)

There will inevitably be snags and unforeseen circumstances along the way toward completing the IDP. This is when your mentor can be an invaluable resource, offering suggestions and telling you how others have proceeded before you. I have been asked the following questions frequently, and they may apply to you as well.

What if I move to a new state before I complete my records?

IDP is a national program administered by NCARB that has been adopted by nearly all U.S. and Canadian jurisdictions. Therefore, as you progress through your internship period, your council records will follow you as well (as long as you keep NCARB updated as to your current address). The training reports should be completed as you move from office to office and state to state. Prior to the completion of your requirements, you will need to send a letter to NCARB indicating which state you would like your completed records to be sent to. A sample letter can be found on the NCARB Web site.

What if I can't get my employer to sign my forms?

While it should be the goal of every registered architect to mentor and help interns progress toward licensure, there are exceptions to the ethical norm. There are cases where vindictive employers have withheld signatures from interns. There are also situations in which the only registered architect at the firm has left with no forwarding address, or has passed away. While these situations are rare, they do occur. Specific scenarios like this are best submitted in writing to NCARB for individual evaluation.

Will my IDP enrollment allow me to defer my student loans? [1]

Repayment of federally insured student loans granted prior to July 1, 1993, may be deferred through participation in IDP. You should contact your lending institution for eligibility criteria and deferment forms. Most deferment forms require two certifications. Your supervisor ("program official") must certify that you are employed in an acceptable training setting, and a registration board official must certify (1) that an internship is required for architectural registration, (2) the required length of the internship period, and (3) that a baccalaureate degree is required before entering the internship program.

Questions regarding loan repayment and deferments should be directed to your lending institution or to the agency that has guaranteed your loans. The American Institute of Architects and the National Council of Architectural Registration Boards are not authorized to sign deferment forms.

Participation in a required professional internship program no longer qualifies for deferring repayment of most federally insured student loans granted after July 1, 1993, except in cases where significant economic hardship can be demonstrated.

---

[1]Source: www.ncarb.org; see IDP FAQs

Taking Matters into Your Own Hands

This posting, from Archinect.com, is from an anonymous intern who found that his firm was not supportive of his IDP or licensure objectives. He reminds us that IDP is ultimately the intern's responsibility, and there are times when you have to take your professional destiny into your own hands and create opportunities.

> As an intern, I had the toughest time getting IDP hours in the construction administration areas. Some of that could be attributed to working in a large firm with many out-of-state projects, but my opinion was that the firm cared more about my productivity in the office than my professional growth. While my employers were eager and excited to work with me on my IDP hours in the design/CD categories, they were reluctant to spend money teaching me something I hadn't yet learned. At first, I brought up these concerns with my direct supervisors, who claimed they supported IDP and wanted to help me out but made little effort to do so. Eventually, I went directly to our construction administrative staff and asked to ride along to construction meetings. They were very amenable, and I had soon completed my hours, although I also spent many overtime hours making up time on my assigned projects. This experience made me realize that nobody is going to hold your hand and complete IDP for you.
>
> That first firm I worked for wasn't very proactive with IDP. In a firm with more than 50 architects, there were very few interns. Some of the younger principals were eager to set up a proper IDP plan, but senior management wasn't very receptive, probably because of the small intern population. Unfortunately, I feel that IDP was a step in our education that, although just as necessary as obtaining a college degree, wasn't much fun.

The AIA conducted a survey of firms in preparation for the 2004 NAAB Validation Conference, which revealed that only 50 percent of firms participate at any level with IDP. Unfortunately, this statistic does not indicate that the firms were proactive in any manner other than having supervisors sign off on completed forms.

Navigating the Process Successfully

While IDP may at first seem daunting, it can be a linear process if you utilize the tools available. The NCARB Web site has a timeline that outlines the approximate duration of each of these steps. The IDP timeline can be downloaded from www.ncarb.org. The following flowchart provides a simplified overview of the IDP process and how it transitions into the ARE.

The IDP/ARE Process

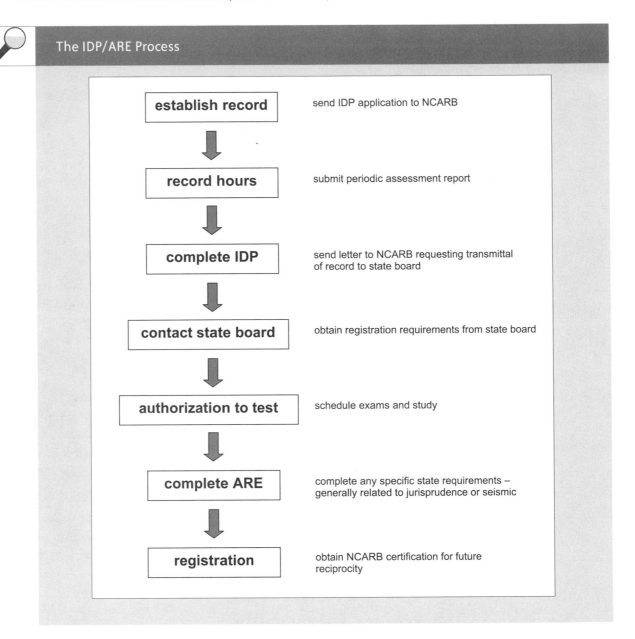

establish record	send IDP application to NCARB
record hours	submit periodic assessment report
complete IDP	send letter to NCARB requesting transmittal of record to state board
contact state board	obtain registration requirements from state board
authorization to test	schedule exams and study
complete ARE	complete any specific state requirements – generally related to jurisprudence or seismic
registration	obtain NCARB certification for future reciprocity

IDP Web Sites

www.ncarb.org — NCARB—IDP general information

www.aia.org/idp — IDP-related information notes

CHAPTER 5 | # THE ARCHITECT REGISTRATION EXAM

The Changing Culture of the Exam

The culture of the Architect Registration Exam (ARE) has changed dramatically since the mid-1990s. In the past, the exam was only offered once a year; people signed up in advance and took the exam regardless of their level of preparedness. It was quite common for people to realize a few weeks before the exam that project deadlines, family, or other distractions had prevented them from studying; but since it was only offered once a year, they would go ahead and take the exam to "see what happened."

As a result, pass rates were significantly lower than they are today. In addition, the format of the exam (all nine divisions offered over a four-day period) was more about physical and mental endurance than a test of one's knowledge of architecture. Many "war stories" have been traded about being overwhelmed when walking into the warehouse full of candidates sitting at their desks the first day of the exam, or of candidates sweating bullets when colleagues began stippling their finished building designs several hours before the end of the exam. Those individuals intimidated by any examination generally experienced a great deal of anxiety at the thought of taking the ARE for four straight days. Others found it difficult to study for nine exams at once; they would set aside a whole year to prepare, and by the time the exam rolled around, they had forgotten what they had studied nine months earlier.

A Look at the Numbers

In 2003, there were 37,011 ARE candidates but only 32,500 divisions of the ARE administered, indicating that on average, less than one ARE division was taken per candidate. For the sake of reference, between 1999 and 2002, the number of ARE candidates increased by 7,800 (52%), while the number of divisions of the ARE administered increased by 5,300 (only 21%). In 2002, the number of candidates increased 14%, while the number of divisions administered increased just 3%.

Source: Archvoices.org

Photo by Grace Kim, AIA, 2004

In 1997, NCARB abandoned the four-day, paper-and-pencil exams for a computerized exam. With this change, candidates had more control of their destinies, with the possibility of taking the nine exam sections one at a time. This has allowed candidates to schedule the exams at a rate convenient to their project deadlines and appropriate to their study habits; for some that means taking one every two weeks, and for others it is one every other month. In addition, candidates can reschedule exams (for a fee.) This allows individuals to avoid taking an exam for which they are ill prepared. Consequently, the pass rates for the ARE have increased dramatically since the switch to computerized examinations.

ARE Basics

The Architect Registration Exam was established by NCARB to assess whether a candidate has the skills and knowledge required to provide the varied services of an architect. However, given the breadth of our profession today, the ARE is not all-encompassing. NCARB maintains that the ARE is intended to protect the health, safety, and welfare of the public, and it does so by establishing minimum competencies for the profession.

The ARE has nine divisions—six multiple choice and three graphic. The multiple-choice divisions are Pre-design, General Structures, Lateral Forces, Mechanical & Electrical Systems, Building Design/Materials & Methods, and Construction Documents & Services. The graphic divisions are Site Planning, Building Planning, and Building Technology. Detailed information about the ARE can be obtained by downloading the ARE Guidelines from www.ncarb.org.

The ARE is computerized and can be taken Monday through Saturday. At press time, the exams are administered by Prometric[2], an independent company that operates computerized testing centers throughout North America. A list of those nearest you can be found on the Prometric Web site (www.prometric.com).

As the only examination adopted by NCARB and the Committee of Canadian Architectural Councils (CCAC), the ARE is exactly the same across the United States and Canada. As with IDP, the standards are universal between the two countries, and you can take the examinations wherever you are. However, you must first be granted authorization by the state or provincial registration board from which you seek licensure, which can take anywhere from a couple of weeks to a couple of months. While it doesn't matter in which state you initially obtain registration, you must ultimately be registered in the state in which you practice architecture. The title of architect is a legal acknowledgement by each state signifying that you have satisfied the requirements for licensure. This title is not automatically recognized across state boundaries.

Note: The terms *registration* and *licensure* are synonymous in the context of architectural registration.

---

[2] Prometric operates and maintains test centers that administer various computer-based examination programs. There are more then 350 Prometric test centers, with over 4,000 ARE workstations in the United States, its territories, and Canada available to ARE candidates.

Survey Results on Licensure

- Regardless of career plans, 94% of respondents indicated an intention to get registered.

- 63% of respondents who completed all nine divisions of the ARE did so within two years, with the average duration being one-and-a-half years.

- The most common reason for taking the exam was personal fulfillment (79%), while peer pressure (5%) and firm pressure (12%) were the lowest motivations.

- Of those eligible to take the ARE, lack of time to prepare was the most common reason for not taking it.

Source: 2003 ArchVoices/AIA Internship and Career Survey

Photo courtesy of Schemata Workshop, 2005

The Application Process

Before you submit your final IDP training report, you should send a letter to NCARB requesting that they transmit your completed records to your state registration board. This can take up to 30 business days. As noted in Chapter 4, a sample letter can be downloaded from www.ncarb.org. Don't twiddle your thumbs while you wait for NCARB to "do their thing." Contact your state board to request an application for architectural licensure. In fact, the old adage "no news is good news" certainly does not apply here. If you have not heard from NCARB within 30 days, be sure to follow up. There have been instances where interns have called their state board several months after submitting their final IDP training reports only to learn that the reports had not been received, and then to learn from NCARB that the records had been transmitted and then lost by the state. Be proactive and follow up on your records in a timely fashion to ensure that everything is in place.

Completing your IDP requirements and having them transmitted to the state board does not immediately make you eligible to take the ARE. While each state may have a different name for it, the license application or application to test must be submitted and approved in order to obtain an "authorization to test" from the state board to proceed with your examinations. While it may seem redundant, you may be required to submit your education and employment information as you did for IDP registration.

There are still several states that require specific examinations (such as seismic or jurisprudence exams) in addition to the ARE, and still others that require oral interviews. Some state boards meet every other month, so be sure to understand their schedule and organize your paperwork while you wait for NCARB to transmit your records. While many states request that you read the state laws regulating the practice of architecture, some boards actually require that you retype the laws and submit them prior to licensure.

After your application has been reviewed and accepted, you will receive an authorization to test along with an instruction packet from the Chauncey Group[3] describing the process for scheduling an exam. Information from your "authorization-to-test" letter will be needed to schedule your exams.

---

[3]The Chauncey Group serves as NCARB's test development and operations consultant. Their responsibilities include processing the eligibility information sent from various boards of architecture and distributing the test information package that includes the ARE Guidelines, a list of test centers, and your authorization-to-test letter. The Chauncey Group also issues your test results directly to your state board of architecture.

Several jurisdictions allow candidates to take portions of the ARE prior to completing IDP. Some interns are electing to obtain their initial license in these jurisdictions and later applying for reciprocity in their home states. At press time, seven jurisdictions allowed this: Arizona, California, Florida, Texas, Vermont, Wisconsin, and Puerto Rico. Contact these state boards directly if you are interested in starting the examination process prior to completing IDP. Archvoices.org has written about this process. Generally speaking, you still need to complete your IDP requirements before the state will award you registration.

NCARB.org provides a summary of all member board requirements. It is a comprehensive and clearly organized matrix that allows you to quickly compare the requirements for all 55 registration jurisdictions.

Costs

As you will soon learn, there seems to be a fee for every step involved with registration. States generally have an application fee, although a handful do not; check with your state board. This application fee is generally independent of the licensing fee that is paid upon successful completion of the ARE and satisfaction of all state requirements. The licensing period ranges from one to three years, and the renewal fee varies depending on the period.

Registration Fees (as of 2006)	
Examination (ARE) fees:	
six multiple-choice divisions	$102 each
three graphic divisions	$153 each
exam rescheduling	$35
State application fees	$10 to $345* (varies by state)
State registration fees	varies by state

*New York includes the first three years of registration with the initial application fee.

Photo courtesy of Schemata Workshop, 2005

Getting Your Employer to Pay for It

Firms support licensure in many ways. Some firms pay for the actual exams (usually just once, so it's really worth passing it the first time around). Other firms pay for the time off to take the actual test. Some firms may just pay for the licensing and renewal fees. In any event, it is worthwhile to find out what the office policy is. If no policy exists, it doesn't hurt to suggest one. The lack of policy may simply mean that the company never had to address licensure in the past.

Remember that your registration can benefit your employer. Here are just a few reasons why:

- If your company pursues public work, the key personnel it lists are often required to be licensed professionals.
- Licensure increases credibility with clients. Generally speaking, clients want to work with registered professionals, not just interns. In some cases, your licensure may allow the principal to reduce his time on a job while maintaining the client's trust (especially if you were doing the work already).
- Having licensed employees presents a marketing opportunity. A firm will sometimes bill itself as the largest employer of registered architects in the city or region.

Which Part to Take First

I've heard many interns say they are going to "study for them all and take them when I'm ready". Years later, they are still "studying" and haven't taken a single one. Establish a schedule for yourself and be disciplined about studying. Setting a schedule ensures that you stay on track upon initiating the exam process. Many states have a five-year maximum time frame in which to complete the exam; NCARB has recently adopted a national standard for the five-year "rolling clock." As an example, if you've passed only seven of the nine divisions and it has been more than five years since you began your examination process, you need to start the entire application and examination process over again.

While there is no prescribed sequence for taking the exams, evaluate the subjects in which you are weakest and take those exams first. If you take an exam and fail, you will have to wait six months before you can take that particular division again. By waiting to take the most difficult divisions last, you run the risk of failing an exam and having to anxiously wait out that time. However, if you take the most difficult divisions first and happen to fail, you can focus on the other exams during the six-month waiting period and take the failed divisions afterward. If you feel that all divisions seem equal, then use another measure, such as overall pass rates, to help you determine which exams to take first.

ARE Pass Rates by Division (in %)						
	1999	2000	2001	2002	2003	2004
Multiple-Choice Divisions						
Pre-Design	69	73	76	77	77	75
General Structures	74	76	76	77	73	73
Lateral Forces	86	89	90	93	92	77
Mechanical & Electrical Systems	85	78	73	74	74	67
Materials & Methods	89	90	90	88	86	76
Construction Documents & Services	84	85	86	86	85	79
Graphic Divisions						
Site Planning	72	72	64	68	70	71
Building Planning	69	61	62	68	68	64
Building Technology	75	78	67	67	65	63

Source: www.ncarb.org

Moving from State to State

Unlike the IDP, where the end of the process establishes the state to which your records are sent; your ARE progress is tracked by the state in which you initiate the registration process. Now that the exam is standardized and computerized, you can take portions of it at any authorized testing center throughout the country. For example, let's say you start taking your exam in Alabama, but before you complete it you are offered a position in St. Louis. Rather than having to return to Alabama to finish taking your exam, you can take the remaining portions at any Prometric testing center in the country. Your exam scores are forwarded by Prometric to the Alabama State Registration Board.

Preparing for the ARE

Some useful study guides are available for purchase. The Kaplan ARE Exam Preparation Series has been the standard ARE prep resource since the days of the paper-and-pencil tests. A volume is dedicated to each division, so it is comprehensive.

Quizzes at the end of each chapter and a final test reflect the type of questions on the actual exams—in both content and phrasing. The Kaplan series is a very good way to get into the mindset of the exams.

NCARB also publishes two guides, one for the multiple-choice divisions and one for graphic tests. Since NCARB is the administrator of the ARE, the sample questions found in these guides may match the actual ARE question formats most closely.

Kent Ballast has also authored a series of review books. Like the NCARB guides, they consist of a couple of succinct volumes. These are a good supplement to the Kaplan series and NCARB study guides.

Norman Dorf has written a study guide called *Solutions*. Dorf has a long history with NCARB. He has served as an ARE grader, helped to write ARE test questions, and chaired the NCARB committee that developed the computerized testing format. He offers seminars across the country as well as a "home-study" program based on his book.

Archiflash cards are a useful supplement to the aforementioned study guides. Their portability makes them perfect for studying on the bus to and from work. However, the questions on the cards are quite different in content and phrasing from the actual ARE questions, so they may not be ideal as a primary study source.

ARE Study Guides and Workshops

- Archiflash. Nalsa, Inc. 1,152 cards. www.archiflash.com

- Ballast, David Kent. *Architecture Exam Review* series. Professional Publications, Inc., 1999, 2002, 2005

- Dorf, Norman. *Solutions*. www.are-solutions.com

- Kaplan ARE Exam Preparation Series (formerly known as ALS guides or Architectural License Seminars). www.kaplanaecarchitecture.com

- NCARB. *ARE Study Guide: Multiple-Choice Divisions Version 3.0*. www.ncarb.org

- NCARB. *ARE Study Guide: Graphic Divisions Version 3.0*. www.ncarb.org

- Prep ARE structures workshops — www.prepa-r-e.com

- William Amor Study Guides — www.amorstudyguides.com/index.html (four sections)

ARE-Related Web Sites

- ARE Forum — www.areforum.org
- NCARB ARE guidelines — www.ncarb.org

Prep Courses

Another method of study is through local ARE prep seminars. Some AIA chapters sponsor courses at modest cost. In other cities, local architecture schools provide courses through their continuing education or evening extension programs. These courses tend to be more in depth and cost a bit more. In some cases, the instructors will encourage the formation of study groups.

As mentioned previously, Norman Dorf also conducts an intensive weekend study course. Check his Web site (www.solutions.org) for a current schedule of seminar dates and locations. His seminars may cost more than a study guide but are well worth the investment, particularly since he can be contacted for last-minute questions long after the seminar is over.

Start a Study Group

One way to build personal discipline in studying for the ARE is to form a study group. Scheduling a study period with others is an easy way to set aside the time to do so. Moreover, the financial burden of purchasing current study guides can be shared by the group.

Online Resources

In April 2004, a group of interns started an online bulletin board for obtaining ARE advice from peers who have recently taken the exam. Upon entering the site at www.areforum.org, you'll find discussions organized by exam division. A general section provides access to discussions on the overall exam process as well as jurisdiction-specific exams, the Leadership in Energy and Environmental Design (LEED) certification exam, and IDP.

Within each exam division, test takers solicit advice or share stories by posting their comments on a bulletin board. Previous responses can be viewed in the order of posting. In addition to tips and personal accounts, some users have elected to post useful links and study resources. While it is great to see such a healthy and positive dialogue occurring virtually across the continent, I will pass along a tip from an intern currently using the site for a study resource: Check the sources. Don't take everything posted as the absolute truth.

Note that on the ARE forum home page there is a link to the ARE Confidentiality Agreement that is displayed at the outset of every ARE exam division. While it is the intent of the Web site to share information about the exam process, the reminder from NCARB states that the sharing of actual exam questions is considered cheating and, thus, subject to disciplinary action.

Multiple-Choice Test Taking Tip

The figure below indicates the duration of each multiple-choice exam and the number of questions to be asked, so it is easy to determine prior to the exam how much time you can devote to each question. For example, the Lateral Forces test has 75

Multiple-Choice Division — Duration and Numbers of Questions

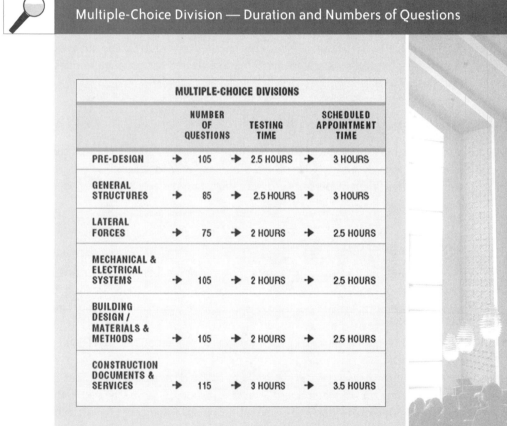

MULTIPLE-CHOICE DIVISIONS			
	NUMBER OF QUESTIONS	TESTING TIME	SCHEDULED APPOINTMENT TIME
PRE-DESIGN	105	2.5 HOURS	3 HOURS
GENERAL STRUCTURES	85	2.5 HOURS	3 HOURS
LATERAL FORCES	75	2 HOURS	2.5 HOURS
MECHANICAL & ELECTRICAL SYSTEMS	105	2 HOURS	2.5 HOURS
BUILDING DESIGN / MATERIALS & METHODS	105	2 HOURS	2.5 HOURS
CONSTRUCTION DOCUMENTS & SERVICES	115	3 HOURS	3.5 HOURS

Photo courtesy of Grace Kim, 2004

questions and the exam length is two hours, or 120 minutes. This translates into only 1 minute 40 seconds per question. In taking any of the multiple-choice exams, you should make a mental note that if you get to a particularly difficult question, you should skip it and go back to it at the end, if you have time. Remember that you don't have to score 100 percent; the grading is pass or fail. If you've spent five minutes trying to figure out a crazy formula, you've potentially taken time away from answering a couple of other questions that are more simple.

Familiarity with the Software

If you use a computer regularly, you will likely have no difficulty navigating the multiple-choice portions of the ARE. The graphic divisions, however, are another story. Instead of using a proprietary CAD program, and thereby giving some candidates an advantage over others, the developers of the exam developed a generic program that was intended to be intuitive and easy to learn. In theory, this was a great idea. However, this dumbed-down computer program feels extremely clumsy and imprecise to most CAD users. While it is relatively easy to learn how to use the program, the graphic user interface can be cumbersome, and many candidates have or wasted time trying to get the program to do what they were accustomed to using a familiar CAD program.

 For the graphic portions of the exam, the most important preparation is to download the program from the NCARB Web site and practice using it — a lot!

Scheduling Your Exam

You can schedule your exam online at www.prometric.com or by phone. Either way, you must pay for the exam at the time of scheduling and will need the following information ready:

- Your credit card or prepaid voucher number
- Your authorization-to-test letter
- The division or divisions you want to schedule
- The date and time you want to schedule each division
- An alternate date and time

A prepaid voucher can be purchased by check; a form is included in your information packet from the Chauncey Group. If you want a Saturday time slot, you are advised to call at least a month in advance. You will receive confirmation for each scheduled exam. Put that confirmation number in a safe place; you will want to bring it to the testing center along with your authorization-to-test letter.

Once you schedule your exam, your test fee cannot be refunded. However, you can reschedule your exam as many times as you wish within one year from the date of payment processing. In order to do so, you must call the Prometric Candidate Services Contact Center at (800) 479-6215 no later than 12:00 noon EST, three business days prior to your scheduled exam. At that time, you will be asked to reschedule your exam for a later date, and you will be charged a $35 fee. Failure to take the exam within one year of payment or failure to show up for a scheduled exam will result in forfeiture of the exam fee.

What to Expect at the Testing Center

When you take your exam, the testing center will also be administering a variety of other tests to accountants, barbers, and pharmacists, as well as college entrance exams such as the SAT, GRE, and LSAT. You will need to show two pieces of ID and your authorization to test. If you purchased a voucher, you must submit this to the test center adviser when you arrive.

Don't bring much else with you. The center will provide pencils and scratch paper. You cannot bring notes or textbooks into the exam room with you. For the multiple-choice divisions, you can bring your own calculator. However, it will need to be a simple, nonprogrammable type (the kind you might pick up at the grocery or drugstore). The testing center may have a small locker for you to store your valuables, but it will probably be too small for most briefcases, book bags, or totes. There will be a place to hang your coat, but it will likely be unsupervised. If you want to wear your coat during the exam, at most testing centers you will not have the option of putting it on and taking it off repeatedly during the exam.

The room in which you take the test may be filled with numerous cubicles. You may be distracted by loud or frequent mouse clicking, air-conditioning, or doors opening and closing. While such noises may seem benign, it is quite possible for sleep-deprived, stressed-out candidates to be overly sensitive to them. The testing center should have a supply of earplugs on hand, but if you are concerned, bring your own. A personal note about earplugs: I recently took an exam at a testing center and requested a pair. They were so good that they blocked out all exterior sounds; as a result I became conscious of all my internal sounds—my heart beating, my eyelids closing, and my throat swallowing. You may consider bringing your own so you can try them out prior to the exam and make sure they provide just enough sound isolation. As best you can, try to anticipate some of these environmental issues and come prepared.

The temperature of the room can also be a problem. Testing-center rooms seem to be air-conditioned year round. If you get cold easily, bring a sweater. But as with your coat, you'll probably have to keep it on, or if you want to take it off, take a break and put it in your locker. Depending on the staff at the testing center, if you take your jacket or sweater off and drape it on your chair, someone may come and hang it up in the waiting area. So plan accordingly.

With the multiple-choice divisions, you do not have scheduled breaks. A break can be taken, but the clock will not stop running. The longer graphic divisions have required breaks, so you should bring a small snack in case you get hungry. Be careful not to eat too much before or during the exam, as you could become sluggish. On the other hand, you won't want to be distracted (nor will your fellow testers) by your growling stomach.

After Your Exam

Within a few weeks of your exam, you will receive a letter from your state registration board indicating whether you passed. All test scores are reported as pass or fail, and you will receive limited diagnostic information for each failed division. If you don't see your scores after two months, you should contact ARE Operations to ensure that there are no problems. (Contact information can be found in the ARE Guidelines.)

The Last Exam

When you successfully complete your last exam, some state boards will send you a letter of congratulations indicating that you have passed the ARE. In other states, there is no notification other than the standard letter stating that you've passed. It's pretty anticlimactic.

Note that passing the ARE does not automatically mean that you are licensed. In fact, the State of Texas sends those who have completed the exam a packet of information along with a warning that states: "You Are Not Yet Licensed to Practice Architecture in the State of Texas." Many states send a similar information packet (minus the warning); it should include an application form for registration. You will have to return the completed application along with your registration fee. For some states, such as Florida and Montana, that's enough, and they will send you a certificate and wallet card. However, many other states require additional information, ranging from work history to letters of recommendation from practicing architects. Some states also require an interview; it may consist of an intense battery of questions from a three-person panel, as in California, or an informal group orientation, as in Oregon. Interviews are generally held in conjunction with the meeting of the state board, which in some states occurs every other month. Since you will be anxious when you finish your last exam, you should look into this process early on so that when you receive your final exam scores you are prepared for the next steps.

Now That You're Registered

The fact that you are licensed doesn't mean you should start stamping any or all of your drawings. By stamping drawings you are ensuring the health, safety, and welfare of the building users—potentially assuming liability for the project, including any future injuries or claims.

At a large firm, certain individuals are allowed to bind the firm to these risks. These individuals are usually identified by the firm's insurance policy. In a smaller firm, the insurance policy may allow any registered architect employed by the firm to stamp drawings. However, the firm will generally have a policy that only principals have this responsibility. As a rule, you should not stamp any drawings while employed at a firm without fully understanding the legal ramifications of your actions and the insurance coverage in place to minimize your risk in the event of lawuits.

At the same time, licensure is a major accomplishment, so be sure to share your success with your employers. While many employers don't automatically grant you a salary increase, your licensure may open up new promotion and leadership opportunities. Licensure can also open up opportunities for starting your own practice (refer to Chapter 12).

AIA versus RA—What Do the Titles Mean?

Once you are registered, you are entitled to put the letters *RA* after your name. But what does that mean? *RA* stands for *registered architect* and is an indicator that a person has passed the licensing requirements of the state in which he or she practices architecture. However, the letters *AIA* more frequently follow the name of many registered architects, causing much confusion both within the profession and outside it about what the acronyms mean. The letters *AIA* represent membership in a professional organization—the American Institute of Architects. While the designation implies registration (nonregistered members of the institute are called associate members), it is not the sole indicator of registration status. An easy way to think of it is that although an individual can be a registered architect and not be an AIA member, one cannot be an AIA member without first being a registered architect.

Success Stories

While the process of completing the ARE may seem overwhelming and perhaps even daunting at the outset, remember that there are thousands of other interns experiencing the same situation. The following two contributions are from newly registered architects who had vastly different study approaches but were both successful in completing their exams. They describe some of their frustrations with the process and the personal challenges they encountered along the way. While you may not be fortunate enough to pass each division on the first try, perhaps you can glean some tips that will help you develop an approach for conquering the ARE yourself.

I waited nearly seven weeks to receive the results of my final two ARE exams. By that time, I had grown rather impatient with the process. How could NCARB, Prometric, my state board, or the U.S. Postal Service be so cruel? After the many years of school and internship, the countless hours studying for each exam, falling asleep at 2 A.M. beneath the mammoth study guides, hadn't I been through enough already?

It was a Saturday when I received my final scores—exactly 2 years, 17 weeks, and 5 days after I took my first exam. Upon opening the letter and seeing that sweet word—pass—I felt as if a tremendous weight was lifted from my shoulders. No more exams. No more waiting for my career to advance to the next level. No more explaining to people, "I'm not really an architect, but I act like one at work." Finally, I could call myself an architect.

Admittedly, I did not find it particularly easy, comfortable, or convenient to get to that point—in fact, it was completely the opposite. Simply finding the time to schedule, study for, and take each exam was a challenge. The ultimate goal of licensure seemed so distant at times that I had to focus on short-term milestones to keep myself going. I found it helpful to think of the information gained from my studies as useful knowledge for the day-to-day practice of architecture. I viewed preparation for each exam as preparation for practice, seeking a compre-hensive understanding of the material instead of temporary memorization. From that perspective, it was easier to justify each additional hour I spent studying and each book or download I obtained.

Deciding what to study was a difficult task. I felt as if I had been placed at the base of a mountain and told, "Get to the top," but had not been told how or what tools to use—and, making things worse, the summit was shrouded in clouds. Fortunately, NCARB provided some direction in the form of the content areas and a list of references in the ARE Guidelines—so that was where I began. Though I treated each division as a separate entity, I found several resources that were helpful for multiple exams, including Architectural Graphic Standards, Building Construction Illustrated, A Visual Dictionary of Architecture, Solutions, *and the postings and other material found on ARE Forum.*[4]

The two words that best describe my approach are holistic *and* redundant. *I used multiple sources for each subject, as investigating a topic from multiple perspectives gave me a more meaningful understanding of the content. I collected everything I could get my hands on in an effort to immerse myself in each subject area. I began by breaking down study content into categories, and then concentrated on one category at a time. I read general resources on each subject to familiarize myself with the material, then used detailed resources to supplement my basic understanding with more-specific principles and applications. Approaching the subjects with a conceptual understanding provided a comforting familiarity that not only boosted my confidence but also kept the material interesting. I drew from my professional experience and likewise incorporated the knowledge I gained from studying into my professional practice. For example, I took Construction Documents & Services while developing and working with contracts for my firm. Learning to deal with problems related to a contractor's request for a time extension on one job proved especially pertinent to both my practical experience and the exam. When evaluating the relevance of a study resource, I asked myself, "Is this really something an architect should have to know to 'safeguard public health, safety, and welfare'?" When I encountered complex mathematical equations with symbols that looked like squiggles, I moved on. Architects have to know enough about a subject to make sound judgments in practice, not perform our consultants' jobs. On the other hand, some exams seemed to cover such a broad range of subject areas within a single test that I was glad I had spent so much time studying. I found Mechanical & Electrical Systems to be one of the most difficult exams for this reason. Striking the proper balance between too much and too little study can be difficult. Common sense and the ability to learn from the experiences of others are helpful here.*

I found it invaluable to reflect upon my experiences and share my insights with others while I took the exams. Though I didn't have a study partner or group to

---

[4]Ching, Francis D.K., and Cassandra Adams, *Building Construction Illustrated,* 3rd edition (New York: John Wiley & Sons, 1996); Ching, Francis D.K., *A Visual Dictionary of Architecture* (New York: John Wiley & Sons, 2000); Dorf, Norman, *Solutions,* www.are-solutions.com; Ramsey, Charles George, et al., *Architectural Graphic Standards,* 10th edition (New York: John Wiley & Sons, 2000)

help me, I participated extensively in the online ARE Forum. Sharing the struggle with others definitely provides encouragement. And every bit helps—sometimes just saying (or being told) "good job" or offering tips on strategy can make a difference when preparing for an exam.

Before an actual exam appointment, there are several things to keep in mind. First, get sufficient sleep. Do not underestimate—or overestimate—the difficulty of any division. Relax and stay focused. Also, before you begin, calculate approximately how much time you will have to spend on each question based on the total time divided by the number of questions. Establish basic milestones to avoid falling behind.

For the multiple-choice divisions, pay attention to the phrasing of the question, as it often provides a clue to the answer. I found this particularly important for the Pre-Design exam, where many questions required me to exercise professional judgment to provide the most appropriate solution to a specific problem. Complete familiarity with every question is not required; your understanding of the concepts should allow you to find the best answer from the choices given. The first time through, answer all of the questions you know immediately, marking and saving the more difficult questions and calculation problems for last. Remember, a perfect score is not required to pass the exam.

For the graphic portions, it helps to enter with a plan of action for the order of the vignettes and a strategy for solving each one. Practicing with the test software and following directions are the keys to passing. To some degree, systematic strategies can be established for all the vignettes by practicing beforehand. This preparation eliminates the need to improvise during the exam and leaves you with more time to check your work. Remember that the difference between a pass and a fail is not so much what you answer, but what you miss.

The ARE is as much a test of will and perseverance as it is a test of knowledge and experience. The nature of our work often makes it difficult to find or justify the time to begin and keep up with the process. Yet I can now answer the one question that all of us embarking on this journey of internship and licensure ask ourselves: Is it worth all of the trouble?

Absolutely.

Eric A. Booth, AIA
Partner, A•ES ArchiTech
Cornell University, Bachelor of Architecture 1999

Ranking of ARE Divisions

The following rankings were provided by Eric Booth in a posting on the ARE Forum.

Relative difficulty for me, easiest to hardest:

1. Building Technology
2. Site Planning
3. Building Planning
4. Construction Documents
5. Pre-Design
6. General Structures
7. Lateral Forces
8. Materials & Methods
9. Mechanical & Electrical Systems

If I were to do it all over again, I would take the exams in the following order:

1. Construction Documents (to get used to the exam format)
2. Building Technology, Site Planning, and Building Planning in the same week (to get them over with and wait for results)
3. Mechanical & Electrical Systems (one of hardest; take it early in case of failure)
4. Materials & Methods
5. General Structures
6. Lateral Forces (immediately following General Structures)
7. Pre-Design (good summary exam)

Photo courtesy of Schemata Workshop, 2005

Unlike Eric, the following contributor started off without a systematic approach. However, in the course of her examination period, she gained confidence by attending seminars and found great benefit in the camaraderie she found by participating in the online ARE Forum discussions.

> *It took me two years and two weeks to finish the arduous journey of the ARE. I'm a task-oriented person, and this was my first experience with hitting a brick wall and being unable to complete a goal in a timely manner. Becoming an architect had been my dream since age 10, and I had previously done everything in my power to satisfy the prerequisites of licensure.*

I began IDP as soon as I was eligible, during the senior year of my undergraduate studies at the University of Florida. I spent the year working for a local architect and then went to work at another firm in Orlando the following summer. I worked as a graduate assistant during my master's program, so by the time I graduated in May 2001, I had a nice foundation of IDP hours to start off my career. Less than a year later, I had acquired enough IDP credits (235 training units) to be eligible to take my exams in Florida. I was energized! I was going to get my license and start my own business lickety-split.

My authorization to test was dated May 9, 2002. My first tasks were to figure out which exam to take first and then what study materials to use. The office where I was working (and where I am still employed) had only one other employee besides my boss. Since I had few associations with any newly registered architects or other interns, I was pretty much on my own. At the time, I didn't know about prep seminars or online resources like the ARE Forum. But I had seen an advertisement for Archiflash, so I ordered a set.

Making what seemed like an obvious choice, I picked Pre-Design as my first test.

As I began to study, it dawned on me that it was going to take time to gain confidence. Pre-Design covered many different topics. And because I had been given no other advice, I simply continued to study lackadaisically for almost a year before I told myself that I had to buckle down and schedule a test. I realize now that I would have benefited in those early days by getting support from other interns, the way I later did through the ARE Forum.

I took the Pre-Design exam almost a year from the time I began to study for it. It was surreal—I felt like I was guessing at so many of the questions. I kept asking myself, "Does this question really show that I am ready to be an architect? These are so random and obscure!" I remember deliberating over one question at the end that had some calculation in it, and finally changing my answer—to the wrong one. You should always go with your first instincts, unless you are absolutely sure it's wrong. It's amazing how often the first guess is right. I received my letter a few weeks later indicating that I had passed, and it felt really good.

With this positive reinforcement, I made a plan to take one test a month. So, I scheduled Construction Documents next. Since the topics are more relevant to the issues we face daily in practice, this would have been a great test to start with. I studied from the student version of The Architect's Handbook for Professional Practice. *This was a great resource! I took the test on May 12, 2003, and felt good about it. I received my second passing letter. The dream was getting closer.*

With the start of summer, I became less motivated to study, and I didn't take my next test—Mechanical & Electrical Systems—until August. I studied Architectural

Graphics Standards *and attended an evening seminar conducted by my former employer in Orlando. That seminar encouraged me to schedule my exam. Seminars are great! I recommend them to everyone. In a room with other interns studying for tests, receiving good information and sharing stories, you're bound to do better than if you go it alone. Although I have heard many interns say that Mechanical & Electrical Systems was the hardest exam, I don't even remember the test, and I was blessed with another pass.*

Then life happened. I had a lot going on in my personal life and didn't have time to think about taking another test. I even contemplated not finishing the exams. I was over it. Life was rough, I wasn't having any fun at work, and I wasn't sure why I was torturing myself with all these tests if I wasn't going to enjoy my career. Fortunately, I eventually found renewed inspiration for finishing the ARE.

In order to catch up, I took a day seminar on Materials & Methods and Building Technology and decided to take these two tests back to back. My advice is: Never take these two like that! Because I was so gung-ho to get going, I scheduled the tests before I started studying and then realized that Materials & Methods was a big exam, with lots of information to memorize. I used the flash cards (which I don't recommend using as your main study materials because they don't cover enough) and Kent Ballast's book. I spent so much time studying for Materials & Methods that I had less than a week of practice time for Building Technology.

I practiced on the NCARB computer program and used an old NCARB graphic exam book with hand-drawn examples of real tests and the graders' comments. Sadly, I still didn't know about ARE Forum—that would have been a huge help.

The graphic section of the forum is the best part. You can post your practice answers and obtain input from others, which I found really helpful. During the actual exam, I realized that I was very weak in roof design. Our firm specializes in commercial projects, and I had designed only flat roofs. Roof design is easy if you have a few pointers and a little practice. I had neither. But it was Friday and time to take Materials & Methods. The test went favorably. I was scheduled for Building Technology on Monday at 8 A.M., so I figured I had the weekend to study.

Unfortunately, over the weekend, I found out my mother-in-law had a brain aneurysm, and I was so distraught I could barely study. By Monday morning, I was an emotional mess, operating on very little sleep. After a physically and mentally grueling five and a half hours, I left the testing center with a sinking feeling.

I had 12 weeks to wait for that test result. Typical wait times for graphic sections are 4 to an unbearable 8 weeks, but somehow mine reached an excruciating 12 weeks. It was a long wait, but I received another pass!

I didn't start studying again until I received those results. I also started to look for a seminar for my last two multiple-choice sections: General Structures and Lateral Forces. I enjoy structures, but I was in no position to take either exam without a refresher. I was given a flyer for David Thaddeus's structures seminar in Miami, which I attended. I felt so good after the seminar that I went right home and scheduled both exams. Both tests went smoothly. Since math is my strong suit, I was happy to see those questions, but they comprised only a small portion of the questions overall. I had felt positive about these two exams, and I passed them both—receiving those test scores in two weeks, which almost made up for my extra-long wait for the Building Technology exam results. Seven down, two to go!

By now I recognized the high value of weekend seminars and had heard good things about Norman Dorf's seminar. Although I wanted to be finished by February, I knew it would be worthwhile for me to wait until his seminar on April 1 and take the test with confidence immediately thereafter. It was at this seminar that I finally learned about the ARE Forum, and I subsequently became a frequent visitor to the site, posting my practice exams and helping check those of others. I took Building Planning on April 12, 2005, and Site Design two weeks later.

When the mail came on May 8, 2005, I received my final pass and entered into the wide world of architects. I was overjoyed. This was the day I had been working toward for so long. It was like a dream. I turned in my final IDP hours later that month and am waiting to receive my registration number and conclude this chapter of my life.

I'm glad that I decided to persevere with the exams, and that my husband, family, and friends continually supported me. Admittedly, I would never want to take the ARE again. It's possible that I could have been content had I pursued another career, but I am thankful for where I am now and that I can be called an architect.

Sharon Migala, Assoc. AIA
Project Architect, Spacecoast Architects P.A.
University of Florida, Master of Architecture 2001

CHAPTER 6 PROFESSIONAL PRACTICE

> 39% of former interns report they have at some time considered leaving the profession (or have left) because they were "not making enough money."
> — 1999 ARCHITECTURAL INTERNSHIP EVALUATION PROJECT

Compensation

Chapter 2 touched briefly on compensation in the context of job interviews. But how do you make sure that your salary is competitive with others at your level, both within the office and at other firms?

As stated in Chapter 2, if you start low, you stay low, and conversely, if you start high, you stay high. The percentage of salary increases tends to be similar regardless of the starting salary, so keep that in mind as you negotiate your initial salary. For this very reason, it is not uncommon in large firms for interns to make more than experienced staff if the economy is good. It is the responsibility of the individual to monitor how his or her salary and performance compare to that of colleagues or national averages.

To help, the AIA conducts a compensation survey every couple of years; the salaries are listed by job description, firm size, and region. With this information, you can compare how an architect of your experience level is being compensated in your city (if you are in a large metropolitan area) or region, as well as how that might vary based on the size of your firm. This document is available for purchase online at the AIA Web site or through the national AIA bookstore. As it is a fairly expensive document, inquire at your local AIA office whether they have a copy you can peruse. The table below, from the Emerging Professionals' section of aia.org, provides salary information pertinent to interns.

Salary Comparison				
	Firm A	Effective Salary	Firm B	Effective Salary
Annual Salary	$36,500	$36,500	$30,300	$30,300
Effective hourly rate (annual salary/2088 hours)	$17.48		$14.51	
Medical/dental insurance ($250/month × 12 months)	deducted from paycheck $3,000	$33,500	paid by firm $3,000	$33,300
8 holidays (8 days × 8 hours × hourly rate)	$1,119 taken without pay	$32,381	included in salary	$33,300
10 vacation days (10 days × 8 hours × hourly rate)	$1,398 taken without pay	$30,983	included in salary	$33,300
5 sick days (5 days × 8 hours × hourly rate)	$699 taken without pay	$30,284	included in salary	$33,300
10% bonus (annual salary × 10%)	n/a		$3,030	$36,330
3% match for 401(k) plan (annual salary × 3%)	n/a		$909	$37,239
Effective Salary		$30,284		$37,239

Source: aia.org

If you feel comfortable discussing salaries, you can also ask your friends in other firms. When comparing salaries, remember to consider what benefits are provided along with the salary. For example, Firm A on page 122 offers a starting intern $36,500. However, the firm deducts insurance premiums from each paycheck and provides no paid holidays or sick days. There are no yearly bonuses or retirement savings plans. Firm B, however, pays its starting interns $30,300. While on the surface this seems lower than Firm A, the employer pays for medical and dental premiums, eight holidays, eight vacation days, and five personal days along with the base salary. In addition, Firm B has historically paid a 10 percent annual bonus and provides a 401(k) retirement plan with a 3 percent employer match. Firm A may initially appear to pay better, but considering the entire salary package in detail would prove that Firm B provides higher take-home pay and possibly lower tax liabilities with 401(k) participation.

Overtime

> More than 33% of interns who are paid hourly were not being compensated for overtime, which is a violation of the Federal Wage and Hour Law.
>
> —2003 ARCHVOICES/AIA INTERNSHIP AND CAREER SURVEY

It has been common practice for architecture firms to argue that interns are "professionals" earning a salary. However, according to the Fair Labor Standards Act (FLSA), professionals consistently exercise discretion and judgment and perform work that is predominantly intellectual in character. As attorney Carl Sapers points out in the seminal Progressive Architecture article, "The Intern Trap," an intern is not an exempt professional, according to the U.S. Department of Labor, and, therefore, is eligible for overtime pay. An intern fulfilling the requirements of the Intern Development Program must be supervised by a licensed architect and, therefore, is not free to exercise discretion and judgment. As nonexempt hourly employees, interns are entitled to overtime pay. Overtime pay is defined as 1.5 times one's regular hourly wage for any hours one is scheduled to work beyond 40 hours per week. While many firms have shirked their responsibilities, their FLSA violations can be reprimanded through fines issued by the Department of Labor.

Despite the law, firms have consistently taken the fall-back position that "this is the way it's always been." So it is up to each individual to decide whether to stand up for his or her rights. Some firms will say, "If you don't like it, there is someone else equally qualified that will accept our terms." If this is the response you receive to questions about your nonexempt status, perhaps you should reconsider whether your goals align with those of the firm.

While interns may not want to rock the boat for fear of losing their jobs, it is in the interest of the profession that we all understand the law and take a firm stand on the treatment of interns. Ultimately, whether you choose to confront your employer

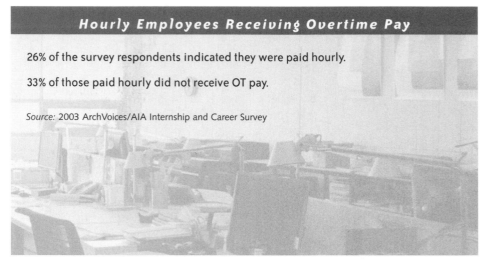

Hourly Employees Receiving Overtime Pay

26% of the survey respondents indicated they were paid hourly.

33% of those paid hourly did not receive OT pay.

Source: 2003 ArchVoices/AIA Internship and Career Survey

Photo courtesy of Schemata Workshop, 2005

is a matter for you to decide. When first published in 1994, Fisher's article incited much discussion in the architectural community. In subsequent years, many large firms were fined and ordered to compensate employees with back pay for overtime hours; yet few changes were made to compensation practices. In reading the article today, it is amazing to see the clarity and magnitude of the abuse, and yet firms still refuse to pay interns overtime.

If in doubt as to whether your firm views you as an hourly or salaried employee, consider whether a reduced number of hours on your time sheet would affect your paycheck. If writing down fewer than 40 hours on your time sheet would result in a lower paycheck amount, then the firm does not count you as a salaried employee. Salaried employees are paid the same amount each pay period regardless of the number of hours worked.

Compensation Time

Many firms partially address the issue of overtime by providing compensation time (commonly referred to as "comp time" —paid time off to make up for additional hours employees work above 40 hours per week. While this practice varies from office to office, the most straightforward rule is that the hours worked in excess of 40 per week can be taken, one for one, at some point in the future as paid time off. Let's say, for example, that your company has such a comp-time policy and you were asked to work 55 hours one week to meet a project deadline. Under such a policy, you would be allowed to take 15 hours of paid time off the following week to compensate you for the extra time you worked.

Some firms with comp-time policies put a limit on the number of comp-time hours you can accrue (to encourage staff to use them rather then letting them accumulate). And others limit how many successive days you can take at once (prohibiting the practice of "banking" hours to be used as future vacation time). Generally, individuals are responsible for scheduling these comp-time hours with their project team to avoid conflict with project deadlines.

A project manager might also put a cap on comp time by stating that the team will be expected to put in additional hours as necessary for the next two weeks but would get three paid days off after the project deadline. This is more of a reward to the entire team for their hard work and uncompensated effort than an actual comp-time policy.

Contract Employees

Another practice to which architecture interns (as well as other exempt-status workers) have fallen prey is contract employment. To put it simply, the employer does not deduct income taxes, Social Security taxes, or other employer obligations from a contract employee's paycheck, and in return pays a higher hourly wage to compensate the employee for having to pay those out of pocket. At face value, the practice appears to benefit both the employee and the employer, and many small to mid-sized firms use this employment structure to reduce their payroll costs. However, there are hidden costs to the intern that only become apparent at tax time, as well as legal repercussions for the employer should the practice be noticed by the IRS.

While the employer does not deduct income or Social Security taxes, the employee is still obligated to pay them. In addition, the employee will be issued a 1099-MISC form rather than a W-2; therefore, the IRS and state treasury will consider the employee to be self-employed and expect payment of the employer's portion of Social Security and income taxes. By hiring the intern as an independent contractor, the employer has effectively left the intern to pay the employer's share of those taxes.

Here is the story of an anonymous intern who learned after several months that she was a contract employee and unfortunately had not negotiated an adequate salary to compensate her for the taxes.

> *The architect who hired me for my first internship told me that the most he could pay me was $7 an hour. Even in 1995 that was a meager wage; however, I needed the internship in order to complete my degree, so I agreed. I had no idea what I should or could be paid or even how to find such information. It was my first job in the profession and I needed the experience more than I needed the money. Later, it was disheartening to discover that a classmate of mine, who became a coworker, asked for $11 an hour and got it.*

Every week, I was required to provide an invoice documenting the hours I had worked so that my boss would write me a check. I realized that taxes weren't being taken out of my paycheck, but I was unclear about the implications this would have at tax time. Since I wasn't making very much money, I figured the more I could take home, the better.

About two months into my internship, I read an article in Progressive Architecture *describing the internship experience. The purpose of the article was to call attention to the fact that interns were being ill-treated—specifically in the area of compensation. Much like me, many interns were being paid as though they were self-employed while simultaneously being treated as full-time employees.*

I realized that my boss had avoided paying his share of employment taxes by paying me in the manner he was. At the same time, I realized that I would end up being responsible for paying his usual payroll taxes. While I hadn't even realized it, I was self-employed. Unfortunately, I had none of the freedoms of a self-employed individual. I was expected to report to work on time, do what my boss told me, work in his office, and rely on him for guidance and, more importantly, supervision. The article was an eye-opener for me.

During the course of the internship, I felt that there was little I could do to change the situation. I needed the job, and this architect hired everyone under these same conditions. Later, I learned that I could pursue compensation; the Department of Labor has avenues through which I could have filed a grievance. Although it was warranted, unfortunately I did not feel like this was something I could pursue, because I would have to rely on my boss to serve as a reference for my next job, as well as to provide documentation of my experience for my licensing exam.

I came away from my first internship understanding two things. The first was that if I didn't ask for what I wanted I would never get it. The second was that it was up to me to understand my rights and responsibilities.

Ava J. Abramowitz wrote an article for the AIA Best Practices[1] series entitled "Employment Status: Independent Contractor—Yes or No?" In the article, she calls attention to the incorrect assumptions that architecture firms make in hiring contract employees. She clearly delineates the characteristics of a contract employee with the question "Are they truly independent?" She notes that an independent contractor must demonstrate that he or she maintains a separate place of business, possesses a skill set not present within the firm, has control over the work being performed, has consulting agreements with multiple clients, and is officially a business entity recog-

---

[1] AIA Best is a compendium of the practical knowledge acquired by AIA members in the real world of architecture practice—knowledge gained from experience, immediately applicable to a task at hand. A list of topics can be found at www.aia.org/bestpractices

nized by state or local governments. The article can be downloaded from the AIA Web site by searching for "Best Practices."

Finally, and perhaps most important for interns enrolled in IDP, NCARB does not recognize work performed by independent contractors as defined by the U.S. Department of Labor. Therefore, you cannot accrue IDP credit for work experience obtained as a contract employee.

Ownership of Work

Some firms have written policies about what is considered company property. Obviously, the physical items provided for the employee, such as phones, furniture, and office supplies, belong to the company. However, data compiled or work created by employees—that is, intellectual property—is also owned by the company unless other agreements were negotiated during the hiring phase.

Photographs and renderings that were created for a project become the property of the firm and, in some cases, the client. You can take credit for producing the work while employed with the firm, but this does not expressly grant you the right to use it. When you leave the firm, you should obtain written permission to use the materials you helped to create for use in your portfolio. When presenting it in your portfolio, you should always acknowledge the company as having originated the work and make your involvement with the project clear. If you are using work that you did not produce directly, such as professional photographs, remember to obtain permission for its use. Reproduction (scanning, color copying, etc.) of professional photography is a violation of the copyright held by the photographer. Generally the firm's copyright agreement with the photographer will permit use by the firm alone, not by its current or past employees for self-promotion.

Nonsanctioned Use of Office Equipment

While at times it may feel that your office is like a second home, it is not. Similarly, the office computers and equipment should not be used freely as if they were your own. Most offices have written or stated policies for using office equipment for nonoffice uses. Some offices may encourage professional growth and have specific arrangements for employee use of company computers and printers for side work or design competitions. It may be that they will deduct printing and supply costs from your paycheck, or that they will allow you to make limited copies and prints at no cost. Whatever the policy, make sure you clearly understand the parameters and make the proper arrangements to avoid awkward situations (e.g., your boss walking over to ask you a question while you are standing at the plotter waiting for a personal project to print out). The best-case scenario would be for your employer to wholeheartedly support your initiative and grant you unlimited use of and access to the firm's resources. The worst-case scenario would be for you to proceed with the work and be terminated for inappropriate use of office resources—or for the company to take ownership of the documents you created on its equipment.

How the Little Things Add Up

If you take a handful of pens for a presentation and forget to return them to the office, this could be considered pilfering. While it may not have been your intent to steal office supplies, if they ultimately remain at your home, this could be considered petty theft.

In a large firm, the cost of such minor losses may be a negligible fraction of the operational budget and, therefore, go undetected. However, for a small firm, these seemingly incidental losses can dramatically affect office expenses if they recur with each employee. As a principal in a small firm, I'm ever so cognizant of the numerous pens that I have accrued over 12 years of practice. It was never my intent to pilfer pens for personal use, but when I worked for a large firm, I recall times when I traveled extensively and treated my briefcase as a portable desk. I would grab a handful of pens in preparation for the numerous client meetings that would occur off-site that week, only to leave them at home to lighten my load to the office between trips. While the firm I worked for at the time did not notice or even care, I know the office manager of my small practice today would question how we could be using so many pens each month. In the short term, this has a direct impact on cash flow by increasing our monthly expense for office supplies. Over the course of the year, if similar losses were realized by several employees at a variety of scales (with a loss not only of office supplies but also of model-building tools and architectural books, and with the reproduction of extra drawing sets or color printing of personal photos), this could have a direct impact on year-end bonuses or other employee benefits.

Moonlighting

Employers approach "moonlighting" or "side work" with a range of responses. They generally fall into the following three categories.

Moonlighting Is Not Allowed

Whether large or small, many companies adopt this position, for a number of reasons. Smaller firms find that there can be conflicts of interest or direct competition for work.

Larger firms want to avoid professional liability for work performed independently by an employee.

Firms that do not allow moonlighting may also want to discourage employees from taking calls or making use of the office for outside work. Outside jobs often require phone calls and meetings during the day, which may interfere with your performance in the office. There is also the issue of physical burnout. If an employee stays up all night to work on a side project, performance the following day will likely suffer.

An intern posted the following on a discussion thread on Archinect.com; his post quite accurately describes the concerns many established firms have about moonlighting:

> My firm (very large) does not necessarily encourage moonlighting. However, the interesting thing is that their position has nothing to do with competition, stealing clients, or lack of productivity at work, but is more about potential liability and diluting the firm's "brand."

Moonlighting Is Your Prerogative

Some firms adopt the attitude that "what you do on your own time is your own business." These firms acknowledge that moonlighting is a prevalent practice, and in some cases they even encourage it. In addition, they may view moonlighting no differently from involvement with other outside activities. Serving on the board of a volunteer organization may also require long hours after work, as would late nights preparing a documentary film or grant proposals for a nonprofit organization. If the employee's in-office performance is not visibly affected and the quality of work is maintained, the employer will not concern themselves over employee activities that occur outside of the normal business day.

It is also the position of some employers that moonlighting is the only way for their employees to make up for their low salary in their chosen field. These firms are indirectly acknowledging that they do not compensate their employees very well.

Moonlighting Is Encouraged

A firm may offer an employee moonlighting opportunities for two reasons: (1) incompatibility of project type, scale, or budget; or (2) client relationships.

It is quite possible for a prospective client to contact your firm with a project that is too small in scope or not in keeping with the design objectives of the firm. The client may ask if the firm can recommend someone else who might be suitable to perform the work. At that time, the principal might offer a staff member the prospect of interviewing for the job on the side.

Alternatively, a prospective client with a small remodel may be referred to your firm by a satisfied client with whom your boss would like to continue a professional relationship. Although your boss is only interested in high-end custom residential projects, she may feel obliged to help this new client and therefore offer you the opportunity to complete the remodel as a side project. The same might also be applicable for a client whose budget is too small for your office to reasonably take on.

Before you accept any moonlighting projects, it's important to understand the firm's policy. Make it clear to the client that your work is being done independently and with no assistance from your firm. Be professional and responsible by not taking calls or scheduling meetings for your side projects during the workday.

Giving Notice

Some states require it while others do not; but as a rule, it is considered professional courtesy for employees to give an employer two weeks' notice of their resignation. This gives the employer time to find a replacement and gives you time to pass on your project responsibilities to another person within the firm.

While it is important to put your resignation in writing, you should meet with your employer or supervisor to tell him or her the news in person and submit your resignation letter. No matter what the circumstances that led to the decision, remember to handle the meeting with the utmost professionalism. The phrase "Don't burn any bridges" is highly applicable to this situation—you may eventually need a reference for a future job or a signature on your IDP forms. A principal or supervisor who was your antagonist throughout your employment could surprisingly become an advocate for you and be highly supportive of your move. Even in the worst of circumstances, where you know you won't ever call upon your employer to provide a reference, his or her opinion of you may be solicited by a friend or acquaintance from the new firm at which you are applying. The global architectural community is extremely networked, so treat your resignation with significant care and consideration.

Regardless of your loyalty or commitment to a firm, two weeks' notice is generally adequate. While it may seem at the time that you have a lot of responsibilities or tasks to complete for a given project, it should be possible to delegate them and bring someone else up to speed within two weeks. I have known some interns who stretched out their departure over three or four weeks, only to realize that they've become the proverbial "lame duck." Lame ducks do not receive any new responsibilities, because they are seen by their colleagues as "on their way out" and can become a burden to the team if they are not productive. There may be special circumstances that require additional notice (i.e., previously planned vacation during the last two weeks), but even then it is advisable to consult with your mentor before giving notice to see if your situation truly requires additional time.

Getting Laid Off

While termination in other fields generally has to do with a significant breach of ethical or professional conduct, being laid off is fairly common in architectural practice. While we all hope to avoid such a situation, it is worth mentioning here. An individual may be laid off for a number of reasons, such as a significant decrease in workload from the time of hire, failure to meet an employer's expectations, or even personality conflicts. Some firms simply embrace the cyclical nature of the business and staff up or down accordingly. While there is no definitive way of knowing if you will be laid off, good communication with the senior people in your office will provide important warning signs. If you are concerned about your performance on a project, it is worth discussing this with your project manager. It may turn out that your performance was stellar or that you far exceeded the expectations of everyone in the firm; if so, you will certainly like to know this, and by asking, you demonstrate your interest in making a significant contribution to the efforts of the firm. If there were issues with your performance on a recent project, the earlier you discuss it, the better prepared you will be for your next project.

7 | PROFESSIONAL DEVELOPMENT

Performance Reviews

Let's say you land the perfect job. What next? Upon starting your new job, you should request a meeting with your supervisors or firm principals to discuss your goals and career objectives as well as their expectations for your performance. This will become the benchmark for your first performance review.

Some firms conduct an initial three-month review, but it is more common to have a yearly review. In nonarchitectural business settings, quarterly reviews are the norm; this frequency provides timely and pertinent feedback to encourage or alter performance—proactive efforts to improve are nurtured and bad habits are not allowed to develop further. If your firm doesn't conduct frequent reviews and you want feedback on your performance, you can always request a meeting to discuss performance with your supervisor.

The review is an opportunity for both you and your employer to evaluate your performance, set goals and expectations, and discuss areas for improvement. While many interns and young architects approach reviews with trepidation, this time should really be considered an opportunity to reflect on accomplishments, identify areas to develop over the upcoming year, and serve as a forum to share your comments and concerns. Remember that your supervisor may also view the review with trepidation. Many supervisors lack formal training in this area and feel uncomfortable providing constructive criticism. Passive-aggressive behavior runs rampant in American society and is evidenced in architectural practice through a lack of communication on performance-related issues.

How to Prepare for a Performance Review

Typically, the firm provides a form in advance that you are expected to complete and bring to the review. Some firms request the completed form before the actual review so they can prepare a response. The form may ask you to:

- List your accomplishments for the past year
- List your strengths and weaknesses
- Describe what you are doing about areas of weakness
- List short-term and long-term goals
- Describe progress you have made on the goals outlined in your previous review
- List ways the firm can support your goals
- List any outside professional or community activities

If your employer does not provide such a form, be proactive and prepare a brief summary of the past year based on some of the questions above as well as topics you would like to discuss.

Asking for a Raise

If you feel you deserve a raise, ask for it before your review. Provide your reviewer with reasons why you deserve the raise, citing the accomplishments that can be acknowledged by your reviewer. This will help the reviewer lobby for your increase over others who feel they deserve increases as well.

Most firms have a specific "pot of money" they can distribute among all the employees. Based on their evaluation of your performance, they will apportion the available funds to those who are, in their minds, most deserving. If you wait to see how much they offer before you counter with an increase, you may be too late, since all of the available funds will have been apportioned already. However, if your expectation for a raise was greater than what was given, you should still make it known during the review so that it is documented in your personnel file.

Asking for a Promotion or More Responsibility

I don't give responsibility, you take responsibility.
—MIES VAN DER ROHE TO AN INTERN IN HIS OFFICE

A performance review is the ideal time to request a promotion or indicate your desire to assume more responsibility. While some may think promotion should coincide with a raise, you may wish to request additional responsibility to demonstrate your readiness for a salary increase. In some cases, it may be that you received a raise and are performing the duties of the next level (job captain, project manager), but have not been granted the title. In other instances, you may have received the title and responsibility without the compensation. Your review is a great time to point out these inconsistencies or inquire about the steps you should take to obtain your desired position or salary.

IDP as a Career Development Tool

The IDP Periodic Assessment Report provides you with a document to share with your supervisors. It can be downloaded from the NCARB Web site prior to your review and numerically demonstrates the training units you have obtained in the past year and where you have deficiencies of experience. Use it during your review as a guide for setting goals in the upcoming year. Develop a game plan with your supervisors for obtaining training in those difficult areas, even if it means attending seminars or taking temporary assignments in other studios. Refer to Chapter 3 for detailed information about IDP and the IDP Summary Report.

Self-Promotion, or "Tooting Your Own Horn"

Without being overly boastful or arrogant, be sure to speak up about your accomplishments and achievements. Regardless of size, in a firm of talented individuals, it is easy to be overlooked for raises and opportunities if you don't tout your achievements. If clients have been complimentary about your work and commitment to a project, thank them and let them know that you would appreciate a note or e-mail addressed to your supervisor expressing their satisfaction. Similarly, firm leaders won't know about your professional awards or community recognition if you do not share the news with them. The firm may even want to share these types of achievements with the professional community by way of a press release to the local business journal or AIA newsletter.

Build a strong working relationship with those around you. An advocate in the firm promoting you at the same time as you promote yourself can go a long way toward increasing your responsibilities and putting you on the projects that you really want to work on. Advocates at a senior level in the firm may ask to have you on their team because they like working with you. These individuals may eventually move on to other offices, and suddenly you may find yourself with a network of future employment opportunities.

Continuing Education

Whether it is an AIA seminar or a product lunch at the office, continuing education seminars can quickly expand your knowledge of current code requirements, trends, and technologies in architectural design and practice. For many interns, practice-related seminars can help provide the background for management and leadership opportunities within the firm. For example, seminars on project management and AIA contracts can provide insight into how your project is being managed and give you a broader understanding of how your daily work fits into the context of the contract and the project deliverables you are responsible for creating.

To maintain a consistent level of quality for continuing education programs, the AIA has developed the Continuing Education System (CES) which provides criteria for the program content and requirements for how to become a CES Provider. Members of the AIA are required to obtain 18 continuing education learning units (LUs) annually, 8 of which must satisfy the health, safety, and welfare criteria. These LUs are currently tracked for the AIA by the University of Oklahoma. They are provided by over 2,500 AIA/CES providers that range from local AIA components to product representatives and individual firms; all AIA/CES providers are registered by the AIA. As an intern, you can accrue learning units for a year prior to licensure; these accumulated hours can then be applied during your first year of licensure. Likewise, if you have obtained more than the required learning units for the calendar year, you can carry up to 18 units forward toward the following year's requirements.

Continuing education requirements are not limited to AIA members. More than half of the states in the United States and almost all of the Canadian provinces require continuing education units (CEUs) to maintain licensure. While the specific number of credits varies from state to state, the CEUs obtained can satisfy both the state and AIA LU requirements.

Building an Area of Expertise

Continuing education can be a good excuse to become an expert in a subject such as sustainable technologies, building envelope systems, or a particular project type. Attending conferences on high-density housing or aging seniors can help you learn about senior housing but also introduce you to a network of other knowledgeable professionals. Your regular attendance at conferences can bring you and your firm recognition in a given field as well as open doors to client contacts. Firms typically address funding requests for conference attendance on a case-by-case basis, but they may pay some portion of the cost. Refer to the section "How to Get Your Employer to Pay" for suggestions on demonstrating mutual benefit.

Another avenue for becoming an expert may lie in the field of sustainable design. Leadership in Energy and Environmental Design (LEED) is a voluntary green building rating system for developing high-performance, sustainable buildings. This national rating system was introduced in the early 1990s by the U.S. Green Building Council and has gained wider acceptance in recent years. Acquiring LEED certification can be time-intensive, but it may make you a valuable contributor to your firm or an attractive candidate in the marketplace. With client demand for sustainable strategies increasing, firms will look toward employees with LEED certification to help market the company in new ways.

How to Get the Most Out of Conferences and Seminars

Conferences generally publish descriptions of the various sessions they offer. Before you sign up, you should scan through the listings to see what programs interest you. Circle them and see if there are enough to warrant the registration fee and time away from work. If tours are offered in addition to seminars, take advantage of both. Events like the AIA national conference or the International Union of Architects (UIA) congress can provide great opportunities to see other cities from a local architect's perspective.

Find out if coworkers or firm leaders are attending. Senior members of the firm may be interested to know that you are attending and may offer suggestions for people to meet or things to do. They may also offer financial support for your attendance.

During the seminars, sit near the front and take notes. Ask questions and try to meet those sitting around you. While the tendency is to write your notes in your sketchbook, seminar handouts are generally the best place to keep notes. When you return to the office, compile in a binder all your notes and insights along with the information distributed. Some firms may request that you share some of your new-found knowledge. If you are not asked, you may want to be proactive and volunteer to present what you learned at the conference.

If you attend the same conference annually, you will start to see familiar faces. Intelligent questions asked during sessions will be acknowledged by others, and over time, you can become an "expert," offering insights and elevating the discussion.

A Selection of Major Annual Architectural Conferences in the United States			
Conference Name/Sponsor	Dates	Location	Web Site
American Institute of Architects National Convention	May or June	Varies annually	aia.org
Greenbuild/U.S. Green Building Council	November	Varies annually	usgbc.org
Build Boston/Boston Society of Architects	November	Boston	architects.org
ULI conferences (based on topics)/Urban Land Institute	Various	Varies	www.uli.org
Congress for the New Urbanism	June	Varies annually	cnu.org
NeoCon World's Trade Fair (interior design)	June	Chicago	merchandisemart.com/neocon
Forum/American Institute of Architecture Students	December	Varies annually	aias.org
Association of Collegiate Schools of Architecture Annual Meeting	March	Varies annually	acsa-arch.org

Photo by Michael Mariano, AIA, 2004

Certificate Programs

Another way to build expertise is through advanced education. Many universities offer certificate programs geared toward working professionals. These intense programs (from one month to a year in length) offer in-depth instruction on specific topics, such as project management, leadership, construction management, and commercial real estate development. They are generally taught by professionals in the field. Additionally, some community colleges offer specialty training in subjects like sustainable design. The cost of such programs varies depending on length and intensity. The knowledge gained can equal the value of the relationships built and contacts made with classmates.

How to Get Your Employer to Pay

Find out if your firm has a continuing education or professional development budget for staff. If so, tap into those resources. If they don't, and you feel the knowledge gained would be valuable, ask your supervisor or a firm principal if the company would be willing to pay for the registration fees and/or time away.

Generally, the best way to approach this is to assemble a letter that describes how your attendance would mutually benefit you and the firm. For example, explain how your attendance at an AIA contract documents seminar could provide you with an understanding of the firm's contracts. Your increased knowledge could help ensure that you only provide your clients with the services for which they have contracted, and your comprehension of contract issues would allow you to alert principals when a client is asking for work that may be outside the contracted scope. Offer to present seminar materials to the office during lunch so the knowledge can be shared with others.

If you really want to attend the conference, demonstrate that you are willing to contribute to your professional development as well: Offer to make up the time out of the office if the firm pays for the registration. Alternatively, you could offer to pay for the seminar if the company provides you with an overhead number so you can bill your time away, instead of using your vacation time. Or, if the conference is in another city, offer to pay for your own travel and lodging in exchange for the registration fees.

It never hurts to ask. The worst they can say is no. And even then, they are at least aware of your interest and dedication to learning.

Going Back to School

Many interns with an undergraduate architectural degree work for a year or two before returning to graduate school. Other interns who never considered graduate school before realize after their first few years that they want to return to school—perhaps to round out their skills or figure out what they ultimately want to do within the field of architecture. And then there are others who, like me, after 12 years of practice and obtaining licensure in 3 states, decide to return to school in order to research a subject and develop a specialization in a specific project type.

Many interns and architects return to school during recessions or slowdowns in the market. These are opportune times to pursue further education. Many architects did this in the early 1990s to ride out the lull in the job market.

Whatever the reason may be, be sure to understand why you are going back to school and what it is you want to get out of it. For example, if you are considering pursuing an academic career, a master of architecture is the minimum degree required for tenure-track positions, but be prepared for an increasing preference for PhDs.

Applying to graduate school after a few years of internship will generally result in a more comprehensive portfolio, demonstrating practical application of the theoretical work you may have done as an undergraduate. It is appropriate to include projects from your professional experience in your application portfolio as long as you acknowledge your role on the team and identify the drawings you produced.

Research the schools you are considering much in the same way you researched firms and cities during your job search. When you graduate, it will probably be easy for you to find employment in the city where your school is located through the contacts you make, so don't settle on a school if you don't like the location. You will be residing in that city for two to three years to complete your studies, so select a city that you will enjoy.

While most architects seeking advanced education will probably focus on architecture, degrees in business management, human resources management, or marketing can be highly beneficial to your work as an architect as well. These aspects of business are central to our practice, and yet little or no attention is given them during our architectural education. In an office, tasks in these areas are generally delegated to firm leaders who demonstrate a propensity for them, or they are assigned out of necessity. Regardless of size, all firms address business management, human resources, and marketing matters to some degree; their success in these areas is evidenced in their profitability, employee retention, and client satisfaction. With a firm grasp of human resource or business management skills, you will be better equipped to successfully manage your own practice if you become a firm leader or owner. Similarly, an understanding of marketing strategies and public relations techniques can help you or your employer achieve a new identity or effectively sell architectural services to an under-served market niche.

Similarly, degrees in related disciplines, such as urban planning and design, land-scape architecture, historic preservation, and construction management, may augment the skills you already possess as well as the services your firm can provide. By obtaining an advanced degree in one of these subjects, you may be able to pursue work in a specialized area of practice, such as renovating historic structures or master planning college campuses. These degrees also provide flexibility in future employment. Some architecture firms take a multidisciplinary approach to their work, and your ability to converse in many disciplines may help you be competitive in the job market.

Finally, depending on your reasons for considering school, ask yourself if there are other ways to achieve the same objective. In some cases, a degree may not be what you are looking for. Certificate programs, as mentioned previously, could provide the knowledge or professional growth you need to reach your goal.

Design Competitions

Design competitions can provide both personal and professional rewards. For those in firms where design innovation is not emphasized, participation in competitions allows for creative investigation and inspiration for the more mundane aspects of daily work. For some young designers, a commission won through a design competition may be the beginning of an independent practice. Being acknowledged by peers and firm leaders also brings personal satisfaction. Whether or not the entry is awarded a prize, a competition submission can become a portfolio piece demonstrating the creative power of an individual or a young team.

While most interns pursue competitions on their own time, you may want to inquire about submitting an entry on behalf of the firm. Some firms may be willing to support the effort should there be potential for a commission as the prize. Other firms may see a design competition as a good team-building opportunity and encourage an office-sponsored team to produce an entry after hours but using company resources. Others might just say that there are no resources available to devote to such endeavors. Unless you ask, you will not know the answer. However, your knowledge of the firm and its objectives will be your best guide in this matter. It may be helpful to assemble a proposal detailing your request for resources from the office (large-format printing, use of computers after hours, etc.) along with a proposed schedule and list of time and materials that the team will donate.

While many organizations may sponsor competitions, the table below lists some of the top Web sites for researching competition opportunities.

Architecture Competition Web Sites	
deathbyarchitecture.com	Death by Architecture
competitions.archiseek.com	Archiseek
competitions.org	*Competitions* magazine
thearchitectureroom.com	The Architecture Room
www.arplus.com	*Architectural Review*
architectureforhumanity.org	Architecture for Humanity
archpaper.com/competitions.html	*The Architect's Newspaper*
builderspace.com/architecture/competitions.html	Builder Space
metropolismag.com	*Metropolis* magazine
ribacompetitions.com	Royal Institute of British Architects (RIBA) competitions
www.acsa-arch.org	Associate for Collegiate Schools of Architecture (ACSA)
aias.org	American Institute of Architecture Students (AIAS)

Photo by Michael Mariano, AIA, 2004

Fellowships and Research Grants

Another way to build an area of expertise or obtain funding for personal research is through a fellowship or grant. While there are many opportunities available, it will take time to find those appropriate for you. Many university Web sites offer links to research grants and fellowships. The following programs represent a sampling of the types of fellowships and grants available in the United States. Refer to the end of Chapter 10 for information on fellowship programs abroad.

Selected Fellowship and Grant Opportunities		
Fellowship or Grant	Description	Web Site
Loeb Fellowship	Promotes leadership potential of mid-career design professionals	www.gsd.harvard.edu/professional/loeb_fellowship
Graham Foundation	Research grants for the promotion of architecture and the built environment	www.grahamfoundation.org
Fredrick P. Rose Architectural Fellowship	$40,000 stipend for new architects to work with community-based organizations to serve low- and moderate-income communities	www.enterprisefoundation.org/rosefellowship
Tradewell Fellowship	Paid, one-year program in medical planning	www.whrarchitects.com/tradewellfellowship.cfm
AmeriCorps	Network of national service programs that meet critical needs in education, public safety, health, and the environment	www.americorps.gov
National Endowment for the Arts/Graham Fellowship in Federal Service	One-year, $40,000 position for recent graduates and young design professionals interested in national design policy and advocacy	www.nea.gov
Detroit-Mercy Intern/Teaching Program	Two-year fellowship for professional degree holders to engage in community design work	www.udmercy.edu
Community Design Opportunities	Online resource linking students, architects, and designers with local, community-based efforts	www.designcorps.org

Loeb Fellowship

The Loeb Fellowship was established in 1970 through the generosity of the late Harvard alumnus John L. Loeb. Based at Harvard's Graduate School of Design, the program offers ten annual postprofessional awards for independent study. Through the fellowship, participants have access to the Graduate School of Arts and Sciences, the Graduate School of Design, the Graduate School of Education, Harvard Business School, Harvard College, Harvard Divinity School, Harvard Law School, the Kennedy School of Government, and M.I.T.

The Loeb Fellowship aims to nurture the leadership potential of the most promising men and women in design and other professions related to the built and natural environment. It enhances the excellence of the Graduate School of Design by exposing students to some of the most exciting mid-career professionals in their fields. Now entering its fourth decade, with over 300 alumni, the fellowship has made substantial progress toward John Loeb's goal of increasing the practical effectiveness of the design professions.

Graham Foundation for Advanced Studies in the Fine Arts

Based in the historic Madlener House in Chicago, the Graham Foundation seeks to nurture and enrich an informed and creative public dialogue concerning architecture and the built environment.

Graham Foundation grants are offered to individuals and institutions in support of activities that focus on architecture and the built environment and that result in public dissemination of ideas through publication, exhibition, or educational programming.

In the past, the foundation has supported a variety of scholarly endeavors, including individual research; grants to architectural schools for special projects, enrichment programs, or new curricula; grants to museums, schools, and libraries for exhibitions and catalogues; and support for publications, usually to help make an important publication better or more affordable. Lists and abstracts of previous grants can be found on the foundation's Web site.

Applicants must send a proposal, résumé, three letters of reference, and any supplemental visual information as well as a work plan, schedule, and budget to complete the project.

Rose Fellowship

The Frederick P. Rose Architectural Fellowship is offered by the Enterprise Foundation, an organization that provides support to community development organizations. The fellowship is designed to promote architectural and community design in low-income neighborhoods with a focus on improving the quality of life through design.

The fellowship fosters productive partnerships between architects and community development organizations and encourages architects to become lifelong leaders in public service and community development. Fellows have played key roles in completing community-based child-care facilities and community gardens, as well as rehabilitating and creating new affordable housing.

Each fellow receives guidance and support from local professionals. Fellows also receive ongoing training from national experts, a $40,000 annual stipend, and benefits including health care.

Each fellow identifies a community development mentor (working outside the partner organization) with whom he or she will meet on a regular basis. The mentor provides the fellow with the opportunity to discuss the scope and scale of community development issues within the community.

Each fellow is also responsible for identifying an IDP supervisor and an IDP mentor, if necessary. The supervisor and mentor will work with the fellow over the three-year period to supervise the fellow's work and comment on the fellow's workplan. While the Enterprise Foundation can't guarantee IDP credit for the work experience, the intent of the program is to enable fellows to apply the experience they gain toward IDP requirements.

Tradewell Fellowship

The Tradewell Fellowship Program is a privately funded fellowship offered by WHR Architects. Named in honor of the company's former vice president and medical planner, the late Gary Tradewell, the Tradewell fellow participates in the development of innovative health facility projects through marketing, research, planning, and design. The fellow works directly with senior leadership at WHR and is expected to support project work as well as complete a project suitable for publication. Benefits include conference attendance, frequent exposure to clients, rapid knowledge transfer, access to senior mentorship, and the opportunity to work on front-end project phases. The fellowship was inspired and founded by D. Kirk Hamilton, FAIA, FACHA, founding principal of WHR Architects.

Invitations to apply are sent annually to universities in North America. Application requirements include a written statement of intent, two letters of recommendation, portfolio samples, and an application form. Applications are reviewed by a committee comprised of the current program director and former fellows currently employed by WHR.

Former fellow Lia Johnson shares her story about how her fellowship helped to shape her career. For her the Tradewell Fellowship nurtured mentorship, learning, and core relationships early in her career, capitalizing on her energy, creativity, and curiosity to foster her development into a talented young health-care architect.

During the junior and senior years of my undergraduate education at Texas A&M, I enrolled in design studios focused on health care. I was mesmerized by the complexity of design for health-care facilities and moved by human events such as birth, healing, suffering, and death. Simultaneously, I was drawn to the aesthetic and philosophical issues related to the environment. In hindsight, I find it difficult to distinguish boundaries between my thoughts on nature and healing, but these interests clearly led to my current specialization.

After my junior year, I secured a summer internship at RTKL Associates in Dallas. It was a typical internship, rife with redlines and construction documents. I was fortunate enough to work alongside design teams assisting with presentations, performing site analysis studies, and building conceptual models. Pay was hourly, with no benefits (typical for short-term employees), but the added value to my résumé far outweighed the financial benefits, in that I was now able to list practical office experience.

The following year, a professor who knew of my interest in health care informed me of the Tradewell Fellowship, and I submitted my application. It was hard for me to get a sense of my chances of winning the award, since I was unable to interview and make a personal connection. Additionally, I didn't know who my competitors were or how I stacked up against them. The national pool from which the fellowship draws its candidates is diverse, with a broad range of skills and backgrounds. Fortunately, I was successful.

During my fellowship, I was responsible for assisting Kirk Hamilton on the vision, planning, and schematic design of a 500-bed replacement hospital in Royal Oak, Michigan. I helped organize a conference and served as editorial assistant of the conference catalogue. In addition, I designed and managed the renovation of a prototypical intensive care unit for an older facility as a pilot prior to the facility's full renovation. These are just a few of my fellowship milestones, clearly unique experiences for a recent graduate of a four-year architecture program.

Following my fellowship, I ventured to Portland, Oregon, and, through another Aggie, secured an interview at the ZGF Partnership. ZGF was targeting me for their health-care studio; however, I was so fearful of committing to a specialization at such a young age that I talked my way out of that studio and was placed on the Oregon Convention Center Expansion team. This was my first experience working on a large-scale project. I concluded my time at ZGF with a decision to return to graduate school at Montana State University.

After completing my master's degree, I secured a job at a high-end residential design firm in Bozeman, Montana. During my tenure at JLF & Associates, I com-

pleted the Intern Development Program and began testing for licensure. My experience was analogous to an apprenticeship. I learned a great deal about residential design and, more important, about craft and design with basic materials and complex detailing.

A holiday visit to Houston and a conversation with my former supervisor, Kirk Hamilton, convinced me to rejoin WHR. It was clear that my skill set, combined with my knowledge and experience in health care, made me a valuable candidate for a firm seeking to hire a young health-care architect. I had missed the deeply sociological aspects of health care and the wonderful, mission-driven clients who made the participatory design process so enjoyable, so I accepted the offer to return to WHR. I was now a "boomeranger," having moved from Houston to Portland to Bozeman and back to Houston.

When I returned to WHR, my résumé included six years of well-rounded general experience, as well as specialized, architectural typologies. Because of this background, I was able to approach my interview and salary negotiations with specifics such as areas of interest and requests to work on front-end project phases. My second-term salary at WHR was almost double my starting salary as a fellow. Since my return, I have I felt valued and supported in my career. I have had the opportunity to work on the initial design phases of health-care projects. I have also been encouraged to lead a sustainability initiative at the firm, which allows me to continue to pursue my environmental interests. Approximately one year after my return, I was promoted to associate.

While it is difficult to distinguish among good luck, timing, and strategy, it is easy to see the correlation between relationship, mentorship, and dedication. Interns may be strategic and opportunistic in their job search, but those elements are worth little without the dedication, support, and wisdom of a mentor. Mentors convey faith and trust; they hone talent and pass on decades of wisdom and knowledge. They provide parameters for success as well as failure, helping young interns steer their careers in clear directions. It is difficult for interns to break free of stifling career paths without the guidance of a mentor. For the holistic success of our profession and the environments we build, it is crucial that interns be matched with committed mentors who openly convey a sense of caring for them and their future. The Tradewell Fellowship is one example of a program in which a firm helps to build relationships, contributing to the careers of young architects as well as to health care.

Lia Johnson, LEED AP, AIA
Associate, WHR Architects
Montana State University, Master of Architecture 2002
Texas A&M, Bachelor of Environmental Design 1998

CHAPTER 8 | HOW DO OTHERS GET THROUGH THIS?

Approximately 25% of respondents felt that their professional satisfaction (24 percent), the type of work (29 percent), and the hours worked (29 percent) were worse than expected.

—2003 ARCHVOICES/AIA INTERNSHIP AND CAREER SURVEY

According to the statistic above, there is a one-in-four chance that you will feel frustrated and disenchanted by the profession during the course of your internship. And you may possibly wonder, "How am I going to get through this?" or "Is it even worth it?" Just remember, you are not alone. Issues surrounding internship are recurring topics for the collateral organizations described below, and professionals and academic institutions are making a concerted effort to remedy internship malaise. Such effort has been slow in coming, however, so creative interns have also been adapting and finding their own means of "survival," initiating support groups in their local communities as well as on the Internet.

The Five Collaterals

The five main bodies representing members of our profession are known as the collateral organizations, or simply the five collaterals: AIA, AIAS, ACSA, NCARB, and NAAB. The five collaterals work together to address issues pertinent to the entire architectural profession. These organizations have served our profession for many generations.

The American Institute of Architects (AIA) was founded in 1857 and represents those who are engaged in professional practice, including emerging professionals. Since 1956, architecture students have been represented by the American Institute of Architecture Students (AIAS). The Association for Collegiate Schools of Architecture (ACSA) was founded in 1912 to advance the quality of architectural education, and its membership consists of American and Canadian architecture schools and programs. Founded in 1919, the National Council of Architectural Registration Boards (NCARB) is responsible for establishing model legislation and programs for adoption by state boards. It represents the registration concerns of the profession. Members of these four collaterals all serve on the National Architectural Accrediting Board (NAAB) to maintain standards for architectural education and accredit architecture schools. The figure below shows how the five collaterals relate. These organizations shape the national debate on all topics related to architecture. The presidents of each organization are often referred to as the Five Presidents' Council.

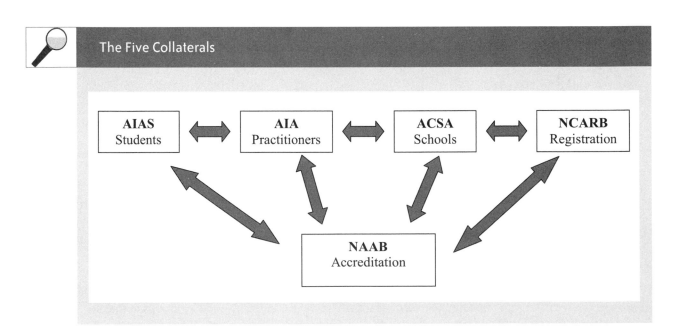

The Five Collaterals

AIAS
Students

AIA
Practitioners

ACSA
Schools

NCARB
Registration

NAAB
Accreditation

In the past decade, interns and young professionals have come into their own, requesting a voice at the table. Through major initiatives involving the collateral organizations, significant strides have been made toward improving the status and acceptance of younger members of the profession. The AIA has devoted energy and attention to the Young Architects Forum (YAF) and created a National Associates Committee (NAC), both of which fall under the umbrella category of *emerging professionals.* The AIA has also developed Web resources for emerging professionals, including a mentorship Web site, an online mentor matching program, and the Emerging Professionals Companion. The NAC and YAF have local, regional, and national programs and serve as voices for emerging professionals within the AIA. These groups meet at the local and national level throughout the year.

The collaterals' work has historically been slow, perhaps too slow for the constantly evolving issues faced by interns. In direct response to this concern, interns have created their own infrastructure of support groups. Two such groups, ArchVoices.org and Architect.com, have become venues for architectural discourse on a national level. On another Web site, InsideArch.com, interns share information about office culture from an insider's point of view. In addition to providing general information, members can anonymously rate their firms and provide comments about what it is like to work in them. All three groups were started by interns who wanted to provide interns across North America with a voice. These groups exist almost exclusively on the Web and are comprised of thousands of subscribers. There is no physical membership that meets collectively on a regular basis.

To fully appreciate the role of such groups as ArchVoices and the National Associates Committee, it is important to understand the discourse that led to their inception. Much of the recent focus on intern issues can be attributed to the publication of *Building Community: A New Future for Architecture Education and Practice,* by Ernest Boyer and Lee D. Mitgang of the Carnegie Foundation for the Advancement of Teaching. This seminal book, published in 1996, came to be known as the Boyer Report and was the seed for several committees that reviewed its recommendations.

One such committee, the Collateral Boyer Task Force (CBTF), was comprised of representatives from each of the five collateral architectural organizations. The CBTF recommended a summit to focus discourse on the transition between education and practice.

The first Summit on Architectural Internship convened in April 1999, after defining several objectives: reconsider the term *intern;* allow the ARE to be taken upon graduation; integrate practice and education; allow alternative paths for practical experience; foster a culture of lifelong learning; enhance reciprocity; and increase accessibility to the profession. The collateral organizations appointed 11 summit attendees to a serve on a new task force to review the objectives and develop implementation strategies. This group, called the Collateral Internship Task Force (CITF), discussed and expanded upon the seven objectives of the summit. The work of the CITF was presented to the five collaterals in a report for adoption and action.

In January 2001, the Five Presidents' Council "accepted with appreciation" the final report of the CITF but did not adopt the recommendations. Several months later, an open letter to the 5 collaterals written by 17 interns and young architects, frustrated by the bureaucracy, pointed to the need for an additional internship summit and requested support from the other collaterals.

The 2002 National Summit on Architectural Internship was hosted by the University of Oklahoma and organized by ArchVoices. Fifty members of the profession, representing all collateral organizations and a wide range of experience levels, were invited to attend. Summit participants identified a series of quantitative metrics to measure the current status and future progress toward the CITF recommendations. A successive summit was held in San Antonio in September 2005.

ArchVoices: Started *by* Interns *for* Interns

When John Cary, cofounder of ArchVoices, submitted this contribution, he acknowledged that the architectural profession and the world at large have changed radically over the past decade. The Internet and e-mail have given professionals, both young and old, the ability to stay connected and share ideas. The following account from John, which can also be found on the ArchVoices Web site, speaks to the latent power in these intern-led organizations. He describes the events that resulted in the founding of ArchVoices, beginning with the 1999 Summit on Architectural Internship.

The Moon Shot

The room was packed. An opening statement by well-known educator Wayne Drummond cautioned that the summit was just the start of what would necessarily be a long process. Drummond's analogy was to Kennedy's moon shot: Kennedy didn't know exactly how to get to the moon, but he set a ten-year goal and inspired people to meet it. Entirely new technologies had to be developed that no one had even considered in 1960. Drummond's point was that truly meaningful change would take time and would require new structures that no one in 1999 had even considered.

The Journey Begins

One intern, Casius Pealer, was convinced that the moon shot was the right analogy. However, he wasn't confident that the collateral organizations would be able to successfully tackle the challenge. He didn't know what the answer was, but he felt it started with better communication. So he sent out an e-mail to 200 friends and colleagues and hoped for a response.

To his surprise and amazement, the response was overwhelming, with interns responding to e-mails that had been forwarded by friends 10 or 11 times. The young people who responded were in a complete void of information about internship, such that a random e-mail from a complete stranger was welcome relief. So Casius sent out another e-mail. And another. Then he moved to a banana field in a remote village of a developing country.

About a year earlier, Casius had volunteered to teach carpentry in the U.S. Peace Corps. In July 1999, he got on a plane with 54 young people he didn't know, to spend the next two years living in an island nation he had never heard of, with people he had never met. Although there was no electricity, Casius had brought a laptop computer. As work got underway, soon there was running water and electricity, as well as phone service and even Internet access. Meanwhile, e-mails continued to pour in from young professionals throughout United States wanting information about architectural internship. Casius had expected someone else or some established group to start coordinating these e-mails, but that didn't happen. And thus ArchVoices started—from a developing country.

At the time, I happened to be serving as the AIAS national vice president, working out of the AIA headquarters building in Washington, D.C. This was in the wake of the 1999 internship summit, but you would never have known it; for the collateral organizations, it was business as usual. Frankly, I was both confused and impressed that the only regular source of information about internship was coming from a banana field in the West Indies. Wanting to do my part, I began to contribute whatever time, energy, and ideas I could to ArchVoices. Our almost-monthly newsletter soon became monthly. Then, in November 1999, we added a monthly resource issue, and in August 2000, twice-monthly editorial issues.

Believe in the Future

More than six years after its establishment in 1999, ArchVoices exists as an independent nonprofit organization and think tank focused on young professionals and the future of the profession. In addition to sharing ideas and information with thousands of people each week via our e-mail newsletter and Web site, we host regular conferences, cosponsor a biennial survey, and coordinate an annual essay competition.

Our mission remains the same as it was in that very first e-mail years ago: We seek to increase communication among and about young professionals, as colleagues who are facing similar challenges with similar hopes and aspirations. ArchVoices is clearly not the definitive word from interns or young professionals, and we would hardly expect such a disparate group to speak with one voice. However, we continue ArchVoices in the interest of having our peer group become less disparate and more involved.

The same factors that necessitate a "survival guide for architectural internship" continue to reinforce the need for ArchVoices. Through these efforts, we can only hope that we're guiding the profession to a point where young people won't have to worry about "survival," but can focus instead on the things that drew them to architecture in the first place.

John Cary
Cofounder, ArchVoices
University of Minnesota, Bachelor of Arts in Architecture 1999
University of California, Berkeley, Master of Architecture 2003

2003 ArchVoices/AIA Internship and Career Survey

As a think tank, ArchVoices collected and disseminated information about the profession; it also conducted surveys among emerging professionals. The 2003 Internship & Career Survey, cosponsored by ArchVoices and the AIA, was intended to expand our knowledge and establish some common ground. It is a unique snapshot of the experiences and opinions of young professionals working in a wide array of settings throughout the country.

In developing the survey, a work group drew upon several preceding internship surveys as well as ongoing market surveys like the AIA Compensation Survey and Firm Survey. What these other efforts consistently show is that the traditional path to registration is changing in significant ways. This is an exciting but critical time for all members of our profession to study and respond to significant trends in internship and registration.

The survey was delivered by e-mail to 19,912 interns and young architects and elicited 4,816 responses. It was divided into ten broad sections: (1) Career Path, (2) Current Employment, (3) Education, (4) Prior Employment/Careers, (5) Firm Support and Mentoring, (6) Internship, (7) Architect Registration Examination, (8) Licensure/Registration, (9) Professional Involvement, and (10) About You.

This entire effort was the result of a collaborative partnership between two unique but related groups: ArchVoices and the AIA National Associates Committee (NAC). A follow-up survey was conducted in 2005, in preparation for the 2005 internship summit. Results of this survey were not available at press time.

Vicky L. Boddie, Assoc. AIA
Project Manager, Studio Five Architects, Inc.
University of Minnesota, Master of Architecture 1999

Archinect.com: Virtual Mentoring

The mission of Archinect is to make architecture more connected and open-minded, and to bring together designers from around the world to introduce new ideas from all disciplines. Archinect was initially developed in 1997 by Paul Petrunia, and the site has since become a top online destination for progressive, design-oriented students, architects, educators, and fans.

This Web site provides an interactive environment for asking questions and receiving advice. It's a great example of peer-to-peer mentorship; participants can actively solicit responses or passively review what others have posted. The postings occur at all hours of the day and night, and topics range from computer help to politics. Interns solicit advice on salaries and the job search. Students ask professionals whether all the hard work and insanity is worth it in the end. Since the posting is instantaneous, it's quite possible to have a pretty lively discussion in almost real time.

A single query can result in hundreds of responses from diverse points of view. However, as with other bulletin board Web resources, it is difficult to gauge the validity of the advice at times. The experience level of the person providing the advice is not always evident. On the other hand, the advice is likely to be timely and vitally relevant.

Users of the site range in experience from students to architects with their own practices; however, the postings to the discussion threads suggest there are more students and interns than practitioners. This site offers a valuable service to emerging professionals and will continue to grow as the user demographic expands.

American Institute of Architecture Students

For those still in school and recent graduates trying to make a transition to internship, there is the American Institute of Architecture Students. Its mission is to promote excellence in architecture education, training, and practice; foster an appreciation of architecture and related disciplines; enrich communities in a spirit of collaboration through community service; and organize students and combine their efforts to advance the art and science of architecture by encouraging them to serve on the boards of the AIA, ACSA, and NAAB.

Opportunities for dialogue and collaboration include publication in the student journal *CRiT;* attendance at the national AIAS convention, FORUM; participation in public service projects at the local and national level; participation in design competitions; and active involvement with the decision-making process of the other collateral organizations.

CRiT *Magazine*

For more than three decades, the AIAS has been publishing *CRiT*, the only national source of published student work. Each issue is focused on a theme and encourages dialogue on current debates in architectural education and the profession. Student projects selected for publication represent some of the best work being completed in North American architecture schools.

As a publication written by students for students, the topics are of greatest relevance to them. However, feature articles about faculty members and schools as well as practitioners and professional practice also appear in each issue. The "News" section lists announcements for design competitions, programs, and other opportunities. In addition to its other functions, *CRiT* provides a recorded history of the AIAS by chronicling the accomplishments of the membership while exposing the ongoing challenges they may face as they transition into the profession.

Photo by Michael Mariano, AIA, 2004

AIA Young Architects Forum

The Young Architects Forum is a leadership development program of the AIA. It was started in 1989, when the AIA became concerned about the future of the profession, and today there are over 30 active YAF groups across the country. With names such as ENYA (Emerging New York Architects) and BAYA (Bay Area Young Architects), they all have a similar mission: to gather and sustain architects through dialogue and a supportive peer network early in their careers.

The YAF is generally known for local programs that address a wide variety of issues, from construction administration and project management to mentorship. Its programs are not only relevant to young architects (those licensed ten years or less) but also interns. Construction tours, competitions, exhibitions, and discussions with up-and-coming firms are all examples of programs organized by YAF. While the combination of intern and young architect programming on the local level can be confusing to some, by blurring across the line of architectural registration, the YAF has been able to achieve its three main goals: leadership, mentorship, and fellowship.

Involvement in the YAF can be passive or active and range from simply attending an event to organizing one. At both the local and national level, leadership opportunities are abundant. The YAF is affiliated with the College of Fellows[1] and promotes mentoring relationships between young architects and Fellows. You can be mentored by a more seasoned professional or choose to mentor an intern or student in your local area. The network that you build throughout your career can be strengthened by your involvement in the YAF.

AIA National Associates Committee

The National Associates Committee is a relatively young group. In 1991, the AIA Board of Directors created the Intern/Associate Committee with the purpose of selecting an associate representative to the AIA board each year. By 1999, that group had determined that they were inadequately representing the rapidly growing associate membership (the fastest growing category of the AIA). They agreed to dissolve and proposed a new group consisting of 18 regional directors, calling it the National Associates Committee (NAC). The NAC's first meeting was in October 2000.

---

[1] The College of Fellows is composed of members of the AIA who are elected to fellowship by a jury of their peers. Fellowship is one of the highest honors the AIA can bestow upon a member, recognizing the individual achievements of the architect as well as his or her significant contributions to architecture and society.

The NAC is charged with representing the associate members of the AIA. Associate AIA membership is available to anyone who is an unlicensed architectural professional. This includes graduates of professional degree programs in architecture, those working in a professional capacity under the supervision of a licensed architect, faculty members in a university program in architecture, and those we know best, interns. Of the 13,000 associate AIA members, 80 percent are on the path to licensure. The rest do not have plans to obtain licensure for a variety of reasons, most likely because their career paths do not require it.

Reaping What You Sow

With any organization, what an individual receives is usually commensurate with the effort that person puts in. It is easy for architects to sit back and complain that the AIA doesn't satisfy their needs or that any other organization isn't doing a good job. However, if all those individuals were to take positive action and participate to make their organizations satisfy their needs, our professional community would be much richer and relevant to all. Although the following contributor is currently employed by the AIA, her earlier contributions to the Institute on intern-related issues can be seen in programs that she now oversees. She explains how her previous involvement with NAC helped shape the future for emerging professionals within the Institute.

I had the privilege of serving as a Regional Associates Director (RAD) for the mid-Atlantic region in 2001 and as the National Assoicates Committee's first chair. The group was so energetic, I spent most of my time trying to keep up with all of their ideas! In 2002, I served on the AIA board, where I faced the challenge of representing a viewpoint very different from that commonly heard at the AIA. The average AIA member is 55, white, and male. NAC leaders are, on average, in their early thirties; about 50 percent of us are women, and we represent an ethnic diversity more in keeping with the population we serve. The ideas planted by the first RADs in 2001 were beginning to take shape while I was on the board. We proposed a national survey, codeveloped with ArchVoices; contributed to the dialogue about an appropriate title for interns; and began an awards program to recognize associates and their service to the profession.

Today, I serve as the staff director at the AIA national component overseeing the NAC, the YAF, and pretty much anything having to do with internship, IDP, and the ARE. It is an enormous portfolio of work. But when I decided to leave my job with a great firm where I had a lot of opportunity for growth, I knew that the NAC and YAF were in the best position to make lasting changes in the architecture pro-

fession. Now in its fifth year, the NAC continues to represent a more culturally, ethnically, and gender diverse leadership than the AIA board of directors. For me, this is a testament to the unique contributions that interns and other nonlicensed architectural professionals make to the profession.

Suzanna Wight, AIA
Emerging Professionals Director, American Institute of Architects
Carnegie Mellon University, Bachelor of Architecture 1999

Other Groups

While the five collaterals dominate the U.S. architectural scene and interns work to find a collective voice, a number of other organizations continue to serve the needs of diverse groups within the architectural community. The Canadian counterparts to the five collaterals are listed in the table below.

Canadian Counterparts to the Five Collaterals

American	Canadian
AIA	Royal Architectural Institute of Canada (RAIC) and Provincial Architectural Associations
NCARB	Committee of Canadian Architectural Councils (CCAC) and Provincial Architectural Associations
NAAB	Canadian Architectural Certification Board (CACB)
AIAS	Canadian Architectural Students Association (CASA)
ACSA	ACSA (same organization for both the United States and Canada)

Described below are just a few examples of the various organizations that serve our profession. In addition, as you develop specific areas of interest or expertise, you will find other organizations, each addressing a particular project type or delivery method, such as the American College of Healthcare Architects (ACHA) and the Design-Build Institute of America (DBIA). Information for these other groups can be found on the Internet.

Society of American Registered Architects

An alternative to the AIA, the Society of American Registered Architects (SARA) was formed in 1956 as a professional society that includes the participation of all architects, regardless of their roles in the architectural community. SARA follows the Golden Rule — treat others as you would like to be treated — and supports the concept of profitable professionalism for its members. SARA offers a variety of membership services and programs, including a professional referral service, seminars in conjunction with its annual convention, professional and student design competitions, and efforts to strengthen and protect the interests of practicing architects.

Docomomo

This international organization derives its name from its objective: to promote the *doc*umentation and *con*servation of buildings, sites, and neighborhoods of the *mo*dern *mo*vement.

Until recently, the architectural heritage of the modern movement, which glorified the dynamic spirit of the Machine Age, was at risk. By the end of the 1980s, many modern masterpieces had already been demolished or had changed beyond recognition because they had not been designated heritage sites. (The time lapsed since their construction had not rendered them historically significant in the eyes of local and national landmark boards.)

Docomomo's mission is to act as watchdog for important modern movement buildings under threat; exchange ideas relating to conservation, history, and education; foster interest in the ideas and heritage of the modern movement; and encourage responsibility toward this recent architectural inheritance.

Docomomo holds an international conference every two years, selecting venues of significance to the modern movement.

International Union of Architects

The International Union of Architects (UIA) is a nongovernmental organization founded in 1948 in Lausanne, Switzerland, to unite architects from all nations, regardless of race, religion, or architectural school of thought. All practicing architects of member countries (including the United States and Canada) are granted member status in the UIA. The organization conducts the UIA Congress every three years, at rotating international venues.

Association for Women in Architecture

Founded in 1923, the Association for Women in Architecture (AWA) provides support to its members, especially those starting out in their professions and running their own firms, by developing educational programs, lectures, and tours, and by providing opportunities for mentoring and mutual support. The AWA also raises money for annual scholarship awards to women students pursuing degrees in architecture or allied fields. The national organization saw its peak in the mid-1950s; after this time, more women were admitted to architecture schools and eventually to the profession. The AIA broadened its membership to be more inclusive of women and, thus, the AWA began its decline. Today there are only two professional chapters surviving, in Los Angeles and Seattle, with a similar organization in Chicago called Chicago Women in Architecture.

National Organization of Minority Architects

Founded in 1971 by 12 architects from across the United States, NOMA exists to encourage communication and fellowship among minority architects; to work with local, state, and national governments on issues affecting the development of the built environment; and to provide motivation and inspiration for minority youth pursuing architecturally related careers. NOMA's mission is to build a strong national organization, strong chapters, and strong members to minimize the effects of racism in our profession. The association consists of 18 professional chapters and 33 student chapters.

Arquitectos

Started in 1995 in Chicago, Arquitectos is a membership organization that unites Hispanic architects to promote professionalism, economic development, and mentorship. Arquitectos is comprised of individuals with diverse backgrounds united by a professional, artistic, cultural, social, and political interest in architecture and community. The association consists of a professional chapter and two student chapters.

Boston Society of Architects

The Boston Society of Architects (BSA) is one of the oldest and largest chapters of the AIA. However, at times it may seem like a separate entity from the national AIA, sponsoring annual conferences and trade shows (such as Build Boston and Residential Design). Since its establishment in 1867, the BSA has administered programs and provided resources that enhance the practice of architecture and the public and professional understanding of design.

Architecture Radio

A nonprofit organization devoted to publishing audio/video recordings of important lectures, interviews, and discussions on the Internet, Architecture Radio (AR) was founded to promote learning and discussion on the pressing issues of design and the built environment. AR works by partnering with schools, nonprofits, professional organizations, and grass-roots groups to assist them in recording and publishing their public lectures and events online. AR helps groups streamline and clarify the process, and then collects the content in an online portal that is searchable and easy to use and encourages discussion and interaction between the audience and the speaker.

Public Architecture

Public Architecture is a nonprofit organization that uses the resources of architecture in the public interest. Public Architecture works proactively, identifying significant problems of wide relevance that require innovative research and design. It seeks to satisfy needs and desires that are palpable but poorly defined, and to take innovative action, from obtaining financing to identifying the client. The organization doesn't just pursue its own pro bono projects; it challenges other architects nationwide to formalize their commitment to public service. The "One Percent Solution" program encourages firms to pledge a small portion of their billable hours to the public interest.

Architecture for Humanity

In 1999, the nonprofit Architecture for Humanity was founded to promote architectural and design solutions that address global, social, and humanitarian crises. Through a variety of means, including competitions, workshops, and educational forums, Architecture for Humanity creates opportunities for architects and designers from around the world to help communities in need. Where resources and expertise are scarce, innovative, sustainable, and collaborative design can make a difference.

Web Site Resources

aia.org—American Institute of Architects

ncarb.org—National Council of Architectural Registrations Boards

naab.org—National Architectural Accrediting Board

www.acsa-arch.org—Association of Collegiate Schools of Architecture

aias.org—American Institute of Architecture Students

aia.org/nac—National Associates Committee

aia.org/yaf—Young Architects Forum

archinect.com—Archinect

insidearch.org—InsideArch

sara-national.org—Society of American Registered Architects

docomomo-us.org—Docomomo

uia-architectes.org—International Union of Architects

awa-la.org and **awaseattle.org**—Association for Women in Architecture

noma.net—National Organization of Minority Architects

arquitectoschicago.org—Arquitectos

architects.org—Boston Society of Architects

architecture-radio.org—Architecture Radio

publicarchitecture.org—Public Architecture

architectureforhumanity.org—Architecture for Humanity

CHAPTER 9 | MENTORSHIP

Origin and Tradition

In the epic poem *The Odyssey,* the goddess Athena disguises herself as a lifelong family friend named Mentor and helps young Telemachus learn the truth about his father Odysseus. Mentor's role is to educate, train, and develop the youngster to become an adult. In this ancient Greek story, we find the origin of the term *mentor*. In the context of architectural internship, mentorship is the key that helps each intern to develop into a masterful architect.

The art and craft of building developed over the centuries, in large part due to trusted master-apprentice relationships. This practice continued into the early part of the 20th century and evolved as architectural education became more formal. Today, this mentoring relationship is experiencing a renaissance and gaining importance as effective collaboration continues to prove essential in our fast-paced and rapidly changing work environment. This renaissance has been aided in part by the Boyer Report and the subsequent summit and Collateral Internship Task Force mentioned in Chapter 8. In their report, the CITF recommended a significant commitment to mentorship (see the sidebar below). In response to this recommendation, the AIA developed two tools to encourage mentorship: (1) a Web site entitled Mentoring: A Journey in Collaborative Learning, and (2) the AIA National Mentor Matching Program. These programs are described in more detail at the end of this chapter. Many large firms have adopted new mentoring programs, and irrespective of IDP requirements, individuals have taken a greater interest in pursuing formal mentor relationships.

84% of the respondents indicated interest in formalized mentoring programs.
—2003 ARCHVOICES/AIA INTERNSHIP AND CAREER SURVEY

CITF Report Recommendation on Mentoring

Excerpt from the 2001 Collateral Internship Task Force Report

The nine recommendations are presented as goals, objectives, and (possible) implementation strategies. The strategies are not exclusive; they are meant to provide guidance points for accomplishing each objective.

Recommendation VII. Continuous learning and mentorship are fundamental to the profession.

The demands of the architectural profession require a lifelong pursuit of knowledge, and acceptance of the obligation to be leaders and teachers.

1. Continuing education should be required to maintain registration.

2. Mentoring guidelines for all peer groups should be developed;
   for example, between students and graduates, between graduates and emerging professionals, and between emerging professionals and practitioners.

3. Mentoring networks should be established.

4. Incentives for individual and firm participation in defined mentorship programs should be provided.

Photo courtesy of David Sachs, 2005

The Impacts of Mentorship

As described in Chapter 3, mentors are required for IDP. However, mentors and mentorship can have a profound impact on career development throughout your professional life, not just during internship. It is possible to have many mentors at a given time, with each mentor providing guidance in specific areas: professional practice, design, project management, or social responsibility. Mentors may also change over the course of your career.

As an intern, you may need a mentor to help navigate IDP and the ARE. As a newly licensed architect, you may seek a mentor with strength in project management. As the principal of a firm, you may be seeking guidance in leadership and marketing. While mentorship should occur naturally, having some guidelines for what to expect can help you get the most from a mentoring relationship. The following account from an architect in Chicago describes how a variety of mentors have shaped her professional career.

You're Never Too Old

During my 14 years of architectural practice, I have worked in various-sized firms and even had a four-year stint in corporate America. I have taken on a variety of roles on project teams, from design to construction administration to project management. Although I have participated in formal mentor/protégé programs and believe them to be important, my most valued mentors have been those I have met on my own and with whom I have established relationships over time. I have found that you may not always seek out your mentors; some come and go, while others stumble into your life and remain. Regardless of how you meet, your mentors will play a key role in your professional development. I have already had several influential mentors in my career, and from them I have learned that you are never too old for a mentor.

There are no specific criteria for choosing a mentor. Mentors can be found in both genders, at all ages, and in all professions. You can have several mentors at the same time, assisting you in different facets of your life, both professionally and personally. As your needs and experiences change throughout your career, so will the qualities you value in a mentor.

Some mentors enter your life in unexpected ways. The office in which I currently work is an architecture and engineering firm. My architect peers are an obvious resource, but it's my engineering peers who mentor me on project communication and organization. Early in my career, I realized that I could learn a lot from engineers. Although they are in-house, they consult with other architecture firms. They often share with me specific successes and failures on other projects so that I can learn from their lessons as well. As a project manager, I have found engineers to be a great resource for discussing effective team motivation, communication, and processes. Serving in the dual role of in-house consultant and objective third party, the engineers provide me with a great perspective on our profession. Unlike my architectural peers, who might be reluctant to volunteer criticisms, the engineers have an uncanny knack for cutting to the chase and telling me how it is.

Mentors can also provide insights on your personal life. One of my current mentors inspires me to create a balance between work and home. She has been in the architectural field for 17 years and has learned to juggle her roles as wife, mother, and architect gracefully. She can seamlessly transition from conducting a client meeting to hosting the perfect birthday party for her five-year-old. Professionally we are equals, but with respect to our personal lives, she is truly my role model.

My longest mentor relationship has been with my first boss in Chicago. Our relationship has evolved during the 14 years I have known him. When he first hired me to work in his 20-person office, I was straight out of school and possessed the stereotypical "ready to conquer the world" intern attitude. I craved knowledge and experience and was ready to do almost anything on a project. In addition to my project responsibilities, I would sit for hours soaking up his stories about the the firm's history, its projects, and the profession in general. Many of the stories he shared were about his experiences at my age. Some of my favorite memories of working with him are of sitting around after hours when the phones had stopped ringing and asking the right question to start a story or two.

It was at this office that I followed my first projects from design through construction. Every week, after I returned from my field observation trip, he would patiently listen to my observations, answer my questions, and coach me on how to respond or, more important, teach me where to look for my response. Even when there was an error in my work, he never yelled but instead simply explained why it was a mistake and how to correct the situation, or advised me how to avoid making the same mistakes in the future.

It was also during this time that I took my architectural exam. My mentor was supportive, lending an ear to my concerns but not lecturing on how or when to study. Knowing the pressure I was putting on myself, he countered with good-natured chiding about how the test was so much more difficult when he took it. Long after I left his office, I could always count on him to listen patiently and offer advice when I called to discuss my next challenge. Some of his stories and the lessons I learned from him still pop into my head when I'm discussing a change order with a contractor or coordinating details with an engineer. Over time, the line between mentor and friend has blurred, and I look forward to our lunches, knowing that I can still ask a question that will lead to a great story.

I've realized that at some point, mentorship comes full circle, and you find value in advising someone else—you gain the opportunity to learn from that person as you pass on your experience. The bottom line is that you are never too old for a mentor, because you are never to old to learn.

Teri Wright, AIA
Senior Associate, OWP/P Architects
University of Michigan, Master of Architecture 1990

Like Teri, the following contributor benefited from many mentors early in his career. His account demonstrates how interns can actively identify mentors throughout the various stages of their professional development, starting with architecture school.

Mentoring: As I Knew It Then and Now

Since the beginning of my architectural career, I have continued to refine my definition of mentoring. Early in my career, I was mentored by everyone around me but did not realize it. During that time I learned the intricacies of pen-and-ink drafting and running blueprints. My early mentors provided advice on a variety of topics, including which colleges to apply to and how to set up a credit union account. After some time, my mentors became integral to the development of my career. Mentoring occurred day to day, but more important, it became the basis for a series of lifelong relationships. Sometimes finding a mentor seemed like the greatest challenge. I asked myself, "Can I just pick someone?" In retrospect, I realize that finding a mentor just happens, and you will know when it does. The most prominent mentors in my life have helped shape my career and have enabled me to become a mentor to others.

In college, one of my professors became my mentor, friend, and colleague. He became licensed during his second semester of teaching, and he always had time to help. Many students valued his perspective and ideas. While I was learning about architecture, I was also learning what made a good mentor. He would help us with our English papers, math, and physics problems. He went above and beyond what students expected from a professor.

He guided me through my first four years of college. I always knew I could count on him—at any time, I could pick up the phone, and he would be willing to help out with anything. My lesson about mentoring from this period is that a mentor helps you not only through school but also through your career and your life.

My next mentor was my greatest mentor and teacher of all. He guided me in my activities with the AIAS and through graduate school, helping me open doors that I had not known existed. These opportunities furthered my education by exposing me to new experiences, and I was able to pass them on to other students in the AIAS. He was also instrumental in getting me to serve on numerous boards and committees within the college and AIA. I received more than an architectural edu-

cation from him. He guided and mentored and educated, always hoped the best for all his students, and enjoyed seeing us succeed and fulfill our dreams.

Two architects I met through AIA became my next mentors. I have relied on both of them to answer questions about the ARE as well as about professional situations. During this time, I was learning how different offices operate, and I was questioning what was right and what was wrong, or the best way to approach a situation. While I was taking my ARE exams, I began to understand the concept of cradle-to-grave mentoring. I began the subsequent phase of my journey with the ability to give advice and mentor others in the profession.

The most significant event in my career was meeting my next mentor, an inspiring architect, contractor, and interior designer with her own firm. Under her guidance, for the first time in my professional career I felt like someone was putting sizable challenges before me. She provided me with the opportunity to do the work I knew I was capable of and to be actively involved with the management of the firm. I recognized that this was a great opportunity and a great place to be as a young professional. She quickly became one of the people I respect most in my profession.

This was also a time in my life when I began to question whether I was on the right path. I questioned the type of work I was doing, the city I was living in, the city I was working in, and the people around me. These contemplations led me to one of the most difficult decisions of my life. I decided to leave the firm—a place where I could realistically have grown and fulfilled many of my career aspirations. The realization that this was not where I wanted to stay for the duration of my career was a major turning point in my life. The owner of the firm and I have remained in touch, and we still share the successes and burdens of our work and lives. She has helped me gain knowledge and experience, and she continues to mentor me in my career. She taught me about running an office and managing projects, and she shared my ideals about giving back to the profession. I also learned from her that mentoring requires a willingness to let go of your own ideas. For my mentor, that meant abandoning her thoughts, plans, and future goals for me and supporting the changes I decided to make.

In a sense, I am still being mentored by all of these people. In some cases, it is through lessons learned; in others, it is through regular contact. I currently work full-time in a firm and mentor staff in ways I learned from my own mentors. I am also able to apply my skills and ideas about mentoring to my work as a professor at a local community college. I have been mentored all along my path and am now mentoring others as they pursue theirs.

Douglas Whiteaker, Assoc. AIA, LEED AP
Designer, Boulder Associates, Inc.
Southern Illinois University, Bachelor of Science in Architectural Studies 1994
University of Nebraska, Master of Architecture 1997

Roles and Responsibilities

Nearly all respondents indicated an interest in mentoring, while only half indicated satisfaction with the mentoring they were currently receiving.
—2003 ARCHVOICES/AIA INTERNSHIP AND CAREER SURVEY

A successful mentoring relationship requires effort from both parties. While there will be times when a mentor is "assigned" to you by your firm, your IDP state coordinator, or an AIA mentor-match program, the quality of the mentoring is generally much more rewarding if you are proactive in the selection of your mentor. If you are not satisfied with the quality of the mentoring you are receiving, talk to your mentor, evaluate your individual expectations, and brainstorm how the relationship could be improved. Take active measures to change those circumstances, and if no change occurs, seek out new mentors that satisfy your needs.

While it is typical to think of the mentor as someone older than you—a seasoned veteran or wise sage—there are times when your peers or even those with less experience can serve as mentors as well.

A mentor is someone who provides insights, instruction, and advice in a variety of settings. This relationship may be formal or informal. An informal relationship is one that develops naturally from working on a project or committee. No actual agreement is made to mentor or be mentored, but advice is sought and freely given. As evidenced by Teri's story, a mentor can be a personal acquaintance or coworker.

While interns may directly benefit from their advice, mentors don't always realize how much—they may not even be aware that they are serving as mentors. It is quite common for an informal mentor to be pleasantly surprised when an intern cites him or her as a mentor. Be sure to thank your mentors and let them know that you appreciate their guidance.

If the relationship is a formal one, meaning that you have both formally acknowledged it via a matching program or a verbal request, it is important to clearly define your expectations. It is generally not the job of the mentor to initiate the contact or discussions. As the one seeking out mentorship, the intern should always be proactive. It is *your* career that your mentor is trying to help you develop.

To ensure continuity, establish a regular meeting time (either monthly or quarterly) to discuss issues and seek advice. This might occur casually over beer or more formally with a predetermined agenda during lunch. By establishing a predictable meeting date, you can both schedule your time around meetings and, thus, reduce disappointing cancellations.

Mentor Meeting Checklist

☐ Discuss and agree upon the intern's expectations for his or her internship

☐ Establish the intern's "game plan" for completing the IDP training requirement

☐ Establish a procedure for the intern to use when contacting you

☐ Schedule future meetings

☐ Establish a joint commitment to the intern's successful training

☐ Establish a method to document mentoring activities with a diary or other record

Source: NCARB Mentor Guidelines

Photo courtesy of Schemata Workshop, 2005

Considerations for Seeking a Mentor

As a young intern, you are hungry for knowledge, eager to effectively settle into your work environment, and anxious to build relationships that will facilitate your professional development within the firm. As you seek out mentors, keep several factors in mind:

Mutual interests—Look for mentors who have interests and passions similar to yours, people whose work and ideas you respect and find stimulating.

Motivation and direction—Demonstrate to a potential mentor your desire to move on to the next level of professional growth. Share your goals and visions with him or her.

Proactive development—Be proactive in pursuing information and knowledge that will help you grow; take initiative in expanding the range of your responsibilities.

Skills and strengths—Demonstrate why a mentor should invest in you. Let him or her know what strengths you bring to this relationship, including your openness and commitment to learning.

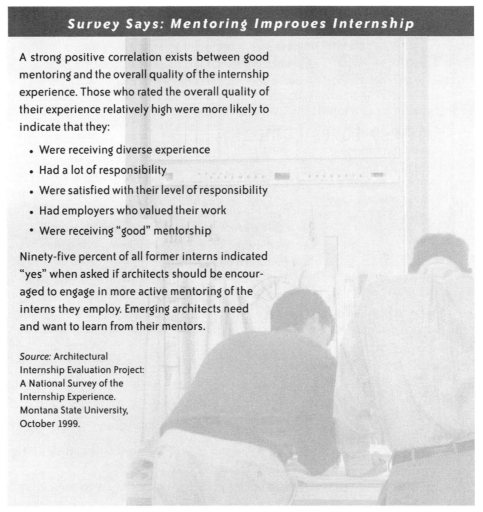

Survey Says: Mentoring Improves Internship

A strong positive correlation exists between good mentoring and the overall quality of the internship experience. Those who rated the overall quality of their experience relatively high were more likely to indicate that they:

- Were receiving diverse experience
- Had a lot of responsibility
- Were satisfied with their level of responsibility
- Had employers who valued their work
- Were receiving "good" mentorship

Ninety-five percent of all former interns indicated "yes" when asked if architects should be encouraged to engage in more active mentoring of the interns they employ. Emerging architects need and want to learn from their mentors.

Source: Architectural Internship Evaluation Project: A National Survey of the Internship Experience. Montana State University, October 1999.

Photo courtesy of InVision

Create Networks

*N*etworking doesn't have to be a bad word, conjuring images of schmoozy sales people and slick corporate gatherings. Think of a network as a safety net of friends and advisers who push you toward further development when times are good and keep you from falling through when trouble hits. In upcoming years, you may be laid off from work, fail an ARE exam, or deal with personal issues that affect your professional career. We all need to have people around and accessible to us who can help advise and pull us out of a funk. And here's what most people forget: The more diverse it is, the stronger the network. In your current situation, you should seek out advisers of different genders, ages, and backgrounds, such as your high school drafting teacher, a professor from school, a young architect you met through YAF, or the architect who liked your work but couldn't offer you a job. All of these people can provide you with an objective outlook.

Misery Loves Company

Remember that you are not in this alone. There are many other interns experiencing the same trials as you. You may find value in forming a peer adviser group. You might find it helpful to learn how others have overcome hurdles and obtained the necessary experiences to move toward licensure. The advice will be recent and probably applicable, since someone else may well have just encountered the same situation for which you seek advice.

How to Be a Good Mentee

Having thoughtfully chosen a mentor or mentoring team, you must maintain your relationships in a professional manner. It is imperative to show through your attitude and actions that you are a responsible colleague. The following tips for mentees have been adapted from the University of Michigan publication *How to Mentor Graduate Students: A Guide for Faculty in a Diverse University.*

- Be respectful of your mentor's time and be efficient with your meetings
- Take yourself seriously
- Be open to criticism and receive it constructively
- Be responsible by showing up on time and following through with commitments
- Respect boundaries and treat the relationship professionally

Drawing Boundaries

A mentor is a guide and resource but should not be regarded as a job prospect. While your mentor may be able to share leads for other possibilities, it would be inappropriate to ask him or her for a job. Be careful to understand the boundaries of your relationship and respect the time of your mentor. Likewise, it would be inappropriate for a mentor to "recruit" his or her mentee or to try to gain professional advantage from a mentoring relationship.

Looking Back at Mentoring

When I got out of school, I thought I was pretty good. Then I got a job.

I quickly realized that I didn't know everything. I was fortunate enough to work for a talented architect who also was a good teacher. He would never admit to the latter, but it was from him that I learned the subtleties of effective line weights, drawing management, and the inherent beauty of a well-organized and well-drawn set of documents. Over time, my skills developed, and I felt pretty good. Then I took a job with another, larger firm.

While I certainly could put my skills to good use, I quickly realized a successful project involved a lot more than a good set of documents. It involved client management, construction budgets, fee budgets, and staff management. I was fortunate to work with a firm with a diverse staff and project type. The firm provided opportunities for the staff to take on significant responsibility, sometimes with success and sometimes not so successfully. In this environment, open communication naturally occurs, and everyone, from the intern to the partner, inevitably learns something. My professional growth came not necessarily from one individual but from the firm as a whole.

Jim Romano, AIA
Architect, Seattle
University of Oregon,
Master of Architecture 1991

Photo by Warren Kim/Richard Meier & Partners Architects, LLP, 2004

Laddered Mentorship

It's never too early to become a mentor. As you advance through your internship, you will always have someone following in your footsteps. While it is easy to continually look forward and forget how difficult the road was behind you, remember to look back and help illuminate the path for those at your heels.

Laddered mentoring is the idea of serving as a mentor to someone while receiving mentorship from another. There is so much diversity in professional practice and changes within project types and technologies that there is always something to learn and knowledge to share. In a field dominated by lifelong learning, an architect should always be engaged as both a mentor and a mentee.

With this idea of laddered mentoring, I started a group that has been aptly named by a former participant as the "laddership" (poetically derived from the terms *leadership* and *laddered mentoring*). The experience level of the group ranges from recent graduates to those about to take their exams. The responsibility of organizing the monthly meetings is rotated among the members of the group, each taking a turn to select the topic. This model was inspired by a mentor group started many years ago by Rob Rosenfeld, NCARB's director of council record services. By keeping the group small, a healthy dialogue can be sustained. By rotating the responsibility, the topics can truly reflect members' interests and concerns. My role is to provide insights and guidance, but not lead the discussion.

Past topics have ranged from how to find a new job to working collaboratively with a contractor. We have toured projects under construction and shared travel photos to discuss how travel informs the design process. We all learn from the mistakes and experiences of one another, and sharing provides us all with a feeling of empowerment. As the mentor, I take away much from the meetings that has direct application to my practice. Hearing interns describe their ideal firm helps me understand the benefits that are important to interns and how I can inspire and motivate my staff. Listening to their frustrations about job responsibilities or poor instructions from project managers helps me consider ways to provide greater opportunities and improve my communication.

Modeling Mentorship

As a mentor, I have found the best method of mentorship is modeling the behavior that you want others to follow. When serving as a mentor, consider those mentors you respect and try to emulate their actions. If you did not receive good mentorship, think about the behavior of supervisors that you didn't appreciate and take caution that you do not mirror their actions.

A skilled mentor can demonstrate that mentorship and leadership are synonymous. Many articles are written about successful leaders in the business community that stress the importance of acting as a role model. These leaders are often considered mentors in their field. As with strong leaders, great mentors are open-minded, willing to listen to intern concerns, and able to help interns find solutions suitable to their needs. Great mentors possess vision, integrity, and the ability to follow through. The following paragraph was adapted from James B. Rowley's article "The Good Mentor," found on the Web site of the Association of Supervision and Curriculum Development (www.ascd.org).

The good mentor is a continuous learner. Interns rarely appreciate mentors who think they have the right answer to every question and best solution for every problem. Good mentors are transparent about their own search for better answers and more-effective solutions. They model this through their openness to ideas from colleagues, including interns, and by their pursuit of professional growth. They lead and attend workshops, develop and experiment with new practices, write and read articles in professional journals. Most importantly, they share new knowledge and perplexing questions with interns in a collegial manner.

Mentoring Resources

Mentoring relationships come easy for some, while others need encouragement or support. The following resources will provide valuable insights into how to establish and nurture a productive mentoring relationship. These tools are specific to the architectural profession. However, the Internet is host to a myriad of other mentor-focused Web sites that delve deeper into the psychology of mentoring as well as providing business models for mentorship.

IDP Mentor Guidelines

The Mentor Guidelines can be downloaded from the IDP section of the NCARB Web site. While it is intended for mentors who are working with IDP interns, this five-page document (with 19 pages of appendix) is a tremendous resource for anyone looking for suggestions on establishing a formal mentor relationship. The topics covered include mentor responsibilities, a checklist for the first meeting, and the benefits of mentoring. If you are asking a mentor to advise you on IDP or further career development, this would be a helpful document to review with him or her to ensure that you are both clear on your expectations.

AIA National Mentor Matching Program

This mentor matching program is a service sponsored by the American Institute of Architects to assist participants in their personal and professional development. The program matches mentors with mentees based on various essential competencies and the compatibility of their attitudes toward learning and work. Matches may be either self-directed or made by the program coordinator. You can simultaneously participate as a mentor and a mentee.

Compatibility is assessed through a variety of questionnaires in which participants indicate preferences for working styles and personality traits. For example, you may be asked whether you are detail-oriented or prefer to keep the big picture in mind, whether you are focused and methodical or dynamic and energetic. These indicators help to assure compatibility in a mentoring relationship. Participants may also consider personal preferences in their search for a mentor or mentee, such as primary type of work (e.g., residential, commercial), years in the industry, ethnicity, gender, age group, and region. The more flexibility you build into your match criteria, the greater range of matches you will be offered for consideration.

While the mentor match service was free for new registrants through 2005, the fee to use this program now ranges from $20 to $100, depending on your AIA or AIAS member status.

Mentorship: A Journey in Collaborative Learning

This mentorship resource is the product of the national AIA Mentoring Task Group and is unfortunately difficult to find on the AIA Web site. The simplest way to access it is to type "Mentorship: A Journey in Collaborative Learning" into the AIA Web site's search engine. Alternatively, you can click on Mentoring in the Emerging Professionals section of the Web site and find the title there. The site is an outstanding resource for those who are seeking effective mentorship as well as for those who want to become better mentors. It provides tips on a variety of topics, including how to select a mentor, common pitfalls to avoid, the benefits of being a mentor, and how to start a mentor program for your firm.

CHAPTER 10 | CHOOSING THE NONTRADITIONAL PATH

> Each year, roughly 4,000 students graduate from professional degree programs in the United States. Anecdotally, about 50% of those graduates go on to complete licensure.
>
> —1999 AIA Survey on Internship

So where do all of these graduates go? In order to answer that, we should first look at where they start. While 82 percent of respondents to the 2003 ArchVoices/AIA Internship and Career Survey indicated that they were currently working in traditional internships, 21 percent of them did not plan on a traditional career in architecture. This means that more than a quarter of the respondents have likely already left traditional practice and that a significant number of interns start in traditional internships and leave prior to licensure. Some move on to become project managers for contractors, real estate developers, and public agencies. These are relatively obvious roles for architects; oftentimes, the employer has had the opportunity to see them at work prior to hiring them. There are others, however, who become social workers, writers, and software programmers. It is generally harder to guess how these individuals broke into their new professions.

An argument is often made that an architectural education prepares an individual for a number of career paths beyond that of the traditional practicing architect. Architecture provides ample opportunities for creative problem solving, a skill that is incredibly helpful in a variety of professions. The ability to "think outside the box" has allowed architects to excel as visionaries in other fields. For example, the former mayor of Curatiba, Brazil, is the architect Jaime Lerner. By thinking innovatively, he has been able to transform a relatively unknown, polluted and crowded South American city into a model of inexpensive sustainable urban design strategies. His low-tech solutions included rapid bus transit and a citywide recycling program; their success and the city's ability to generate revenue to pay for these programs has piqued the interest of other cities and nations around the globe.

Nontraditional Career Paths

Robert Douglas, FAIA, refers to those graduates who pursue nontraditional career paths as "maverick architects." In his study of Harvard graduates with a degree in architecture, Douglas found the following careers represented*:

Advertising	Imagineers
Arts and illustration	Industrial light and magic
Construction and program management	Law
Congressman, deputy mayor	Management consulting
Design-build	Manufacturers' representative
Digital photography	Manufacturing
Editors, authors, and critics	Photography
Environmental graphics	Private investigator
Environmental planning	Product development and marketing
Executive search	Public relations
Facility management	Real estate development
Facility planning consultation	Theatrical, scenic, and production design
Fashion design	Rock tour manager
Financial services	Video animation
Forensic architecture and investigations	Virtual-reality imaging
Furniture design	Yacht and cruise-liner design
General contracting	
Historic preservation	

*From Andy Pressman, *Professional Practice 101.*

Photo by Grace Kim, AIA, 2005

Alternative Career Options

In 2003, the Corporate Architects Group of the AIA produced the publication *Career Options for Architects*. The following career paths were highlighted: (1) corporate architecture, (2) public architecture, (3) facility management, (4) writing/criticism, (5) education, and (6) land development.

Nontraditional Career Paths

Similarly, the AIA publication *Career Options: Opportunities through Architecture* found individuals with an architectural education were employed in these occupations:

Architectural critic	Graphic designer
Architectural photographer	Illustrator
Architectural programmer	Interior designer
Architectural renderer	Landscape architect
Building inspector	Lawyer
Building pathologist	Market researcher
CAD coordinator	Model maker
Campus planning	Museum curator
Carpenter	Printmaker
Cartographer	Professor
City planner	Property assessor
Civil engineer	Publisher
Construction inspector	Real estate agent
Construction manager	Researcher
Contractor	Set designer
Corporate consultant	Structural engineer
Developer	Technical writer
Document designer	TV/film producer
Furniture designer	

Together, these lists represent a wide array of potential careers.

Photo by Grace Kim, AIA, 2004

"Career Decision Strategies: Looking beyond Architecture," an article published in the 12th edition of *The Architect's Handbook of Professional Practice*, detailed the following career fields: (1) landscape architecture, (2) interior design, (3) lighting design, (4) acoustical design, (5) engineering, (6) construction, (7) urban and regional planning, (8) architectural history, theory, and criticism, and (9) environmental and behavioral research. "There are no limitations on where or how far an architect may migrate from the field," the article states.

Shaping the World around Us: Other Roles for Architects

Architects influence a greater sphere of the built environment than they often acknowledge. The design phase is a small period of time in the overall life of a building. Given the problem-solving skills honed during their broad education, architects are well suited for many other roles. Architects have the potential to influence a project from start to finish in a much broader sense than just the traditional design process.

For the sake of illustration, let us look at a hypothetical new central library for a major U.S. city. The city public library decides to build a radically new building for the 21st century and holds an international design competition. Given the enormity of the budget and significance of the project, the library hires a development consultant. From this consultant's staff, a project manager with architectural experience is assigned. The library itself also has architects on staff, one of whom will serve as project manager. In addition, the library has an advisory board comprised of local business leaders and community members; two architects currently serve on this board. This team of representatives for the library, advisory board, and developer—all with architectural backgrounds—decides how the Request for Qualifications (RFQ) process is to be organized.

Subsequently, a respected, internationally renowned architect is selected from the competition entries, and design begins. Both the foreign and local architects meet with various manufacturers and product representatives to discuss materials and finishes that would be appropriate throughout the building. The curtain wall manufacturer has technical staff to facilitate the curtain wall design. Interior designers assist the architect with interior finishes, colors, and furniture. It's possible that all of the roles mentioned are filled by design professionals who were trained as architects.

As the project progresses, permit drawings are reviewed by the city's building department staff, of whom some were trained as architects. In addition, the project manager for the general contractor was recruited from his previous architectural job to oversee this project. While this scenario may be a bit exaggerated, it illustrates the many roles that an architect can play on large-scale projects. The following personal accounts describe a number of different career paths that have been taken with an architectural education.

Reasons Cited by Those Not Working in Traditional Practice

46%   better salaries, benefits, advancement opportunities

30%   increased respect for their skills

20%   personal or family circumstances

17%   path to registration is too long

11%   never wanted traditional career in architecture

Source: 2003 Archvoices/AIA Internship and Career Survey

Photo by Michael Mariano, AIA, 2004

Architect as Owner or Contractor

A common role for architects to assume is that of the contractor or owner's representative. A satisfied owner or contractor may recruit an architect who has successfully led a team through challenging circumstances on a project. It is less frequent, but not uncommon, for an architect to have the opportunity to play the three roles—architect, owner, and contractor—providing a comprehensive perspective for future projects. Steve Tatge, who has had this opportunity, explains why he chose to leave an award-winning architectural practice and how he has since applied his architectural skills in newfound roles.

After 13 years practicing architecture and working on a variety of challenging projects, I made a difficult decision to leave a senior position at a great firm to manage capital projects for a large bio-tech company. I had, in effect, decided to stop being "the architect" and start being "the client." Despite years of experience and numerous projects, I admittedly did not have a very good idea of what owners' representatives did when they weren't meeting with the architect. I did, however, have a growing interest in understanding what makes a project happen—before, during, and after the "architecture." That's ultimately why I was open to making the change when approached with the opportunity. Since that initial change in career trajectory, I have worked as a project manager for a major contractor, and I am currently managing capital projects at a major university.

The change entailed an adjustment not only to the actual work I performed but also in how I identified myself. Although it's been four years since I left the firm, when people ask what I do, I still answer, "I'm an architect." The next question is "What type of architecture do you specialize in—houses or office buildings?" I then explain that I serve as the "owner" for a large public university, managing construction projects rather than designing buildings. Admittedly, much of my personal self-image is tied to being an architect, and I haven't been able to get past that. However, I would argue that although I no longer practice architecture, the skills I learned as an architect have greatly informed how I perform.

I look at projects and architectural design from a different perspective when it's "my" money being spent. In an architecture office, I can clearly remember being frustrated because our fabulously designed project was two percent over budget. I thought, "Can't they just get some more money?!" I now know that in the case of public institutions, there is often no more money to be had. I also know that budgets are sometimes spent on "design elements" that, while laudable on an architectural level, do not meet the needs of my constituents.

Having been in the architect's shoes makes me a better client in many ways. I know when a design looks great but will be difficult to maintain, or when the architect is not really exploring all options early in the design process. I know when the architect is being asked to make too many presentations or attend too many meetings, and whether the architect is really listening and responding to our needs.

The key to being an "architect-turned-owner" is being able to keep my own design preferences out of the projects I oversee; after all, my responsibility is to ensure that the architect and contractor are meeting the project requirements, not to play architect myself. An architecturally trained owner can provide enlightened direction to the design without dictating it. It's been helpful to think back to good clients I've had and how they contributed to the success of a project.

I've also had moments when I've realized that I have a greater impact on a project's design than I did as an architect. Once you achieve a certain level of experience and seniority as an architect, more of your time is spent in management — fee negotiations, consultant coordination, responding to permit corrections, meetings, and the like — than in active involvment with design.

In addition, if the design partner wants to do something that you think is a bad idea, as a project manager you will not likely change his or her mind; your job is to make the designs real. However, as the owner, you have ample opportunities to provide design direction. If you don't agree with the design, it can be changed. I've found personal satisfaction in being able to ensure that the building design is everything that it should be for the people who use it. This has been as rewarding for me as an owner as it was when I was producing the design.

I'm also fortunate enough to have worked for a large contractor. Along with two other architects, I served as a quality-assurance/quality-control manager for a major construction company, which is another way of saying that we were responsible for ensuring that the documents from which we would build were as complete and correct as possible before we started building. I also made sure that we and the subcontractors were executing the work properly.

In a job that was not too different from what architects normally do, I redlined a lot of drawings, sketched details, raised questions, and offered solutions to problems while working for the general contractor. Because our company negotiated all our work up front, we were often onboard early in the project and provided input all along the way as the design was developed. In many cases, I felt that I was doing much of the architects' work for them. Frankly, I was often shocked and embarrassed by the poor quality of the drawings that architects produced for construction.

During my time in traditional practice, I heard many "dumb contractor" stories swapped by architects and told at seminars, with chuckles all around. I've since learned that contractors have just as many equally true and equally amazing "dumb architect" stories; and I've personally seen more than a few such cases myself. It seems that some architects are more adept at creating a 3-D fly-through of their project than at developing the documents to actually build it. Architects would likely do a much better job if they spent some time working for a contractor, trying to determine how to price and build projects designed by someone else.

It's unfortunate that there is often a certain adversarial relationship between architects and contractors. Architects often fault contractors for not understanding the "design intent," but it's important to note that contractors are not trained that way, nor are they present for any of the design presentations the architect makes to the owner, where the design intent is discussed. Contractors, at least the good ones, are honestly trying to figure out what the architect intended and always seem to be operating in an information-starved state. Somewhat perversely, the contractor is also sometimes criticized for asking too many questions, particularly during construction. An experienced architect can be invaluable in helping a contractor understand the design better, as well as suggesting more economical and buildable ways to realize the design.

Architects react much more favorably to "help" from a contractor who is also an architect. I've taken a lot of satisfaction in improving the way architects and contractors work together on projects. Few contractors have staff architects providing this service, but my experience has been that design architects welcome such input and understand that it makes their lives, and the projects, better.

Steve Tatge, AIA
Project Manager, University of Washington
Knox College, Bachelor of Arts in Psychology 1981
University of Washington, Master of Architecuture Program, 1984–1988

Representing the Building Trades

Like Steve, the following contributor practiced architecture for many years before finding a new career path in the building trades industry. She is a registered architect with more than 15 years' experience working in architectural firms.

My interest in architecture was born out of curiosity. An initial awareness of the physical differences found among cities and countries eventually led me to the pursuit of architecture. To this day, even though I no longer practice architecture, I consider myself fortunate for having known what I wanted to study in college, and I continue to identify myself as an architect. I practiced architecture for nearly 15 years. When I started, I would never have predicted that my experiences would lead to a decision to leave the practice, nor did I realize the value my cumulative architectural experiences would provide in a nonarchitectural career.

I graduated from the School of Architecture at Tulane with the hope of landing a job in one of the larger design firms in New Orleans. Instead, I took a full-time position with a civil engineer interested in expanding into A/E services. I became responsible for everything from initial design to production to construction administration, and my experience can only be described as nervewrackingly thrilling. In time, and thanks in part to the confidence extended to me by my boss, my nervousness dwindled, and the thrill turned into pride in the completed work. Although my first professional architectural experience ended quite a number of years ago, it provided me with two invaluable lessons: (1) an understanding that opportunities return their maximum potential when you have the right match with your personal interests, and (2) it is impossible to overestimate the long-term impact of working for (or with) someone who sincerely trusts your skills and values your participation. My first job as an intern architect taught me that everyone has the potential to make a contribution, whether to an idea, to a process, or to a problem.

Four years of work in an A/E firm were followed by almost three years as a staff architect and owner's representative in the facilities department of a hospital undergoing major renovations and additions. I explain being an "owner's rep" this way: When you make a mistake, people know exactly where to find you. It is a very accountable position. As architects, we often approach design from the point of view of the final user; yet as the owner's representative, you are the final user. In addition, as an architect in the role of the owner's representative, you quickly realize the day-to-day impact of your architectural decisions, large or small. Ironically, it was this firsthand insight into a particular industry that made me most valuable as a health-care architect, the role in which I spent the balance of my architectural career.

I left the practice of architecture to pursue a graduate degree in international affairs and business administration. I was one of three architects enrolled in the MBA program and quickly learned that recruiters found great value in the problem-solving process that characterizes our architectural training. An architect's ability to imagine the intangible and administer its construction leads to better problem solving, team building, and project management. Finished projects indicate an ability to schedule, budget, and plan. These skills are easily transferred and applied in any industry.

Currently, as Director of Program Development with the International Masonry Institute, I am responsible for developing programs that enhance craftworker awareness and improve industry partnerships and future opportunities for the union masonry craftworker. The skills that give me the ability to carry out these responsibilities are deeply rooted in my architectural education and background. I depend on my ability to identify and organize all the pieces of a project, much as an architect identifies the components involved in designing. After years of architectural practice, my mind automatically sees every project as the traditional architect sees his or her latest commission, organizing all the parts of the project and weeding out the solutions that cannot be applied.

I've often been asked why I left the practice of architecture. I left because I realized that my architectural strengths lay in problem solving and planning—I am inherently more of a builder than a designer. I wanted to take these building skills and return to what had originally piqued my interest in architecture many years before: real estate development.

Before I returned to graduate school, my boss and firm principal gave me advice that I'd like to pass along. "Find an outlet to continue to use your architectural skills," he said. "No matter where you go, you'll always be an architect, and you'll always need a creative outlet to keep that side of you alive and well." My path continues to allow me to "build" and, in this manner, stay matched to my true interests.

Maria Viteri, AIA
Director of Program Development, International Masonry Institute
Tulane University, Bachelor of Architecture 1983
University of Pittsburgh, Master of Business Administration 1997
University of Pittsburgh, Master of International Affairs and Economic Development 1997

The previous examples are from individuals who were engaged in traditional practice prior to making a deliberate career change. The following story demonstrates that a change in career path might not be the result of a conscious decision; instead it can evolve slowly as different opportunities present themselves. For her first internship, Candace took a teaching job on a Western Pacific island, which led her down a non-traditional path in architecture. Almost ten years later, she is defining a role for herself as an environmental educator and an expert in *permaculture*—loosely defined as the design of integrated systems for sustainable societies.

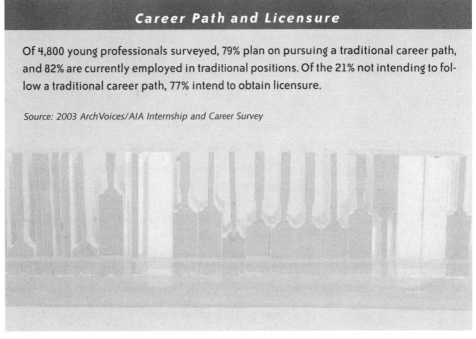

Career Path and Licensure

Of 4,800 young professionals surveyed, 79% plan on pursuing a traditional career path, and 82% are currently employed in traditional positions. Of the 21% not intending to follow a traditional career path, 77% intend to obtain licensure.

Source: 2003 ArchVoices/AIA Internship and Career Survey

Photo by Kristin Cross, 2004

Internship at the Ponape Agriculture and Trade School, Micronesia

After two years of the three-and-a-half-year master's program at SCI-Arc, I was ready for a break. A professor handed me a flyer that read: "Architecture instructor wanted for Jesuit boys' trade school in Micronesia." Coincidentally, I had just bought a book about Micronesian traditional architecture. I applied for the job, and despite their preference for a graduate, I was hired to teach at the Ponape Agriculture and Trade School in Micronesia.

My workday was divided in half: in the morning I taught design development to high school juniors, and in the afternoon I supervised the Pacific Architecture Consortium, a collective of senior construction students who worked on a variety of design projects in the community, ranging in scale from church pews to a marine science lab. The afternoon work seemed familiar enough—I had been around construction my entire life, and for the past 15 years I had worked for a home builder, general contractor, and Realtor, and in the fields of economic development and community organizing—but nothing had prepared me for teaching a 90-minute course five days a week. I had not even taken a design development course myself, but I figured the best way to learn something was to teach it.

When I arrived, I found 38 years' worth of archives in my office and teaching space. After I sorted out what was expected for the junior architect class, I went over my own brief architectural education to see how it might inform what

I was to teach. I felt my education had taught me to observe and synthesize my surroundings, using the site as a point of departure for design. As I prepared my curriculum, I also thought a competition and presentations would be useful. Later, I would learn that I was proposing a very "American" approach to architectural education and that, in the islands, "the nail that stands out gets pounded in." The boys at this trade school were considered the brightest students and were well regarded by the community at large. There were very established cultural norms and attitudes toward what an architectural education should be and the type of work architects should produce.

The semester began, and by the time my students had completed their first design assignment, I had gained an understanding of the school and community. I was able to organize our first field trip to document the site for a bathhouse we would later design. My intent with this assignment was to investigate how one could use concrete hollow block, a widely used construction material, to design a comfortable structure for this hot and humid climate. I was very excited.

I had arranged for a school worker to take all 17 of us to a neighboring atoll in the school skiff. The atoll, a coral island consisting of a reef surrounding a lagoon, was rumored to be the birthing site for women who lived at the neighboring Nan Madol—an enormous area of stone platforms and canals on the edge of the sea that was inhabited by a lost civilization 1,000 years ago. On our tiny atoll, the students, in groups of three, documented the paths, vegetation, visitor huts, fresh water, views, sounds, orientation, land mass, and so on. Within two hours, they had completed the work, so we went for a swim and headed back. Everyone had worked hard, and I felt we had spent a successful day mapping and observing.

The next day, I arrived in class to encounter stern faces and glaring eyes. The boys revolted. After hearing about their day of documenting and swimming, the other students had questioned what they had learned the day before. My students wanted to know how mapping an atoll was related to architecture. They were intent on becoming skilled draftsmen, not surveyors. I had to compile all of their research into a site collage to reveal how the environment could influence their building design. With the collage and a few other, more obvious demonstrations, they came to understand bioclimatic design. We completed the bathhouse and then went on to design the house that they ambitiously hoped to build that summer. By the end of the course, the students had completed a full set of hand-drawn construction documents. They were once again the envy of all the other students and the pride of their families.

So that is where my lesson began. I had gone to teach at the trade school with the idea that Micronesians were like Americans, that these students wanted to build an original masterpiece that would stand out from others. In retrospect, I can see that they would have been satisfied to have all drawn the same house.

However, this idealized house that they all longed for was fraught with controversy. Concrete construction was embraced by islanders after WWII due to its resistance to termites and hurricanes. This new type of construction changed not only the appearance of the vernacular architecture but also communal building traditions, societal roles, and overall human interactions necessary in a reciprocal island society. In addition, the manufacturing process used to produce the concrete hollow block requires the dredging of sand, which causes the erosion of the coastline, leaving the island susceptible to tsunamis and eliminating habitat for fish. The largest loss is the dismissal of the vernacular form that had evolved over time — a vernacular that had respected the ecosystem, contained ritual and societal beliefs, and was culturally appropriate. The form was a symbol of unity and respect for the place and environment. The new concrete buildings promoted a Western ideal of individuality and privacy. This internship taught me that exporting Western ideals to other cultures requires serious consideration.

After my 16 months abroad, I returned to SCI-Arc. Based on the Ponape architecture curriculum and a chapel design I completed for another Jesuit school, I advanced a year, completed my thesis on tropical hybrid architecture, and graduated.

Since 1999, I have been weaving a life that incorporates all that I learned on the islands. I continue to document indigenous structures of the Pacific and have been awarded two fellowships in New Zealand and Australia. When I returned from these fellowships, I designed a curriculum for teaching sustainability at the K–12 level based on subsistence island living. I also founded CyberHuts and continue to work as a sustainable building consultant and designer as well as an environmental educator. I have learned about natural building techniques and permaculture through workshops and experimentation. I am currently writing a book on the Kiribati traditional meeting house, the maneaba, *and am developing educational products that teach youth and adults about indigenous architecture.*

My current goal is to incorporate ritual into the construction and materials production process. Even here in the United States, we have much to learn from the Navajo people, who sang elaborate songs to bring their buildings into existence, and the Plains Indians, whose tepee poles each represent a specific cultural value. Indigenous cultures lived on the land without destroying it; I think we can learn from them before the traditions are forgotten. I believe that when we begin to see our materials and buildings as a sacred "thou," instead of a replaceable "it," there will be hope that we can make buildings that sustain the earth.

Candace Vanderhoff
Ethnoarchitect, Designer, Educator
SCI-Arc, Master of Architecture 1999

The previous accounts are from those who have left the traditional field of architectural practice but are in somewhat related fields. However, as mentioned at the start of this chapter, there are a great number of architectural graduates every year who never enter the profession. Sometimes this is due to a poor economy — for example, in the early 1990s the economy was very poor, and many interns and new graduates were forced to find employment outside the field. Evidence of this trend can be seen nationwide in the low number of architects with 13 to 15 years of experience. Architectural graduates and interns may also leave architectural practice when they find that the profession is not what they expected or when better financial opportunities present themselves in other fields. The following contributors are among those whose occupations are not associated with the architectural profession.

Architect of Virtual Worlds

When I entered architecture school, I never thought it would lead to a career in the video-game industry. In fact, I finished at the top of my class at Berkeley and was captivated by the idea of design and the design process.

However, after interning for two summers at an architecture/engineering firm and also experiencing the challenges of working on (and winning) a national design competition with several of my peers, I became disenchanted with the constraints that real-world architecture placed on creative vision. These experiences, coupled with my personal objections to the apprenticeship system of the profession, greatly diminished my interest in following a traditional career path.

During my junior year at school, I stumbled upon a computer graphics (CG) visualization class offered by the architecture department. The early consumer CG software was difficult to use and challenging to learn, but the moment I had the opportunity to see what was possible, I was ensnared by the sense of creative liberation the medium provided. The nearly limitless inventive potential of CG caught my imagination, and I became entrenched. I had a lot of free time in my last year of architecture school, so I took this opportunity to teach myself 3-D modeling software and the theory and technology behind CG. I also researched the video games and animation industry and the types of jobs available. The more I researched, the more persuaded I was to seek out a career in CG. I had heard of many architectural refugees who were unable to find work during the recession of the early 1990s and who had successfully migrated to the CG industry. I was determined to be successful in this endeavor as well.

As with most of my peers, I enjoyed playing a lot of video games in college and soon made the connection that, with these new skills, I could make a living working in the game industry. I had considered a career in animation/postproduction (i.e., special effects) but found the work too specialized to be enjoyable.

I got my start with a lot of determination and, more important, with a lot of luck. To make a long story short, I put together a computer graphics–focused portfolio and demo reel, mailed these out to as many game companies as I could find addresses for, and landed one interview. I must have left a good impression, because that company decided to hire me. So I packed my bags and relocated to Seattle to start my first real job as 3-D environment modeler.

Seven years later, I am still having fun working for one of the largest companies in the world. Overall, the work is very rewarding, although not on a physical or tangible level. At this point in time, my job involves creating environments for car racing games. These range from real-world circuits to imaginary racecourses. The dual advantage of my work is that I have the opportunity not only to travel, to research and re-create existing race tracks, but also to synthesize these real locations and create new imaginary places. Because they are designed to be realistic, when I'm working on these fictitious tracks, I have the unique chance to be architect, landscape architect, urban planner, and civil engineer all at the same time. This is where I derive the greatest fulfillment. I have the good fortune of being able to allow my creativity to wander without constraints. I can design purely for the sake of design, even if on an entirely theoretical and virtual level. None of this would be possible if I were a traditional architect.

Now, I'm sure you're wondering what the compensation is for this unreal job. On average, the starting salaries for 3-D artists in the game industry are between $30,000 and $40,000. Most full-time work is salaried, and overtime pay is rare. The pay scale differs among companies, but on average, a skilled modeler with several years of experience will have a salary between $65,000 and $90,000. Benefits (i.e., medical, dental, and retirement) also vary greatly, with most small firms forgoing comprehensive plans in lieu of higher salaries. As with most technology companies, stock options are an additional perk.

Like compensation, work hours vary from company to company. You can expect to work longer hours at the smaller ones, since they rarely have the resources or money to fully staff their projects. At the larger companies, eight-hour days are standard, with the occasional crunch period before deadlines. Although full-time salaried positions don't pay overtime, companies may give what's known as "comp time" at the end of a project. Depending on the duration of the crunch, you could expect to receive two weeks to one month worth of paid compensation time.

Looking back, I believe I could not have had a better education than architecture school provided. Even though I will never see my buildings built in the real world, I have no regrets about the career path I chose. Between the liberating amount of pure design I do and the intricate technical (and technological) problems I'm challenged to solve every day, I could not imagine finding more intellectual and creative stimulation. Where else could I be paid for doing something I love, without the stress and worry of liability, regulations, or budget?

Eugene Wong
3-D Environment Modeler for Xbox video games, Microsoft
University of California, Berkeley, Bachelor of Architecture 1998

Architecture through a Camera Lens

Should I become an architect? This was the question I kept asking myself as my graduation approached. As I thought about my experiences in school, more questions arose. How should I interpret the fact that I got straight As in architectural history, construction technology, and structures, but not in my studio classes? Did I really have a shot at being a designer? Should I consider an alternate career?

Throughout school, I had worked for a small construction firm in the city, doing high-end residential and some smaller commercial projects. After graduation, I decided to continue working for the same firm so that I could explore construction management possibilities and devote some serious time to photography. Given the complaints of my older colleagues about endless hours in front of the computer and the lack of compensation, I did not rush to look for work in an architect's office. Furthermore, I was very excited to have more time for photography and wanted to consider that as a possible occupation. Working for an architect would have required a time commitment that I did not desire to take on.

I first studied photography in the former Yugoslavia, where I grew up. After a high school program heavy in math and science, I went on to study electrical engineering in college. As I struggled with subjects in my engineering major—all of which were nonvisual—I quickly realized that I had made the wrong choice. Around that time, I learned the basics of photography and started shooting, processing, and printing my own black-and-white projects. Interestingly, some of my first subjects were architectural. When I moved to the United States a couple of years later, I chose architecture over photography in part because it seemed a more certain occupation. Nevertheless, photography remained an important source of personal fulfillment, and I continued to hone my photography skills while I was in school. I looked for every possible opportunity to use photography in my architectural projects, but I never felt I had enough time for it.

My construction management career was short-lived. I discovered that I did not like staying in the office, looking through catalogues, trying to find the right product for the right price in the right time frame; supervising staff and subcontractors; obtaining approvals from architects and owners; and making phone call after phone call. Equally important, my construction job interfered with my photography projects, demanding too much time and providing no flexibility. I realized I needed to prioritize my interests and put greater focus on photography.

I found a very flexible part-time job doing architectural woodworking. I enjoyed this and was good at it, but more importantly, it allowed me more time for photography. I was able to start assisting some successful photographers and managed to shoot some small jobs.

It took a couple of years to get a really good handle on the profession and to experience all of the pros and cons of architectural photography, but eventually I was able to answer the question that I'd first asked myself back in school: What is it that I want to do?

Through endless hours in the architecture studio, I learned the language of architecture, both verbal and graphic. This is the same language used in architectural photography. I also learned the iterative creative process of design. Just as we had to repeatedly revise and improve our designs on trace paper before producing the final presentation drawings, an architectural photographer will revise a photograph, Polaroid after Polaroid, before the final version is recorded.

All those slide lectures in architectural history created a bank of visual information I constantly refer to as I'm presented with new projects. Even though every shoot is different and every project unique, I draw upon this valuable source to make a strong historical reference or create a completely original composition.

One of my recent shoots was the Clinton Presidential Library in Little Rock, Arkansas. I did not research existing images of the exterior prior to the assignment, wanting to see it with "fresh eyes." When I returned, I looked at the architect's Web site. One of the five images of the building was an elevation rendering showing the whole building as you approach it. One of the dozen images I'd independently created looked like a real-life version of the drawing, a clear indication that I'd understood the architect's thinking about the building.

The lifestyle of an architectural photographer is quite different from the lifestyle of an architect. It is a well-known fact, for example, that all architectural photographers drive Aston Martins. Just kidding. In reality, when it comes to material lifestyle I cannot say there is a clear pattern I have observed, nor do I look to find one. However, there are some clear differences between architects and architectural photographers when it comes to the nonmaterial aspects of life. One major difference I particularly enjoy is that architectural photography has a great connection with nature. Every shoot is in a different location and environment, with a unique set of constraints. I am constantly aware of the light, of varying weather, and of different times of the day. I love the fact that I get to spend beautiful days in the spring or fall working outside. Working outside is not so great when I'm out on a 0- or 100-degree day, which happens every now and then. I have to be extremely flexible, as my plans can change at the last minute just because it is sunny or rainy. There are also a number of days every year that I am up early so I can be on location a good half an hour before dawn. Sometimes I keep shooting until after dusk, only to return home to spend hours preparing for the next day's shoot. This makes for mentally and physically exhausting days. And if I could give only one piece of advice for this situation, it would be: sunscreen!

It was around the time I started focusing on photography that I decided I was going to work only with nice people. Architectural shoots provide a creative, stimulating, and energetic environment. They gather people for a day or two with a common goal: to make the project look as good as possible. However, despite this collective aspect, architectural photography as a creative process also has a solitary component. A degree of mental or physical isolation and focus is necessary for the creation of every image. In addition, I am often alone between shoots, as well as during preparation and postproduction. Although it is intense, and sometimes stressful, I try to ensure that the creative process of architectural photography is enjoyable, productive, and fulfilling for myself and for those I am working with. I always try to remember and remind others: It's supposed to be fun.

Albert Vecerka
Architectural Photographer, represented by Esto
City College of New York, Bachelor of Science in Architecture 1997

Architect as Artist

Seven years after graduating from architecture school, I now know that I was meant to be an artist. As an undergraduate I studied sculpture, and yet somehow I became enamored with the discipline of architecture. Introduction to Architecture was my first exposure to the subject. It left me awestruck. I was intrigued by the multitude of factors that affected architecture and the rigorous exploration of these factors. The university I attended for my art degree did not have an accredited architecture program, so after the survey course, I took architectural history and all the available studio courses focusing on conceptual and schematic design.

After graduation, I felt my art degree was frivolous; I desired to do something I could take more seriously. In addition, I didn't know what to do as a sculptor—how to support myself or get shows—so architecture seemed a logical and more practical choice.

My architectural education proved to be a rich experience—an experience of formerly unrelated subjects coming together and creating a rich kaleidoscopic view of the world. This multifaceted view allowed me to explore subjects from new vantage points with a level of creativity previously unknown to me. From history to conceptual design and from theory to physics, I was exposed to a myriad of fields, from which I developed my design methodology.

Conceptual design held much of my interest during school. However, in practice the concept is revisited throughout the design of the building and is constantly tested as it repeatedly informs decisions. I was more interested in the abstract and representative aspects of the concept. For me, the concept was continually being marginalized not only by budgets, codes, and clients but also by the need for functionality.

My education also taught me the language of drawing. Architectural drawing techniques inform my explorations of ideas. Most of my sketches for sculptures look like architectural details and are often isometric or sectional drawings that help me visualize how a piece will be assembled. To better understand the spatial qualities of larger installations, I often sketch them in perspective or isometric. Drawing becomes a natural means of expression for an architect; it is also an invaluable tool for my communication as an artist.

Through practice I developed an obsession with detailing. In how many different ways can an object be detailed? What materials reinforce my concept? What materials and fasteners are available? Again, there are numerous solutions and endless materials and products with which to design, and that is the endless investigation I enjoy.

I practiced architecture for a number of years in a variety of cities, in both small firms and corporate settings. During that time, I felt that I was an artist masquerading as an architect but was not willing to face that fact. A series of revelations helped me realize my true passion for art and make a major career change.

The first epiphany came when I allowed myself to have a studio where I could really work. Because I work with resin, which is generally toxic, and wood, which needs special tools and a shop to contain the dust, I needed a proper workspace. By obtaining a studio, I validated my practice as an artist in a way that I hadn't before.

The second revelation came when I had my first show, which was attended by my friends and family. Comments from the people who know me best made me realize that I had always seen myself as an artist. The validation I felt from that show made me recognize that I had to be an artist and take my work seriously.

The decision to leave traditional practice was a difficult one. I never worried that I was making the wrong decision, but it was daunting to give up a regular paycheck and benefits. Fortunately, I had a temporary situation that allowed me to quit my job and forgo a regular income. That gave me the opportunity to be fully absorbed in my art, which had been difficult when working full-time. It also allowed me to get to know the art scene more intimately and network with other artists. I had much to learn about how to pay for materials, taxes, and health insurance, as well as how to operate as an artist in general.

Most artists I know need to earn a little money on the side to support their art habit, or they are supported by their families. It is difficult to make a living as an artist, and even if you attain that goal, it will certainly take time and hard work to get established. Many artists work in construction, art supply stores, and restaurants.

The discipline of architecture has informed my view of the world and will forever influence my art. I now know that I could have taken many paths in my education but would still have ultimately ended up an artist.

Kristin Cross
Sculptor
Syracuse University, Master of Architecture 1997

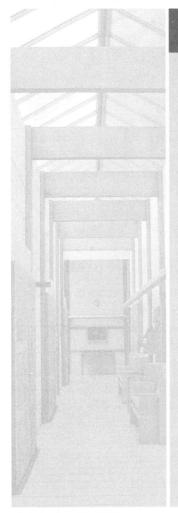

How to Catch a Gallery's Attention: Tips for Aspiring Artists from Kristin Cross

The most traditional avenue for selling your work is through a gallery. Therefore, it is important to understand the art scene in your city. Which galleries do you like? Where do you think your work would fit? Get on the mailing lists for these galleries and attend their openings. Visit them later during the show as well so that you can see the work without a crowd. You need to research the galleries so you do not waste time approaching galleries where your work would be inappropriate.

As a rule, you need 12 to 15 pieces that are united in theme, material, and size before you can start showing your work or approaching galleries. Check with your galleries of choice for specific submission requirements—format, number of images, curriculum vitae, biography or artist's statement. Some only review slides at certain times of the year. You can usually find this information on their Web sites.

You also need to have your work professionally photographed, as a slide or in digital format. The digital format is much easier to manage and quick to send out as well as being much cheaper to produce than slides. Most galleries request slides. It is tempting to take your own photographs, but it is more expensive in the end when poor-quality images hinder you from getting recognition. Unprofessional slides make your work look unprofessional, and galleries are not interested in working with artists who don't take their work seriously.

The Internet will help you locate organizations that support artists: trusts, foundations, and state or county art commissions. An excellent site that I have found invaluable is New York Foundation for the Arts (www.nyfa.org). The site covers any question you might have, from finding a studio to legal assistance. They have a section on setting up your own Web site and a continually updated list of opportunities for artists.

Photo by Grace Kim, 2004

The Art of Awareness: Lessons Leading to a Career in Marketing

Over the past ten years, I've had the opportunity to work in four firms of various size, structure, and culture. Each intern experience provided valuable insight into my personal strengths in visual communication, marketing, and client relations. I am currently a project manager/marketing coordinator with KDF Architecture, leading an expansion into a new market and a new branch office.

Lesson No. 1: Understand What Excites You

The first and largest of the four firms made the greatest impression on me. During a student internship in Portland, Oregon, I was able to witness a well-organized blend of graphic and facility design with the development of six different NikeTown retail stores. Our high-energy designs were based on well-defined client goals that encompassed everything from larger-than-life athletic imagery to the familiar swoosh on the polished door pulls. My first professional design experience really turned me on to the creative potential of graphic and physical design working in harmony. It was also at this early stage in my career that I was introduced to a wealth of creative professionals in marketing, graphic arts, product design, retail display, and lighting design, many of whom had started with an architectural education.

Lesson No. 2: Seek Opportunity

My first postgraduation internship brought me physically closer to home and exemplified a more conservative approach to the practice of architecture. Spokane is a competitive mid-sized market, and I was afforded a tremendous opportunity to observe a large, well-established firm's approach to marketing and management. In this 50-year-old firm, interns were utilized in a very traditional way, and corporate culture was slow to change. I knew that I wanted to be an active participant rather than an observer, and I soon realized that I belonged in a smaller and more flexible environment capable of immersing a young intern in all aspects of the business.

Lesson No. 3: Know When to Say When

The office down the street radiated with enthusiasm. It was a young firm that had recently spun off from a larger office. Aggressive in their marketing, they sought to introduce a fresh approach to design in an otherwise conservative market and had no qualms about challenging the local status quo. They presented themselves differently from anyone else in town and embraced every opportunity that walked in the door—to a disastrous fault. Despite all their success, the organization began to erode from within because of the founding partners' insurmountable personal differences. Comparable to watching a divorce unfold, the environment became painfully uncomfortable, and our relationship quickly came to an end.

Lesson No. 4: Growth Takes Time

I now find myself at a point where the experience, skills, and observations I gained from previous internships are finding their way into my interpretation of the prac-

tice of architecture—specifically, architectural marketing. I am interested in devel-oping and conveying (both internally and externally) consistent firm branding, award-winning design, and high-quality client service. Many of my current daily activities now focus on the pursuit of expanded nationwide clientele, increased profit margins, and team building.

Looking Back

In retrospect, the common denominator of these professional experiences trans-lates into two key words: adaptation *and* awareness. *Architectural graduates need more than great design or technical capacity; they must also have the ability to observe, understand, and enhance the career culture they have chosen to embrace. The internship experience enables you to sample professional diversity, and a mindful approach to the process will assist you in defining, or creating, a career path that's right for you.*

John McLean
Project Manager/Marketing Coordinator, KDF Architecture
Washington State University, Bachelor of Architecture 1997

Writing about Architecture

I came at architecture sideways. Interested in interpretation and words, I have a bachelor's degree in journalism from Northwestern University that's heavily laden with art and architectural history credits. Since earning that degree, I've written for the Chicago Tribune, *the* Associated Press, Architectural Record, Shelter, *and the Graham Foundation for Advanced Studies in the Fine Arts and have served as a studio critic at the University of Illinois at Chicago.*

My transformation from roving reporter to architectural writer and critic took me through a few cities, institutions, and experiences. Always wanting to explore the uncertain and sometimes rough terrain where disciplines don't so much intersect as nudge one another, I knew that eventually my interests would yank me out of writing "hard news." That happened in 1994:

> *Robert Sandifer's 11-year downward spiral of family neglect and juvenile delinquency finally ended in a pool of blood in a pedestrian tunnel on Chicago's South Side. Sandifer is believed to have committed two shoot-ings, killing 14-year-old Shavon Dean and leaving another boy with a spinal cord injury. Police searched for Sandifer for three days before find-ing him. He had been shot twice in the head.*
>
> —Chicago Tribune, *Sept. 2, 1994*

When I was a reporter for the Associated Press in Chicago, I helped cover Sandifer's murder of Dean and his ensuing execution by gang members. I was a few months out of undergraduate school, proud to be working for the AP, but also loathing it. The AP furnished plenty of adrenalin and national byline exposure. It also provided lousy working conditions and memories of so much tragedy.

A few months later, I found myself married and living in Berkeley, California. Instead of applying to the Chronicle *or other Bay Area publications, I sent my résumé to every architecture firm published in the Yellow Pages. I announced that I was a writer and editor and wondered if a design firm could use those skills. I got one reply and became a marketing coordinator, which involved far less death than the Associated Press but required loads of administrative work and late nights. I learned the difference between billable and nonbillable work, and how architects' priorities can be compartmentalized accordingly. Still unsatisfied, needless to say, I wanted to learn how architecture could be used as a means of interpretation.*

So I left temperate Berkeley for humid St. Louis to pursue a master's in architectural design at Washington University. However, after one semester I dropped out, having realized that the program involved countless hours drawing parallel lines with earphones in place, and precious little writing. Out of luck and low on dough, I became a marketing manager for a large A/E/CM firm. Unlike my first job, marketing the megalomaniacal design aspirations of the San Francisco firm's leaders, my second marketing position allowed me to become well versed in terms such as turnkey services, program management, design/build, and liability. Here, architecture wasn't so much about design as it was about managing other architects while hitting the sweet spot between risk and reward.

Two years later, I left and went to Yale, where I earned a master's in environmental design and degrees in history and theory. I wrote my thesis on Rem Koolhaas's McCormick Tribune Campus Center at the Illinois Institute of Technology in the context of Mies van der Rohe's 1938 campus and Koolhaas's rhetoric on Mies in his books Delirious New York *and* S, M, L, XL.

Today, I write the occasional piece for local newspapers, including a recent story on Koolhaas's ideas in conjunction with coverage of the Seattle Public Library's opening in 2004. After writing about him for two years at Yale, I finally interviewed Koolhaas for that article, in phone conversations that spanned four calls, two days, nine time zones, and, for him, two countries. I still appreciate the audience and journalistic rigor of newspapers. If you can write about architectural theory to a lay audience, then you know you understand it.

Architecture has provided me with the analytical framework by which I interpret the world. To earn a living (freelance writing pays only the smallest bills), I use that framework to help commercial architecture and engineering firms set their marketing and public relations priorities. I am a communications consultant, and ten years after leaving the Associated Press, I am happy to be interpreting architecture.

Rosemarie Buchanan
Communications Consultant
Yale University, Master of Environmental Design 2002

Corporate Training: The Development of People versus Buildings

They say pivotal life changes occur in cycles of seven years. This was definitely true for me as, after working seven years in the architectural profession, I packed up my triangles, trace paper, and "architect persona" to pursue other career aspirations. Since then I have dedicated my pursuits to individual and workplace learning. My various roles have included technical writer, presentation skills consultant, personal and leadership coach, and corporate trainer. My current role is training manager for the store development division of Starbucks Coffee Company.

I have a passion for understanding what makes others tick—for human psychology. This curiosity was well matched by my early architecture-school explorations. I was fascinated by the effects of the built environment on self-image, human behaviors, and civilization. What environments help to create a sense of community? How can views of natural light accelerate hospital patient recovery? Why do some places just feel so uplifting? These questions intrigued me. As a lifelong learner, I found there was never a shortage of intellectual or sensual pursuits to be found in architecture, the profession that weaves together art and science.

Looking back on my architectural education and career, I can see some common threads that clarified, predicted, and paved my future direction:

- *During architecture school, I was twice as motivated to spend time organizing student affairs as president of the AIAS chapter as I was to focus on my studies. Leadership roles have always been central to my life.*

- *On-the-job teaching, coaching, and mentoring were always a pleasure and an honor for me. I looked forward to these opportunities. Informally, I taught CAD to coworkers during an era when hand-drafted drawings were being transferred to electronic media.*

- *Early in my career, while employed with medium-sized architectural firms, I found few senior-level jobs I desired to grow into—except for those of the owners and leaders of the company.*

- *When I was a staff architect in design firms, some of my most satisfying work was spent in the 10 percent or less nonbillable time on my work schedule. This time was dedicated to serving on human resource committees, organizing continuing education programs, and other similar "overhead" activities.*

- *I learned about the importance of utilization rates, the feast-or-famine nature of the business, and the need for greater investment in employee development using company dollars.*

- *During my entire career, I was a passionate leader and advocate of workplace continuing education. I formed in-house continuing education committees to provide lunchtime seminars on accessibility, building code, mechanical systems, design, and new products.*

- *Though quite impressed with the design and technical expertise of my colleagues, I was often struck by the lack of attention and recognition given to effective teamwork, communication, development of people, and client service. I often wondered what a difference it would make in client satisfaction, employee retention, and fulfillment of a firm's vision and mission if architects had better interpersonal skills.*

- *While participating in a former employer's all-staff communication skills workshop, I learned about personality styles and their influences on decision making, communication, and personal preferences. The course material made complete sense to me. I became a voracious reader of books and articles on style differences, sharing them with any of my friends and family who would listen to my newfound excitement.*

When people hear that I left a career in architecture, they often ask, "But how could you leave all that hard work, dues-paying, and training?" I smile and remind them of the many transferable skills my architecture experience has provided me. The analytical, creative, conceptual, and project management skills and ability to communicate through visual media all bring value to my current work.

Through my career journey, I've learned to follow what comes naturally, what ignites the passions within me, and to take the paths that bring out my best. Sometimes that means a departure from the path and expectations of others. And it's all been worth it.

Julie A. Kerby, Certified Professional Coach
Training Manager, Starbucks Coffee Company
University of Washington, Bachelor of Arts in Architectural Studies 1992

The Academic World

Think back to when you were in architecture school. How many practicing architects did you know? It seems that most architecture students know very few architects other than professors or possibly family members. With this limited personal interaction, a student's perspective on the profession can be quite limited. It may have been difficult to think about the types of firms and work you would like to be involved with, as suggested in Chapter 2.

As the divide between education and practice has widened, it has become ever more important for practitioners to get involved with universities. Students need exposure to practitioners to provide an alternative perspective than that of their professors, often a prospective that is confronted with the challenges of reality such as building codes and client budgets. Oftentimes, universities are looking for professionals who are willing to donate an afternoon or day to critiquing student projects. Professors will draw on their personal contacts, and in some cases, the school will keep a list of interested jurors that professors can select from. If you are interested in serving as a design critic, make yourself known to the academic community. If you don't know any professors or instructors at the local architecture school, send a résumé along with a letter of interest. The more you get to know the instructors, the more likely it is that you will be called to serve as a juror.

However, you may want to do more than critique final projects; perhaps a full-time position in academia seems attractive. Becoming a full-time professor generally means pursuing a tenure-track position. This is a difficult road, fraught with additional considerations and requirements, and a subject for a book unto itself. These days, a career in academia generally requires at least a master of architecture degree.

Architect in Academic Administration

While the following contributor started along a conventional career path, he later switched from practicing architecture to helping others become architects. He shares the experiences that led to his current position in academic administration.

> *Like many, I became interested in architecture during my junior high years. I had the unique opportunity to meet with an architect in my hometown as well as intern in an architecture firm during my senior year in high school, and that confirmed my career choice. To maximize my options, I followed the 4+2 Master of Architecture degree track.*
>
> *At the end of my graduate studies, I still wanted to become an architect. However, serving as the AIAS chapter president and volunteering in the adviser's office led me to consider other career choices. Furthermore, I had the amazing experience of*

serving as AIAS national vice president for a year following graduation; that year exposed me to the profession of architecture.

My experience with AIAS and then with AIA pointed me in the direction of architectural education. Before pursuing this field, I felt the need to be an architect. I found a good entry-level position with an area architecture firm, but I did not find it satisfying, so I quit.

What came next was unexpected. As I learned about college student development as a professional path, I saw that this was a good fit for my skill sets. I pursued a PhD in counseling and development, with the explicit career goal of combining my education in architecture with student development. My dissertation researched the career development goals of architecture students. Upon graduation, my own career goal was to become an academic administrator within a program in architecture by age 40; I met my goal seven years early when I became Assistant Dean at the Illinois Institute of Technology (IIT).

After seven years at IIT, I now serve as Associate Dean in the School of Architecture, Planning, and Preservation at the University of Maryland. I am responsible for recruitment, admission, orientation, academic advising, and career development. My focus is to assist architecture students in pursuing their goal of becoming an architect. I have no regrets about not becoming an architect myself, because my position as associate dean is more connected to my particular skills and interests. I love what I do and am still connected to architecture.

Lee W. Waldrep, PhD
Associate Dean, University of Maryland School of Architecture, Planning, and Preservation
Author of *Becoming an Architect* (Wiley, 2006)
Arizona State University, Master of Architecture 1986
The American University, PhD in Counseling and Development 1993

Learning to Teach: The Intern Professor

In 1995, the ACSA published the *Junior Faculty Guide to Tenure and Promotion*. This informative guide for new professors is available as a free publication from www.acsa-arch.org. In the following essay, one young professor shares tips learned from his "internship" in the academic workplace.

The Art of Teaching

The best design professor I ever had was an artist. He'd been on the architectural faculty of my school for 37 years when he first taught me, and he had an indelible influence over much of the curriculum. He knew how to teach—how to inspire, enrich, and sculpt the minds of young designers—which is not the same thing as knowing how to put a building together. I realized then that teaching is as much an art as building design is, and I decided to pursue an educational career. As I've moved through grad school, and now that I'm teaching, I've picked up a few tips that have helped me cultivate my teaching potential. I hope they give insight to others who might be interested in pursuing an academic career.

Get Experience

My alma mater, as many schools do, had a graduate teaching assistant program. If you are even remotely considering teaching as a career, get involved. This is the only way to get experience teaching, outside being hired as faculty. Look for graduate teaching assistant (GTA) assignments in subjects you're interested in, and make the most of these opportunities. Offer to take on lectures, lead seminars and laboratories, or write exercises. Your boss will rarely refuse, and you'll go a long way toward forwarding your cause. My school's tight budget necessitated a "team approach" to first-year design. A GTA was paired with a faculty member to teach parallel studio sections. Working side-by-side with a seasoned professional afforded me invaluable on-the-job training.

Identify a Mentor

An informal relationship with a respected professor is a tremendous asset. Faculty veterans can advise you in your teaching career, may guide or collaborate on research, and most important, will be models from which to fashion your approach to teaching. My chief mentor, who taught both design and environmental systems, found a successful balance between design and technology. This stance rang true for me, and I've emulated his attitude since beginning my career. As in business, word of mouth is the best way to find out about jobs. Your mentor will be in the know about potential positions, and his or her recommendation will add weight to your application.

Get Credentials

As in other job markets, extracurricular activities can set you apart from the crowd. Look for creative and scholarly opportunities outside of class. Community design centers, charettes, and competitions are good ways to exhibit design competence outside the studio. Writing articles, attending pedagogical conferences, and coauthoring papers with your mentor (see above) are good ways to ground your teaching objectives.

Develop a Research Focus

A faculty position is not all about teaching. Conducting scholarly research and presenting it for peer validation is a chief measure of advancement for professors, although architecture schools normally have a pretty loose interpretation of "scholarly research" when compared to other fields. Faculty search committees want to know that you've done more than scratch the pedagogical surface. An important function of the academy is to contribute to the body of knowledge the profession draws upon. The chance to continue one's studies is one of the major advantages of an educational career—practitioners have little time to spare for research. Conversely, teaching probably isn't the right choice for those uninterested in scholarship.

Develop a Secondary Specialty

Develop broad as well as deep interests. The ability to teach across subject boundaries is highly prized by faculty search committees. A look at any of the job listings in the back of ACSANews—the newsletter published by the Association of Collegiate Schools of Architecture and the premier reference for job openings—will demonstrate the importance of teaching flexibility. Consider a minor concentration during your graduate studies. Conceptually, having multiple interests is closer to being a true architect—someone who comprehends the totality of design. It may also save you from being pigeonholed early in your academic career.

The Job Search

Timing is an unavoidable component of any job search. Some years there are dozens of schools clamoring for new faculty; other years there are next to none. Start looking in August or September for start dates in the following year. Pay close attention to application due dates (usually December through February) and requirements (normally a curriculum vitae, some type of portfolio, and letters of reference). Aside from the ACSANews, your faculty mentor is another reliable source of information. The educational community is small, and he or she may be privy to inside information.

The Interview

Remember how nervous you were at a traditional job interview? What if that interview lasted three days? That's the standard length of time a potential faculty candidate is under the microscope, meeting with all the disparate populations of the school: faculty, students, and a slew of future bosses. You are also required to perform, by lecturing or guest critiquing, or both. However, if you are invited to visit a school's campus, it means you are one of a few top candidates, and your chances have gone from slim to pretty good.

Having an entire school judge your work, credentials, and potential is a critique to end all critiques. The gravity of the school's decision, though, warrants more than a 15-minute Q&A. The visit is an opportunity for you to get to know the school as well. You will absorb a lot of information about the school's conditions during the firestorm. If an offer is extended, it will be up to you to decide whether the school's mission is a good match with your objectives as an emerging educator. This is not a decision to take lightly.

Before seeking my master's degree, I worked as an intern for a few firms. I've personally found teaching to be far more rewarding than traditional practice. Professors enjoy much more autonomy over their work, are encouraged to do research, and are better paid. Most important, even though I am a junior faculty member, my elders treat me as an equal. By contrast, one of my professional employers readily admitted that he considered interns a liability. My teaching colleagues accept my lack of experience, and my potential is cultivated. That's how all careers should begin.

R. Todd Gabbard
Assistant Professor, Kansas State University
University of Florida, Master of Architecture 2004

Satisfying Architectural Desires through Teaching

Unlike Todd, the following contributor found himself interested in an academic career after many years of architectural practice. As a senior member of the academic world, Paul shares the satisfaction he has found through teaching.

Since becoming a member of the architecture faculty at Washington State University, my focus on practice has been greatly reduced—in part, because of the limited opportunities for maintaining a practice in a small eastern Washington town, but more important, because the conditions of teaching architecture design have been far more pleasurable than those of practice. Upon reflection, teaching design has satisfied two desires that I found hard to fulfill in my own practice experiences.

The following observations speculate on these desires and the influence they may have on the content of architecture design studios.

The Desire to Focus on Architecture Issues of Personal Interest

Under most circumstances, teaching an architecture design studio allows much greater choice as to the focus of the architectural problem. Problem definition allows the instructor to select design issues that are of greatest personal concern. Oftentimes, faculty choose to focus more on theoretical positions and do not include more pragmatic issues, such as budget, HVAC, or code requirements. The downside to this teaching strategy is that it does not represent the more comprehensive design process found in most architecture offices, where issues of cost, codes, and so on must always be considered. Students may learn to deal with only a limited number of design issues and, when confronted with a more complex mix of conditions in practice, may become dissatisfied.

Two colleague relocations provide examples of the potential frustrations of these disparities between school and practice. One colleague left the practice of architecture for graphic design because he felt that the process of creating architecture was too complicated. In his words, "It is impossible to control quality when you have so many people involved." The other individual spent five years working on multiple architecture projects, only to see them all go unbuilt because of cost complications. He is now teaching architecture. I would add myself as a third example. I was constantly frustrated by certain aspects of the design process—cost limitations, client differences, contractor disputes, and so on—all conditions to which I had limited exposure in architecture school.

The Desire for More Exploration of a Selected Architecture Issue

When you are a practicing architect, the time allotted to researching a particular design issue is, for the most part, limited by fee structure. Whether the issue is site analysis, historical precedents, relevant theoretical positions, or new technologies, most fee arrangements severely limit the amount of time a firm can devote to investigating these potential influences. By contrast, in the academic environment, design faculties are given both time and encouragement to explore self-selected aspects of architectural influence. Tenure and promotion, in fact, are largely granted on the basis of this research and according to the scholarly contribution one has made to one's area of interest.

In those rare firms that do encourage extensive research and analysis in architecture, negative economic consequences are incurred. Either employees are willing to do the research without pay because they have "bread-and-butter" projects in the office that are repetitive and lucrative enough to support a research base, or firm profits are reduced to fund research agendas. Practice protocol does not encourage educating the client about the value of in-depth problem research and analysis. Unfortunately, most firms also fail to recognize that investing in research can help establish a firm's reputation for expertise in a particular area of architecture and thus garner long-term economic benefits.

Conclusions

The school design studio devotes a great deal of time to nurturing personal interests and investigation. Projects focus on extensive research and personal creative exploration and rarely go beyond the first phase of design—schematics. In contrast, the architecture office spends little time exploring architecture topics of personal significance, as a majority of time is spent on the design phases after schematics: design development through construction administration. Schools focus on the beginning of the design process and practice focuses on the remainder. Students spend five to six years in school developing a design process (which emphasizes innovation and exploration) that is generally underutilized in the workplace.

Is it any wonder, then, that some students never adjust to this rearrangement in architecture priorities when they enter practice and ultimately decide to return to the academic design studio as teachers? My hope is to find a way to better merge the worlds of professional practice and academia. Through the overlapping of teaching and practice, I believe current frustration and migration will be alleviated.

Paul Hirzel, AIA
Associate Professor of Architecture, Washington State University
Cornell University, Master of Architecture 1984

CHAPTER 11 | WORKING ABROAD

Since the earliest days of the profession, architects have been fascinated by travel and foreign architecture. In order to obtain a worldly appreciation for the arts, 16th-century European aristocrats would embark on a grand tour of major cities, including Paris and Rome. In this tradition, many young architects at the turn of the century looked to European schools such as the Ecole des Beaux Arts for education and European buildings for inspiration and architectural precedents. Over the past century, the evolution of architectural schools in North America has enabled the majority of architectural candidates to seek education closer to home. Yet there is still an emphasis on obtaining a worldly appreciation of architecture through foreign study, travel, or work experience.

The easiest way for Americans to find work overseas is to get a job in a U.S. company with a foreign office. Many of the country's larger firms have foreign offices. If you have language skills in the country in which you desire to work, that may prove very helpful, especially at firms that are opening up new offices in foreign countries. Such firms may have job postings specifically for positions in those foreign offices.

If possible, start out in the U.S. office of an international firm. When you've gained the firm's trust and confidence in your skills and abilities, the firm may be willing to help with the necessary paperwork and relocation costs if you are transferred to one of its offices abroad.

How to Research Potential Jobs Abroad

Start with who you know. Ask around among friends, mentors, and former professors. You will be amazed by how many people know architects working abroad. Obtain contact information and get in touch to find out what unique skills the firms are looking for that you might offer as an intern from the United States (most work visa applications will require you or your employer to prove that a you possess skills not found in the local workforce).

In addition, contact the career center or alumni association at your university. They might have a list of alumni living abroad. While these alumni might not always be architects, they may help you with information on the logistics of living in a specific city, such as obtaining a visa and finding housing. They might tell you about the cost and convenience of public transport, make cost-of-living comparisons, and describe their own experience of living there. In addition, they might know of architects to put you in touch with or the names of well-known firms you can research.

As with any job, consider your reasons for living abroad. Is your objective simply to experience living in a foreign country? If so, which one? Do you want to work on a specific project type? Are there specific skills you are looking to obtain? These questions may help determine the firms you apply to or how to approach the job search.

Also consider the type of firm you are looking for and what you hope to gain from your experience, such as knowledge of a specific construction or project type. Is there a social or humanitarian objective for working abroad? And if so, are there American-sponsored agencies and organizations, such as Habitat for Humanity or the Peace Corps, that could provide you with opportunities?

Visa Requirements

Each country has its own visa requirements. In many countries, if you are a tourist for less than three months, a visa is not required. However, if you seek legitimate employment, a tourist visa will not be sufficient, and you will have to obtain a work permit/visa. Most countries will require the employer to verify that you possess qualifications the firm cannot find in its current applicant pool—a tall order for most interns to fill. You are likely to find interns from many foreign countries working "under the table." Use caution when accepting such a position.

Advice from Those Who Have Done It

The remainder of this chapter is comprised of firsthand accounts from young architects who have found employment abroad. Each individual has taken a different approach to his or her job search, but all have had professional and personal experiences that will last a lifetime. The following young architect received her training in Germany and Switzerland. She has traveled extensively; worked in Germany, England, and the United States; and is currently living in Copenhagen, Denmark. She has typically selected the city in which she desired to live and then found employment after getting settled in her new home. Her essay provides an overview of the situations you will need to consider when working abroad.

Tips for Obtaining Foreign Employment

Whether you've just made the decision to move or have already settled into your new home abroad, research the employment situation in your chosen location. Ask yourself these questions: Do you speak the language well enough to communicate, or will you be able to learn the basics in a reasonable amount of time? Will your qualifications transfer? Where are you in your career, and are you willing to step back a little, if necessary? Generally speaking, it is easier to take this step early in your professional life, when you expect responsibility to come with much supervision. For example, if you're used to managing your own projects, it may be a little harder to achieve this level of responsibility in a new place, where you are not only unfamiliar with local codes and practices but also lack the network that one builds up over time.

If you are fortunate enough to work for a company that sends you abroad, the following advice about visas will not be relevant. The company will deal with the visa procedures for you, and there are special visa requirements for foreign employees of a foreign company.

Visa Requirements

Find out as much as possible about work permits and visa regulations ahead of time. Call the embassy, talk to friends, use the Internet, or look for publications on working abroad. If possible, apply ahead of time for a work visa; in many cases, however, you will be able to submit your work visa application only after you have received an employment offer.

At a minimum, you can organize the paperwork in advance: Obtain necessary forms, translations, or transcripts, and find out how long the process takes and what fees are involved. Several months' review time for an application is fairly standard, and depending on your initial status, you may have to leave the country temporarily during this review period. You'll need to discuss this fact with your future employer during your interview. Be prepared to inform a potential employer how much (or how little) effort and money the process will involve.

Work visas are typically not free. At press time, a three-year H-1B visa in the United States cost the employer about US$1,500 in fees. If an attorney files the petition, it will cost a couple of thousand dollars more but will require less effort on the part of the employer, since the attorney will prepare all the paperwork. It's a good idea to talk to an immigration attorney (look for one who offers a first counsel free of charge) to find out whether the application requires any "informal" papers. So-called "informal" cover letters are often required and should be filled with keywords that a person unfamiliar with the process would not know to include. Sometimes an employer will be required to state your unique skills for the particular position and to document the firm's efforts to find a citizen with comparable skills.

Most countries require that a foreigner be paid at least the average or mean salary applicable for his or her profession. Salary categories may be handled with some creativity, but the salary will likely have to be approved by a government agency.

If you've decided to set sail despite all the red tape, update your CV (Europeans refer to résumés as CVs) and portfolio. If possible, do this while you have access to a computer and familiar software programs. If you have the application forms ready and take them along with you, you will save time when you arrive, and you'll get started more quickly and easily.

Research

Most people will have to look for work after they arrive in their new city. Although you can and should do some research ahead of time — any university or college with an architecture department will have numerous relevant publications — once you have moved, you should also get in touch with local professional architecture organizations, such as the Royal Institute of British Architects or other international organizations. These organizations often have libraries that can provide information sources and may also maintain postings of vacancies or a list of people looking for employment. Asking is free, so always ask — perhaps something will come of it.

It's usually fairly easy to identify the top five big firms in a given place, but to find out about smaller practices you will have to rely on word of mouth or cobble together scraps of information such as photo credits and news articles. Inquire about upcoming lecture series through the local architecture school or professional organizations. Lectures are a great way to learn about the work of smaller offices. Utilize any local contacts you obtain, no matter how remote the connection. Go out and explore; get acclimated to your new environment.

A large, well-established office may have experience with hiring foreigners or may be more willing to go through the necessary red tape than a sole proprietor who needs someone right away and who may not be able to wait out the two-month process. This is not necessarily the case, however, so by all means send an application to any firm that interests you.

Application Format

Familiarize yourself with local customs so you can decide whether—or how—you want to stand out from other applicants. For example, in some European countries, it's customary to include a head shot on your résumé.

Provide an e-mail address and preferably a local phone number, even if it's the phone number of a friend you're staying with, so potential employers can contact you easily. An application with a phone number from the other side of the world may look cool, but you're unlikely to receive a call for an interview.

Interview

You'll probably encounter a mixture of curiosity and reservation from interviewers. On the one hand, you have the "exotic factor" on your side: a potentially interesting, or at least different, background. On the other hand, it may be hard for your potential employer to gauge how much of your knowledge will be applicable or transferable and where your gaps might be. Just keep in mind that this is basically the same situation every applicant faces, and that you'll have to sell the employer on your strengths. Nothing new here, as long as your language skills are good enough to master the situation.

Keep Up Your Optimism

Chances are, you made a conscious decision to move of your own free will. A few weeks of making phone calls may seem like forever, but in hindsight it is just a few weeks, after all. I have never regretted the risks I took in looking for employment in a foreign countriy and have always felt I gained more than I put at stake.

Petra Michaely
Architect, CF Moeller Architects
Technische Universität Darmstadt, Germany, and Swiss Federal Institute of Technology Zurich (ETH Zurich), Dipl. Ing. arch. 1996

All around the World

In an effort to complement his architectural education with varied international experiences, the following contributor has traveled to more than 50 countries, working in 8 of those. He was employed with Baumschlager & Eberle in Austria for two years before moving to Denmark. He shares the following insights on how to find work overseas.

The rewards of working internationally are boundless, and the experience is sure to impact both your professional and personal life. However, your high expectations should be balanced with a healthy attitude toward unexpected cultural challenges. In preparation for working internationally, you might ask yourself a few fundamental questions:

- *Do I want to work for a North American firm with an office in a foreign country?*
- *Do I want to work for a foreign firm that works solely in its local region?*
- *Do I want to seek a foreign office desiring to pursue projects in North America?*

Answering these questions may or may not lead to greater clarity, but it will demonstrate some of the many ways to reach your goal of working abroad.

The Educational Route

Many architects get their first taste of living overseas as a student in a foreign exchange program. These summer- or semester-long programs are an excellent way to determine whether living and working overseas is an adventure you want to pursue. In addition, these programs often give you the opportunity to establish contacts with local architects. Bring your work or, better yet, a portfolio of your best efforts so you'll be prepared to present your skills at any time. If your university does not offer this type of exchange program, it may be possible to join an already established program and have the credits transferred to your institution.

Aside from exchange programs, there are many other opportunities to experience living abroad. For example, you might participate in an overseas archaeological dig to learn about surveying, preservation techniques, and measured drawings. Or you might enroll in a foreign university for a year, using your educational contacts to seek work opportunities. European universities often hire practicing architects as studio instructors, who then cull the best students to work in their offices.

Throughout Europe, there are successful stories of North American students finding a foreign office in which to work after a summer exchange program forever changed their outlook on life. Virginia Tech graduates have peppered the architectural ateliers of the Ticino region in Switzerland since a foreign studies program was begun in Riva San Vitale in the 1980s. Mark Carroll, a principal of the Renzo Piano Building Workshop in Genoa, began his employment in Europe after attending the Clemson University Genoa program. These examples are mentioned to underscore the unexpected rewards of traveling and studying in a foreign country.

In addition, universities function as great venues for researching networking opportunities. Before you attempt to seek work overseas, check in with your university alumni center. It's likely that at least one alumnus or alumna has already set out to blaze the trail that you are considering. Contact these alumni prior to your departure and let them know of your interest in working in the region. Ask them for their honest advice and counsel.

Working Abroad by Looking at Home

As evidenced by Frank Lloyd Wright's Imperial Hotel in Japan, American-based architects have long worked overseas. Through improved travel and communication systems, most large and some medium-sized American architectural firms have a global focus, with branch offices in cities such as Hong Kong, London, and Berlin. By transferring from one of their American offices to an international branch office, an individual can ease his or her transition to a foreign country while enjoying the support and camaraderie of American colleagues.

In order to increase your chances for overseas transfer, study the history of the international branch office that interests you — when was it founded, by whom, and what project types are favored — and meet the branch managers, who may travel back and forth between their American base and their foreign outpost. Learn the language spoken in the region in which the branch office is located, and during your reviews, let your employers know of your interest in living and working abroad. An employer will be much more likely to send someone overseas who seeks out such an opportunity than to take a chance on someone who may not fit in culturally and may ask to be transferred back home after a few months.

Seeking Opportunities Abroad

One of the biggest challenges of seeking work in a foreign office is getting your prospective employer to recognize and understand your prior work experience. North American architects tend to know very little about their counterparts in other regions of the world; likewise, foreign architects often know little about the work in America. Your university's prestige, the coursework you completed, the awards you garnered, your office work experience and its reputation, and the recommendation writers who have vouched for your abilities may not be known to the individuals with whom you will be interviewing, and yet they will very quickly determine the direction of your career abroad. Thus, it will be doubly difficult to compete against the local population, whose education and work references will be familiar. On the flip side, you also have many skills and attributes that local job seekers may not possess. Highlighting these differences will be the key to gaining employment.

Publications offer the best information for researching opportunities with a foreign office, but many other resources are also available. For example, embassies and consulates in North America may have libraries or even curate cultural exhibitions that include architecture. A country's foreign business offices will be able to share recent economic data with you, so that before you invest in a trip to the region where you'd like to work, you can verify that the area is economically healthy and that firms there are apt to be in a hiring mode. Consider prioritizing regions that cultivate many strong and growing offices, instead of seeking out a small town that is home to one "star" architect. In recent years, countries such as China, Holland, Switzerland, and Austria have provided a favorable climate for the design community.

One way to make contacts in foreign offices is to attend lectures, symposia, and conferences in North America that are hosted or attended by international architects. Introduce yourself and make a favorable first impression, ask questions concerning their work and locale, and express your desire to travel to their region.

Nuts and Bolts

Every culture and country has different social customs and norms for presenting oneself to prospective employers. Research cultural business protocols to learn how you should prepare your portfolio, make introductions, dress, and follow up on your interviews. In Europe, for example, it is customary to include a portrait photograph of yourself on your résumé or CV, as well as to state your birth year. Even if you are not fluent in the language of the region, consider having your letters of introduction and résumés translated professionally into the native language. This demonstrates that you will adapt yourself to your new home and that, when it comes to business situations, you can get a job done even if you have certain deficiencies. Most foreign architects will not hire you over the phone but, rather, will require you to travel to their offices so they can meet you and gauge your abilities. Your willingness to travel to meet them increases your chances tremendously, as you are demonstrating the lengths to which you are willing to go to secure a job. Keep in mind the extra costs associated with securing a position prior to moving. These costs may include travel, computer time or Internet connections to write follow-up letters to interviews, establishing reliable means of contact (such as international cellular phone service), and accommodations in each of the regions where you have interviews. Doing a little research before your trip will help you estimate how much time you have to secure a job given your financial resources.

Selling Yourself

Your unique skills may set you apart from others competing for the same position. This becomes even more important when you are pursuing employment in a foreign country, where you may not speak the language. Oftentimes, the prospective employer is considering a whole different set of criteria from those you have assembled in your portfolio. But remember that your fluent command of English is, in and of itself, a desirable skill for foreign firms that are trying to tap into international markets.

Be sure to research the firms at which you are seeking employment. This is more difficult in countries where publications are printed only in the local language. Try to locate former or current employees to ask firsthand about their experiences, visit local bookstores that may carry translated texts on the firms' work, and, should the principals be teaching at the local university, try to attend their lectures. Bookstores, libraries, and local architecture institutes can also help you learn about offices doing great work that may be unknown to a wider audience.

Seek letters of recommendation from individuals who may be known to the foreign offices you are interested in. These letters can often be used as a bridge between two cultures. If you are inexperienced, highlight your hunger to learn and your ability to invest your time and energy in the task at hand. If you have previously worked internationally, then highlight your specialties. Experience in airport, hospitality, and medical facility design is often extremely helpful in opening doors and gaining interviews at prestigious international offices. Once you have been offered a position, be willing to accept a lower level of responsibility and compensation to break into the office. One way to approach this issue is to request a probationary period of three months, at the end of which time the employer will schedule a review to discuss adapting your responsibilities and compensation to your skill set. Remember that the international employer is taking a greater risk by hiring you and that you may not be functioning at 100 percent because of language issues and the challenge of dealing with cultural nuances.

When you do bridge the cultures and become situated in your new office, you will begin to reap the benefits of working internationally. Enjoy your new home, the opportunities of your new work environment, and the new culinary delights available to you.

Kai-Uwe Bergmann, AIA
Architect, CF Moeller Architects
University of California, Los Angeles, Master of Architecture 1993

For Interns Only: Tips for Finding Employment in Great Britain

The following intern architect has had many opportunities to study and work abroad. She shares her insights from a recent experience seeking legitimate employment in the United Kingdom.

Changing Horses

I participated in a variety of study-abroad programs in Europe as a student of architecture and found the experiences transformative. I always intended to return to Europe to work for a time. When my boyfriend gained acceptance to Cambridge University, my deliberations began. How does one know when it is time to leave a great position in a great firm to seek new personal and professional experiences? I have been fortunate enough to have faced this predicament several times. The decision has always been difficult to reach, but I have yet to look back with regret after "changing horses."

I began researching firms in Cambridge and London prior to my arrival. I searched firm Web sites, looking for the quality of work I admired and to which I wanted to contribute. I used the ubiquitous "friends of friends" network to develop contacts for advice and employment leads. And I packed CDs of digital files to create a work portfolio.

Eggs in a Basket

Far and away my first choice of employment in the United Kingdom was the Richard Rogers Partnership (RRP) in London. I put together a tight application with a personal letter describing my interest in the firm, a curriculum vitae, a digital portfolio, and academic and professional recommendations. Months before I intended to relocate, I forwarded my application to a partner at the office I had recently left. He sent a personal letter of recommendation along with the firm's monograph to endorse me. Several months later, I received a gracious note from RRP thanking me for my time, but offering no interview.

Thankfully, in the meantime I had continued the search for other firms whose work I admired. I attended an exhibition entitled "Young British Architects" that helped add to the list of prospective firms to consider. I mailed a version of the packet sent to RRP to the firms that interested me. Responses were slow in arriving. Some firms wrote back explaining that they did not accept digital portfolios, but would keep my CV on file until I sent a traditional portfolio. Several firms contacted me to clarify how my American experiences and degrees compared to the UK system of internship. Unfortunately, I could not answer definitively.

TIP   Learn about the education system in the country where you are seeking employment so you can answer questions about degree equivalencies.

Still other firms that contacted me lost interest when I explained that I did not yet have a work permit in place. My initial impression had been that the responsibility for obtaining these permits lay with the employing firm. I now know that it would have been better to research the process, because most firms were deterred by the perceived hassle of hiring a foreigner.

Around this time, I came across a book on the topic of working in Britain that described a program offering short-term work permits to foreigners who were seeking "training and work experience" leading to recognized professional qualification. As I was only partly finished with my architectural licensing exams and not yet registered, this pertained to me. Armed with information to build upon, I decided to simply go to England and pound the pavement with portfolio in hand. Changing into interview clothes in a youth hostel, I felt strangely like Clark Kent, but I am certain the same has been done before by many others.

The trip to England offered immersion in and access to all the various topics I had researched. At the youth hostel, I spoke to people who advised contacting an attorney specializing in visas and work permits. I found several such attorneys in the phone book, whom I telephoned for initial advice though never contracted. I also called a friend of a friend at KPF and met another at SOM, both of whom had previous work experience at the U.S. branches of these firms. Both described the road to licensure in the United Kingdom and advised me to contact the Architects Registration Board (ARB). I then visited the ARB. Having ascertained that my education and experiences should qualify me as having fulfilled parts I and II for registration, I obtained information on applying to Part III of the professional training program for architects.

I could now speak intelligently during an interview and reassure future employers about the process and feasibility of obtaining a Training and Work Experience Permit. Many firms may be unfamiliar with the permit process, in which case hiring a foreigner could appear more hassle than benefit without your reassurance and explanation. Your determination and willingness to take responsibility for researching the permit process may help demonstrate your value to a potential employer.

Making Tea

My employment opportunity came from Ellis-Miller Architects. EMA is a small Cambridge firm that I had come across and noted as an interesting prospect months prior, while I was searching the Internet back in the United States. I interviewed with the firm on my first trip and left with an invitation to return in a couple of months to begin work on a new English country estate. My previous experience with the design of a custom modern residence was of great interest to the firm. During the interview, I shared my knowledge of the Training and Work Experience Permit, which the firm later successfully obtained.

As with any experience abroad, it was fun to test the accuracy of stereotypes. The length of time I stayed and the variety of experiences I had gave me opportunities galore. From day one there were many references to making tea—whether it was part of my job description, whether the builders would have on-site facilities, or whether the window manufacturer was able to come to the telephone. Meetings rarely began without a cup of tea at each attendee's place.

The best souvenirs I collected were the additions to my portfolio and sketchbook and copies of my e-mail correspondence. These documents detail what I gained from the experience of immersion in an environment where things are just slightly different.

Immersion in a different culture prompted constant questions and a critical eye for all that surrounded me—a critical eye I still carry with me. The immersion experience was facilitated by the development of colleague, client, and consultant relationships; exposure to preservation attitudes, urban sprawl, environmental policies, construction methods, and procurement options; attendance at academic symposia, lectures, performances, and concerts; and numerous pilgrimages to experience architectural sites and art exhibitions. Outside of work, cultural immersion continued through pubs, punting, cricket matches, and affiliation with a local karate club.

The following advice pertains to all interns and practitioners, whether leaving a firm to return to school, to seek an overseas adventure, or simply to experience practicing with another firm: Give plenty of notice, work hard through the end of your stay, and be responsible about transferring your knowledge and the history of your projects to the team. I have worked at many firms where individuals were asked to return after a hiatus, and they most certainly followed this formula. Even if you do not intend to return, you will likely desire a future reference.

Tricia Stuth
Lecturer, University of Tennessee; Cofounder, CURB
University of Wisconsin, Milwaukee, Bachelor of Science in Architectural Studies 1995
University of Wisconsin, Milwaukee, Master of Architecture 1997

Useful Resources for Working in the United Kingdom

Architects Registration Board
www.arb.org.uk/

Provides information on obtaining an assessment of your current credentials as an architect-in-training and continuing on the path to UK licensure. Also provides useful links to other professional organizations.

Home Office (United Kingdom Government Site)
www.workingintheuk.gov.uk/working_in_the_uk/en/documents/all_forms.html

Provides information on training and work experience (notes and forms).

Royal Institute of British Architects (RIBA)
www.architecture.com/go/Architecture/Home.html

The UK equivalent of the American Institute of Architects (AIA); the Web site has job listings, including internships for students, and a salary guide. The headquarters on Portland Place in London offers a great bookstore, café, and exhibition and lecture series.

Hampshire, David. *Living and Working in Britain: A Survival Handbook,* **5th ed. Survival Books, 2005**
http://survivalbooks.net/

Working in London and Berlin

More than a decade ago, the following contributor left Chicago to work in Berlin and London. She has learned many ways for successfully finding employment in the studios of Renzo Piano and Norman Foster in Berlin and SOM in London.

Basic Skills

Overseas employers, especially large international firms, seek applicants with computer skills. The most popular systems for drafting here in London are Intergraph Microstation and AutoCAD. Proficiency in 3-D modeling and rendering for design competitions is also a sought-after skill. Being an expert computer user may help you land a job in a foreign office, as the employer can list this needed skill in the letter that may be required for work permits, as was the case for me in Germany.

Large international firms also look for interns with basic model-making skills. Although the final presentation models are almost always made by professional out-of-house model-making companies, study models are created in-house for design development.

 Get accustomed to working in the metric system!

Interview

When reviewing an applicant's portfolio, employers are less interested in "design philosophy" and more concerned with good drawing, presentation, and model-making skills. As in the United States, employers look for clarity of thought when speaking with the applicant, as well as good organizational skills. The applicant should be able to demonstrate that he or she understands the "big picture" when it comes to working on a project. Although knowledge of how to speak with colleagues and consultants in a professional manner is something that can be learned on the job, the applicant should be aware that this ability may be evaluated during the interview. It is very important for an intern to have a good attitude, possess the ability to work with others on a team, follow through with instructions, and demonstrate a high level of inquiry. Interns should not be timid about discussing design ideas or solutions with team members. Sometimes a fresh eye can see a clear design solution right away.

Overtime

One aspect of being an intern in a large firm abroad is the perception that overtime is expected. Student interns, by definition, are not full-time employees and are not required to work more than full-time hours. However, as in the United

States, the reality depends on workloads and time pressures. Interns should not feel pressured to overwork themselves, but should keep in mind that there are many learning opportunities and a sense of camaraderie to be gained "in the trenches" during deadline periods. In addition, the willingness to put in some late-hours work demonstrates team spirit and is always appreciated by others who stay to work late.

Language Skills

When working in a foreign country, it's best to have some proficiency in the native language, although by no means is fluency absolutely required. It is always a good idea to take language lessons, even if it means taking them after work a few days per week. The effort may be tiring but will be worthwhile, as you will benefit more from your time in the office as well as in social situations. Working in an English-speaking office in a non-English-speaking country provides a good transition, as the drawings usually will be in two languages and the native language will be spoken in the office alongside English, especially during meetings with consultants and contractors.

Keep handy a bilingual dictionary of technical terms specific to architecture and engineering.

Don't socialize exclusively with fellow expatriots; make an effort to socialize with your native colleagues to practice speaking the language and get to know the local customs.

Compensation

When working in a foreign office, it's good to be paid as a full-time employee with benefits, if possible. However, be sure applying for benefits is within your language skill level. I found this to be a big problem in Berlin and, thus, missed out on my unemployment benefits. If you foresee that the language barrier might put you at a disadvantage in compensation negotiations, it's better to be paid as a contract employee, as long as the pay is greater to make up for the lack of benefits. The increased salary allows you to take out your own private insurance, which is usually required by law, and to save up for your own unemployment, taxes, and so on. A contract arrangement also allows you to write off some expenses on your taxes.

Madeleine Lee-Schmid, AIA
Architect, SOM London
Rice University, Bachelor of Science in Architectural Studies 1987
Columbia University, Master of Architecture 1991

Working in Portugal

While Madeleine had work experience to support her move abroad, some interns look for foreign employment straight out of school, with little practical experience to offer. In an attempt to obtain employment abroad, many interns take positions where they are paid "under the table," often working for cash and usually without paying local taxes. While such employment situations are quite common, they are not technically legal. (I personally do not endorse such arrangements, but I acknowledge they do exist and recognize that interns need to be informed in order to make their own decisions.) The following contributor worked in the office of Alvaro Siza in Portugal and shares his experiences working for this renowned architect.

In regard to the research I conducted before leaving, I read and learned as much as possible about Siza's work. It also didn't hurt that a former professor spoke to him on my behalf. Many of the foreign architects in Portugal and Spain were living and working illegally, as I was. Positions were usually temporary, with low compensation and few or no benefits. Most people probably recognized this risk going into it.

One strange thing I found was that I was required to legally register to pay taxes—to get a tax identity number and everything—but was nevertheless working and being paid illegally. Since I do plan to return to live in Portugal, I did not want any tax evasion issues to follow me and, therefore, accepted this contradictory tax situation. Other Americans at the office simply didn't pay the taxes and then left the country. [Author's note: Foreigners complain about similar inconsistencies in taxes and benefits here in the United States.]

Working overseas, you may be faced with a variety of issues, including work visas, different work styles, language barriers, and other cultural differences. The European Union allows its citizens to work freely in any of its member countries, but depending on the country you settle in, overseas foreigners are usually confronted with a barrage of bureaucratic requirements when applying for legal residency and permission to work.

In Europe, and especially in southern Europe, I found that a humble attitude and a genuine willingness to learn from others can take you far in a new culture and work environment. It can also help you establish new relationships with friends and valued colleagues.

You never understand the true status of work or the staffing situation at offices and ateliers until you can confront them firsthand. Persistence is often a necessary weapon, so come well armed. Although it's often difficult and sometimes disrupting to simply show up on the doorstep of an atelier, a person could be pulled from that doorstep and put behind a computer during a crunch.

Immediate availability can be a great asset when you arrive at a new and strange place looking for work; use it to your advantage. Make a point of adjusting as quickly as possible to the situation at hand, and be open to whatever might transpire. It's important to express, as best as you can, your strong interest and willingness to start work whenever possible.

Be portable. As with all travel, it's a good idea to remain modest in your impact on a new place. In the beginning, unless you are specifically asked to teach, it's often sensible to try to focus more on learning from others.

Be open-minded. Observe. Keep your eyes and ears wide open. Many European architects may speak English and several other languages, but when at work they generally prefer to use their native tongue. Language can be one of the largest hurdles to overcome in a foreign office. Although you may be able to communicate with others in English initially, speaking the local language can take you a step deeper into the detailed workings of an office and make you a more valuable asset. If you don't yet know the language, you would be wise to enlist in night classes. Proficiency in the local vernacular can be invaluable, not only for flexibility in communicating within the office but also for integrating quickly on a cultural level.

You may find yourself incredibly frustrated at times, and intoxicatingly transfixed at others. There will be infinitely valuable moments of learning in your new work situation and in this new place. Treasure the similarities you discover and learn from the differences in culture, practice, and methodology.

Brad Kelley
Washington State University, Bachelor of Architecture 1994
Columbia University, Master of Architecture 1999

Fellowships

Another way to obtain work experience abroad is through travel fellowships. While they don't provide a significant source of income, there are ample opportunities for research and introspection — luxuries that are hard to come by with a full-time job. A stipend is often provided that generally covers the cost of living for the given duration. While several foreign fellowships are described in this section, there are many others available both abroad and in North America. Chapter 7 describes some of the fellowship opportunities in the United States, and you will find many more on the Web.

Fulbright Fellowship

The following contribution was written by an architect who spent nine months in Tallin, Estonia, on a Fulbright Fellowship. He describes the intent of the program and the benefits received from his fellowship. Language skills are often a prerequisite, and not every country accepts applicants studying architecture. For more information on the Fulbright Fellowship, see the Institute for International Education at www.iie.org.

Buildings are big things. They are not only physically tied to their sites, but are often products of local culture, materials, and technology. Because of this connection, architects benefit from foreign study and travel as do few others. Yet one of the premier fellowships for foreign study has been traditionally underutilized by architects and architecture interns.

The Fulbright program was created by Congress in 1946 to promote international understanding in the wake of World War II. Named for Senator J. William Fulbright, who felt that the United States needed broader foreign experience commensurate with its growing position as a global leader, the program sends Americans to scores of countries around the world. It also brings citizens of these countries to study in the United States. Though the program is open to students of all disciplines, in the class of 2003–04 only 5 of 1,005 Fulbright fellows were studying architecture.

I had the pleasure of being a Fulbright fellow and count it among the most important experiences of my professional career thus far. Living in the quickly changing Baltic state of Estonia, I was able to observe a vibrant architectural culture in which young practitioners are designing some of the most important projects and running some of the leading firms. This amazing opportunity was an unexpected corollary to my original project (the study of Soviet-era architecture), which I could never have anticipated before leaving the United States. Coupled with the chance to immerse myself in the life of a truly unique country—visiting its tourist sites, eating its cuisine, meeting its people, and speaking (or attempting to speak) its language—this experience amounted to a sort of self-directed graduate education focused on issues that interest me.

This begins to touch on the great benefit of a Fulbright grant—the luxury of having control over your own time. During the grant period, your time is your own, to be spent pursuing those activities that interest you. While in Estonia I freely interspersed research, reading, sketching, and leisure travel. Not only did I learn a great deal about Estonian architectural history and publish an article on the subject, but I also had the chance to read several architectural texts I had been trying to get to for years. Quiet moments allowed time to clarify my own approach to design and even to develop some nascent watercolor skills.

Such an opportunity to spend time thinking expansively about architecture seems a natural and powerful addition to the internship experience, which often requires young practitioners to be increasingly specialized. Though geared toward students immediately out of college, the Fulbright program is open to young professionals as well. While Fulbright fellowships will never be for everyone, surely more young architects should take advantage of the opportunities they afford.

Ted Shelton, AIA
Lecturer, University of Tennessee; Cofounder, CURB
University of Tennessee, Bachelor of Architecture 1993
University of Oklahoma, Master of Architecture 1995
Cambridge University, Master of Philosophy 2003

American Academy in Rome

The American Academy in Rome was first established in 1894 and chartered by an act of Congress in 1905 with an aim to sustain independent artistic pursuits and humanistic studies. Each year, the Rome Prize is awarded to 15 emerging artists and 15 scholars through a national competition. Artists may be working in architecture, landscape architecture, design, historic preservation and conservation, literature, musical composition, or visual arts; and the selected scholars may be working in ancient, medieval, Renaissance and early modern, or modern Italian studies. Rome Prize fellowships are designed for emerging artists and for scholars in the early or middle stages of their careers.

From the outset, the ideal of community has been fundamental to the American Academy in Rome. Fellowship winners come to Rome to refine and expand their own professional, artistic, or scholarly aptitudes. The Academy's Rome Prize winners, the core of a residential community of up to 100 people at any given time, are at the center of a multidisciplinary environment, where artists and scholars are encouraged to work collegially within and across disciplines.

For more information and to apply, visit www.aarome.org/prize.htm.

Skidmore, Owings & Merrill Traveling Fellowship

First awarded in 1981, the Skidmore, Owings & Merrill (SOM) Foundation offers travel scholarships for architects, engineers, and interior designers. Grants range from $500 to $15,000, with two $15,000 fellowships awarded annually to an undergraduate and a graduate student from an accredited architecture program in the United

States. The purpose of the SOM Traveling Fellowship is to allow recent graduates to experience the built environment through independent travel. The foundation works with various accredited schools of architecture, interior design, urban design, and engineering that nominate their best candidates in a variety of processes particular to each institution. Successful nominees are those who distinguish themselves academically while presenting compelling plans for travel.

Information can be found on the SOM Foundation Web site at www.somfoundation.som.com.

CHAPTER 12 | STARTING YOUR OWN FIRM

While this may be down the road a distance for most interns, you may be one of those few who realize in these early years of your career that working for someone else is not going to be enough; one day you would like to have your own firm. For you, this chapter may be a good reality check. Since there are many books devoted to just this topic (a good one is *Architect's Essentials of Starting a Design Firm*), this will not be a "how-to" chapter but a series of anecdotes from those who have taken the journey before you.

Starting out on your own is a big endeavor with many decisions to be made. The first of many questions will be related to your ownership structure. Are you going to be a sole practitioner or will you have partners? If it is the latter, what will your legal business structure look like? And who will your partners be? Will all the principals have their registration? What types of projects will you pursue? Who will be your clients? Will you work out of your home or rent office space?

Forms of Ownership

While there are many books that describe the various legal structures (*Architect's Essentials of Starting a Design Firm* has a section about ownership types), here is a brief overview of legal entities as adapted from the Small Business Administration's Web site (www.sba.gov). Those who are actually trying to select an ownership structure should consult with their attorneys and accountants to understand the legal and tax ramifications of their decisions.

Sole Proprietorships

The vast majority of small businesses start out as sole proprietorships. A sole proprietorship is owned by one person, usually the individual who has day-to-day responsibility for running the business. Sole proprietors own all the assets of the business and the profits generated by it. They also assume complete personal responsibility for any of its liabilities or debts. In the eyes of the law and the public, the individual and business are one entity. Despite this fact, it is advisable for the finances of the individual and business to be tracked separately to establish that the business is not a "hobby" in the eyes of the IRS, especially at the beginning when one is likely to see losses for a given fiscal year. Obtaining a business license, a business checking account, and a credit card is an effective way of demonstrating that you are trying to operate your practice as a profitable business venture.

Partnerships

In a partnership, generally two or more people share ownership of a single business. Like a sole proprietorship, the law does not distinguish between the business and its owners. However, in light of recent corporate scandals, newly established partnership structures can limit the liability of each individual and protect partners from the actions of their counterparts.

The partners should have a legal agreement (generally called a "partnership agreement") that sets forth how decisions will be made, profits will be shared, disputes will be resolved, and future partners will be admitted to the partnership or bought out, and what steps will be taken to dissolve the partnership if necessary. Yes, it's hard to think about a "breakup" when the business is just starting, but many partnerships split in a time of crisis, and unless there is a well-defined process for this dissolution, it may be difficult to decide how to handle the separation without emotions getting in the way. Partners must also decide up front how much time and capital each will contribute to the partnership.

How to Find an Attorney or Accountant

Whether sole proprietor or limited liability company, your new business will require professional services from an accountant or attorney, or both. Much in the same way a client would hire an architect, you must do the research and conduct interviews to find a professional who will provide you with the level of service and expertise you need. You will require that person's services over the life of your practice, so don't simply shop for the best hourly billing rates or lowest quote for articles of incorporation. Remember that you are developing a long-term professional relationship and take your time to find the right team members to assist you.

Instead of opening the Yellow Pages to "Accountants" or "Attorneys," start with referrals. Ask other architects, the local AIA office, your friends, or any other trusted source for referrals. Set up interviews to talk with candidates and find out if they have experience with architectural firms or have a solid understanding of the architectural and engineering professions. If they don't, make sure you are comfortable with their knowledge of business law or accounting practices.

Photo courtesy of Schemata Workshop, 2005

Partners in the firm are called just that: partners. As arbitrary as it may seem, some professionals choose this legal entity for the simple reason that the leaders of the firm can have this specific title. All partners can equally bind the firm into any contractual agreement (whether it be leased equipment, leased office space, or client or consultant contracts).

General Partnership

In a general partnership, partners divide responsibility for management and liability, as well as the shares of profit or loss, according to their partnership agreement. Equal shares are assumed unless there is a written agreement that states otherwise.

Limited Partnership (LP) and
Limited Liability Partnership (LLP)

Limited means that most of the partners have limited liability (to the extent of their investment) as well as limited input regarding management decisions, which generally encourages investors for short-term projects, or for investing in capital assets. This form of ownership is not often used for operating a retail or service business. A limited partnership is more complex and formal than a general partnership. Most architectural firms, as well as firms in other service industries with which we associate (e.g., engineering) that are interested in a formal arrangement opt for the professional limited liability corporation (see below).

Joint Venture

This functions like a general partnership, but is clearly for a limited period of time or a single project. If the partners in a joint venture repeat the activity, they will be recognized as an ongoing partnership and will have to file as such, and distribute accumulated partnership assets upon dissolution of the entity. It is common for architectural firms to team up to complete a large-scale project and formalize this through a joint venture for the duration of the project.

Corporation

A corporation, chartered by the state in which it is headquartered is considered by law to be a unique entity, separate and apart from those who own it. A corporation can be taxed; it can be sued; it can enter into contractual agreements. The owners of a corporation are its shareholders. The shareholders elect a board of directors to oversee the major policies and decisions. The corporation has a life of its own and does not dissolve when ownership changes.

This is a quite common form of ownership for architectural firms. The case law and legal precedents are similar from state to state, so any potential disputes and claims are fairly easy to resolve or defend. Due to its prevalence, incorporation is quite easy, and legal fees are somewhat uniform. For "do-it-yourself" types, there are forms and samples of incorporation documents online.

Subchapter S Corporations (S Corp)

This is a tax election only; the Subchapter S election enables the shareholder to treat the earnings and profits as distributions and have them pass through directly to their personal tax return. The catch here is that if a shareholder works for the company and there is a profit, he or she must be paid a wage that meets standards of "reasonable compensation." This can vary by geographical region as well as occupation, but the basic rule is to pay yourself what you would have to pay someone to do your job, as long as there is enough profit. If you do not do this, the IRS can reclassify all of the earnings and profit as wages, and you will be liable for all of the payroll taxes on the total amount.

The leaders of an S Corp are called "shareholders," with an executive body of officers comprised of at least a president and a secretary. Only the named officers can legally bind the company; therefore, they are the ones to legally execute contracts, leases, and so on. For practical purposes, the officer titles are only used for legal documents, and the shareholders usually take on a title such as *principal* for everyday use.

Limited Liability Company (LLC)

The LLC is a relatively new type of hybrid business structure permissible in most states. It is designed to provide the limited liability features of a corporation and the tax efficiencies and operational flexibility of a partnership. Formation is more complex and formal than in a general partnership. In addition, since it is a relatively new type of ownership entity, the case law and legal precedents as well as the incorporation documents vary from state to state.

The owners are members, and the duration of the LLC is usually determined when the organization papers are filed. The term can be extended if desired by a vote of the members at the time of expiration. An LLC must not have more than two of the four characteristics that define corporations: limited liability to the extent of assets; continuity of life; centralization of management; and free transferability of ownership interests. Architecture firms electing the LLC often opt for incorporating as a professional limited liability company (PLLC). All members of a PLLC must be in the same profession (i.e., members of a single PLLC could not be an attorney, an accountant, and an architect.) The owners of a PLLC are also called "members." A managing member is elected by the other members, and this managing member is the only one who can officially bind the firm in any contractual arrangements.

Hanging Out Your Shingle

While you can prepare and take sequential steps to establish your own practice, there is no science to starting a firm. As one of the following contributors points out, you get to a point where you need to stop preparing and just go for it. While the point of "readiness" can be different for everyone, securing the first project generally provides enough momentum to help determine that you might be ready. *Architect's Essentials of Starting a Design Firm* describes the following ten models for launching a successful firm:

1. **Booster rocket** — A major first client or winning competition entry provides the "big break" for a start-up to rise above the crowd and become recognized.
2. **House for family** — Similar to booster rocket, but a family member provides the first major commission.
3. **Academic incubator** — A teaching position provides income, time, and credibility to lay the foundation for a design firm.
4. **Building a better mousetrap** — A firm fulfills an unmet market niche or pioneers a new method of practice or project delivery.
5. **Supersalesperson** — Exceptional sales skills and client relationships allow a new firm to be selected over more-established competitors.
6. **Sponsor** — An established architect lends his or her name or influence to promote the work of a start-up firm.
7. **Golden handshake** — A former employer provides the initial work (or introduction to work) for a new firm.
8. **Spin-off** — Members of a firm break away to form a new firm based on reputation, skills, and client base obtained from a previous firm.
9. **The phoenix** — The rebirth of an existing firm; members of a firm reinvent themselves by creating a new identity or direction.
10. **Starting small** — A new firm starts small, building a strong project base; the solid foundation leads to larger commissions from satisfied clients.

Checklist for Starting Your Own Firm

There are many things to consider when starting a new firm. Here is a sampling of what you might include in a start-up checklist:

- ☐ Seek out legal counsel and attorney
- ☐ Select name of your firm (even if it's just your name); you will need this for your business license
- ☐ If your ownership structure is anything other than sole proprietor:
    - ▪ File documents establishing your firm as a legal entity
    - ▪ Apply for federal employment identification number (FEIN) — even if you don't have any employees
    - ▪ File with state for unemployment or disability insurance (required in most states)
- ☐ Apply for state and local business license
- ☐ Establish phone, fax, and Internet service and Web site hosting
- ☐ Set up company bank account (even for sole proprietorship)
- ☐ Establish accounts for services — reprographics, courier, offices supplies, UPS/Fed Ex
- ☐ Determine your computing needs; hire an IT consultant
- ☐ Purchase computer equipment and software (IT consultant may be able to secure better pricing than you can)
- ☐ Purchase or lease copy machine, fax machine, plotter, printer (depending on your needs, you can lease a nice machine that combines multiple functions)
- ☐ Obtain general liability insurance (to cover people coming into your office or damage done to others around you)
- ☐ Obtain professional liability insurance (to limit your exposure to legal action resulting from your architectural practice)
- ☐ Distribute a press release or an announcement for the new firm
- ☐ Set up payroll (options: do it yourself, hire a bookkeeper, or enlist a payroll service)
- ☐ Establish graphic identity "collateral" — logo, business cards, transmittals, thank-you cards, and so on.
- ☐ Determine if you are eligible for minority or woman-owned or disadvantaged business status and apply
- ☐ Create marketing brochure for distribution to business prospects
- ☐ Register a Web domain and establish a presence on the Internet

The Business Plan

A business plan defines your business and identifies goals by which to measure your success. The basic components include a pro forma balance sheet, an income statement, and a cash flow analysis. A business plan helps you allocate resources and shows how you will repay borrowed money. A good business plan is a crucial part of any loan application.

Basically, the first half of the business plan is geared toward the development and support of a solid business strategy. Describe your services and how they may be unique to your firm. Describe the target market and the stage of development of your company. If you get hung up on a particular part of the plan, skip it for now and come back and complete it later.

The second half of the business plan is largely a description of how you intend to execute your business strategy. What are the specific marketing efforts you will employ? What will your expenses be and what income will you require to break even? How will you grow?

Don't worry about making a perfect first draft of the business plan. Just get some thoughts down to get the process going and you can always come back and polish it up later. However, as this plan will set the initial direction for the company, think carefully about strategies you will employ.

For detailed instructions on how to write a business plan, search the Internet for samples or make an appointment with the local office of the Small Business Administration for individual guidance.

Three New Firms

The following accounts are from young architects who have recently started their own firms. These contributions do not represent the myriad ways in which architectural firms are formed each year, but they do provide some insight into what it might mean to strike out on your own. Depending on your personal disposition and tolerance for risk, you may find inspiration to open your own practice or realize that you are quite content in a satisfying career in an established firm.

Leaving the "Mother Ship"

The first contributor is a principal in a three-person firm in Chicago. She and two coworkers who met at a previous firm decided to start their own firm shortly after the birth of her son and while she was in the midst of completing her licensing exams.

A Fresh Beginning

Studio3 Design, Inc., started during a time of uneasy flux at our previous firm. I teamed up with two colleagues from "the old firm" who were just as eager as I was to make a positive change and control our own destinies. Of the three principals at Studio3 Design, Inc., one is an interior designer, one is a registered architect, and I am halfway through the ARE process, still attempting to carve out time to complete the exams.

The Magic Number

For us, having three principals is an ideal way of maintaining a balance. Voting is easy; there is always a tie breaker. Pooling the resources of three individuals is much less of a burden than relying on the resources of one or two; likewise, splitting incoming cash into thirds softens the blow of dividing money. We dove into this opportunity headfirst, with only our personal cash contributions and our combined design, technical, and marketing skills. Before the "big leap," we had numerous discussions about our initial time commitment to the firm and set internal goals with a clear understanding of everyone's expectations.

The Start-Up Rollercoaster

Once you commit to starting a practice, events happen quickly — from signing contracts with professional advisers to filling out tax and licensing forms; from setting up accounts with various vendors to completing the first projects. The checklist of start-up tasks seemed to expand indefinitely. We simply tackled those items in our rare moments of downtime. One item to seriously consider sooner rather than later is the business plan. This may be a fluid document that evolves with your firm over time, but at least you will have taken a look at major factors affecting your decisions and internal relationships without assuming too much in the beginning. Writing the business plan will aid your review of the big picture and help determine whether starting your own firm at this time is a sound investment.

Project Selection

Amazingly, our initial marketing efforts were minimal, and our first projects were acquired via referral or other personal contacts. We decided to begin with a focus on the familiar, a niche market with immediate but lower-risk needs: space planning, tenant improvement, and property management marketing collateral. We plan to expand toward more architectural projects after our business is running smoothly and we have enough cash reserves to be able to pick and choose our projects and clientele.

The Future

We feel lucky to be busy enough to keep moving full speed ahead and to be able to pay our mortgages. We look forward to an ever-expanding portfolio of project types, with the added practical knowledge of running a business. Our office is based in my loft; the only negative aspect of this setup is that my work is never out of sight. There is simply no leaving the work behind, since the office is physically inside my home. The flip side of this is that I can have "family time" at five o'clock and then complete more work later in the evening.

So if you and a highly trusted colleague or two are willing to "sacrifice" a long commute, a politically charged office atmosphere, and insurance benefits, and are willing to put a lot of extra energy into the seed of a practice, then I definitely recommend spinning off into your own firm. You're getting everything back that you invest, with the additional bonus of gaining invaluable experience that may not otherwise come your way.

Jennifer Svastisalee, Associate AIA
Cofounder and Principal, Studio3 Design, Inc.
University of Illinois at Chicago, Bachelor of Architecture 1996

Former Classmates

Unlike Jennifer and her two colleagues, the following contributor met his practice partner in architecture school. Their extracurricular efforts led to a unique collaboration that became the genesis for the new firm.

My Background

I came to architecture the long way around. My six years of undergraduate education resulted in BS degrees in civil engineering and architectural engineering from Drexel University. After graduation, I took a job with a small structural engineering firm that specialized in forensic engineering, most notably the structural assessment of historic structures. I worked during the day while continuing an architectural education in Drexel's evening architecture program. After four years, I made the decision to pursue architecture as a career. My wife and I moved to Seattle, and I enrolled in the graduate architecture program at the University of Washington. During graduate school and for six years after graduation, I worked at several architectural firms in and around Seattle. In May 2001, I formed Hutchison & Maul with my friend and colleague, Tom Maul.

How We Started

Tom and I were classmates in the graduate architecture program. Following graduation, we formed a collaborative called Rectifier along with several other former classmates. Together, we developed several conceptual projects related to the city's infrastructure. Since all of us worked at firms during the day, we met during the weeknights and weekends. The collaborative allowed us to investigate and explore architectural issues and ideas in a setting outside of the workplace, among peers our own age and with a similar educational background. As Rectifier faded due to the inevitable difficulties of getting eight individuals to meet on a regular basis, Tom and I continued our conversations about architecture and worked together on several competitions. Out of this relationship developed a conversation and, eventually, a decision to form our own partnership.

How We Work

All of the work in our office is a collaborative effort between Tom and myself. This is particularly the case with design. We are not interested in a partnership in which projects are designed by individuals. This being said, most of our projects, especially the smaller ones, involve assigning one of us as the lead. Once a design direction has been established, the assigned person becomes project architect or project manager. This provides our client with a primary contact person and ensures that one person is responsible for managing the project. As our firm grows and the project size and complexity increases, we anticipate that future employees will fill the project architect and project manager roles.

How We Get Work

Almost all of the work that has come into our office has resulted from referrals. Typically, we find ourselves listed with two or three other architectural firms and are interviewed by the potential client. Our marketing material includes a portfolio with all of our firm's work to date, as well as the competitions completed by Tom and me before we formed H&M. Depending on the client or project, we may also show work performed with our previous firms. In this case, we always make clear the architectural firm responsible for the design of the project, and our individual roles on the project. We also list as references those firm principals who were responsible for the work, which provides the potential client a way to clarify our roles and experience on the project.

We try to remember that, when considering work, it's to our advantage to interview the client as well. We have turned away work that does not seem a good fit; for example, in certain cases, we feel that the client doesn't need us, or vice versa. We try to make our architectural interests and motives clear to potential clients, and we encourage them to ask any and all questions.

How We Keep Our Costs Down

As is the case with most new firms, we began H&M with little work (and therefore little cash flow). We have been careful to maintain a low-overhead company. Our studio is in a converted garage behind my house. We have resisted costly purchases, in particular, technology-related items such as computers. I still use my own ten-year-old computer that I sold to H&M. We have established a drawing format in the office so that most of our documents can be printed from our laser printer.

Larger documents are sent out to a reprographics firm and are billed directly to the project. Although we are interested in growing as a firm, we are proceeding cautiously. Typically, all of the workload is handled by Tom and me; when we need additional help, we hire people on a contract basis.

Registration

While both Tom and I had applied for and were eligible to take the Architect Registration Examination when we started our firm, I had not started the examination process, and Tom was halfway done. This was never a concern for us. At the time, we were most interested in working on small projects (not requiring architectural registration) that allowed us to further develop our working relationship. As a result, our work has consisted primarily of residential and retail projects. Interestingly, our lack of registration did not prevent us from doing public work. We have completed two small public projects that involved interior renovation work. Nonetheless, our intent is for the firm to grow, so we have since both become registered and are actively pursuing larger and more complex projects.

Robert Hutchison, RA
Principal and Cofounder, Hutchison & Maul LLC
University of Washington, Master of Architecture 1996

Going Solo

Sole practitioners make up almost a 33% of all firms. About 66% of firms have 2 to 49 employees, firms with 50 to 99 employees make up 2% of firms, and another 2% of firms have 100 or more employees.

—THE BUSINESS OF ARCHITECTURE: THE 2003 AIA FIRM SURVEY

While the majority of architects decide to start a firm with former colleagues or classmates, a large number of architects decide to strike out on their own. The following contributor is one such architect.

How Do You Begin?

I am not sure if anyone is ever "ready" to start a business, but there are some clues that may suggest your readiness for firm ownership. My clues were a desire to leave a comfortable job I had been in since graduation, an inability to find satisfaction in subsequent jobs, and the knowledge that I had developed a solid network of friends and clients who knew my talents.

The first firm I worked for provided me with the opportunity to be involved with organizations such as the AIA and the local chamber of commerce. I took it upon myself to participate at various levels, often in leadership positions. Through time spent in these organizations, I learned how to be a leader, and I was able to con-

nect with people whom I would otherwise never have met. It was a backdoor way of meeting company executives who were potential clients. Although I didn't know it at the time, the effort I spent participating in these organizations has paid dividends in my subsequent venture as a sole proprietor.

What You Need to Know

By the time I knew I was ready, I still didn't know what it took to start a firm. While there is a lot of information out there to help guide a person through the process, there is no substitution for actually doing it. I did my research, but without a doubt, despite how much I read, the majority of what I learned was "on the job."

What I did know at the outset was that I needed a project to get me started and that I needed to possess the ability to perform all the tasks on a project, from executing a contract to conducting a punch list for construction completion. Until I was in a position to hire someone to help me, I would have to undertake every aspect of the project. To cushion the blow of going from having a salary to possibly having no income, I took a teaching position in the architecture program at the local community college.

What I didn't know was how to run a business. This is a very complex undertaking, especially when your business is an architectural practice. In California, there are many city, state, and federal regulations, as well as requirements from the California Architects Board. To learn what was required, I enrolled in a community college course on starting a business. Although I learned much about the pitfalls of starting a business, most of the information was generic and bore little relation to professional service industries such as architecture. So I then purchased books on marketing, contracts, and business essentials for architects interested in starting their own businesses. One of the more specific and most helpful books was The Complete Idiot's Guide to Starting Your Own Business, *by Edward Paulson. I continually refer to this book as a resource when I am unsure of how to deal with things. Also, the State of California has a great Web site (www.calgold.ca.gov), which provides a checklist of "need-to-know" items for those starting a new business, along with links to other resources such as the Small Business Administration Web site (www.sba.gov).*

Beyond Preparation

There were a few things I wish I had known prior to starting the venture—foremost, how much cash was needed to start the company. Starting from scratch, I found that my weekends were filled with purchasing everything from computers to paper clips. Fees from my initial projects were not enough to cover both my expected salary and the equipment and supply purchases, so I often went with a little less pay in favor of investing in the company. Some of these initial purchases have proved to be money well spent. For example, I purchased a professional version of QuickBooks (accounting software for small businesses) and a second-party software package that is tailored to set up an accounting system for an architectural practice. The total cost was minor compared to the benefit of having end-of-year records in order for tax time and tracking my budgets.

Business Finances

I didn't know at the outset that I should keep my business and personal finances separate. I had always assumed that as a sole proprietor, you got all of your money—business and personal—from the same pot. While this is true in practical terms, for tax purposes it is much easier to prove that you are a legitimate business if you separate the two. At the suggestion of my accountant, the business opened bank and credit card accounts along with local supply and reprographics company accounts. This allowed all of my project income to be matched with my business expenses for the year—a necessary accounting function.

I also realized that I wanted to spend more time doing architecture and less time on human resource activities like figuring out payroll taxes and medical insurance benefits; as a result, I outsourced these business functions to a local firm. The amount I spend on outsourcing tasks I don't want to perform is much less than it would cost me to learn all of the related issues and apply them well. I choose to focus on what I do best, and I let professionals in other fields assist me by doing what they do best.

Balancing Work and Family

In hindsight, I wish that I hadn't started my firm in a year in which I would eventually have a life-altering event. About halfway through the first year of my company, my mom died. She had been fighting off a major illness, and while the family was with her for the whole ordeal, I was not. I had been quite consumed with the business, trying to figure it all out, which left little time for my wife and kids or for my parents, brothers, and sisters. Although I could not have planned for this, I wish that I could have waited a year so that I would have had more time to spend with my family during this event. The difficult lesson I learned is that your work will always be there, with the pressure to do things better and faster, but your loved ones may not—and they should always take priority.

Just Do It!

At some point, you just have to take the plunge. Although starting out may be frightening, your dream cannot become a reality without that first step into the unknown. It is somewhat like design, in that you can spend a lot of time planning. In starting my firm, I was realistic in understanding that there was a lot of work to do and that everything could not be perfectly aligned at the outset. The business began with certain elements in place — such as my architectural registration, a business license, and a project — but also with many elements in flux. My firm has changed and evolved over the past year and half, with much of my business strategy still in transition. As the business grows, I will develop these strategies and, I hope, foster new ones. I have recently decided to make the firm's philosophy focus on the process. For me, the business is not so much about achieving a single goal as it is about thriving in the process of creating.

Ed Mojica, AIA
Principal and Founder, mas | mojica architecture studio
California State Polytechnic, San Luis Obispo, Bachelor of Architecture 1997

CONCLUSION

If you just read this book cover to cover, I congratulate you. Hopefully you will know what to anticipate in the upcoming years, while understanding that there is not a definitive answer or single solution to any of these situations. As with any design problem, there are many possible ways to design one's architectural career. The various factors that inform one intern's career may be vastly different from that of another intern. The types of projects you work on, the size of firm you work for, the supervisors you work under, the mentors who guide you all influence your career decisions along the way. Thus, this book should be just one reference point along your journey. The topics covered in this book are always in a state of flux, not only as you progress through your career, but also in the broad spectrum of the profession. When you graduate, the idea of taking portions of the ARE right away might seem very important, and so you research the states that offer this possibility. This topic has been much debated by members of the profession for many years and will continue to be for many more. And yet at some point, you will complete your exams and your attention will move toward concerns of career advancement and personal growth. Or maybe after five years, you'll decide that registration is no longer important because you anticipate a career in a large office that doesn't require a license for senior staff or reward you for obtaining it. The relevance of each career decision changes for you over time, as it does for the entire profession.

As with any guidebook, you will likely refer to individual sections as needed. While this book could serve as a basis for discussion with your mentor, supervisor, or peers, adapt what has been written to suit your needs. There may be suggestions that are entirely appropriate and helpful without too much modification for your specific situation. There may be other suggestions that simply don't apply because of your personality or approach to your career. Pick and choose what you think will work for you. As you learn methods that work better, write them into the margins. Thus, when you become a mentor to someone else, you can relay what was successful for you.

Good luck!

BIBLIOGRAPHY

Articles

ArchVoices.org: A comprehensive bibliography of intern-related articles.

Fischer, Thomas. "The Intern Trap: How the Profession Exploits Its Young," *Progressive Architecture,* July 1994, pp. 69–73.

Books

The American Institute of Architects, ed. Joseph A. Demkin. *The Architect's Handbook of Professional Practice,* 13th Ed. New York: John Wiley & Sons, Inc., 2001.

Anthony, Kathryn H. *Designing for Diversity.* Urbana, IL: Univ. of Illinois Press, 2001.

Boyer, Ernest L., and Lee D. Mitgang, *Building Community: A Future for Architecture Education and Practice.* Princeton, NJ: The Carnegie Foundation, 1996.

Klein, Christopher J. *AEC WorkForce Guide to Finding the Right Job in the Design & Construction Industry.* Natwick, MA: AEC WorkForce, 2002.

Kliment, Stephen. *Writing for Design Professionals.* New York: W.W. Norton and Co. Inc., 1998.

Piven, Peter, and Bradford Perkins. *Architect's Essentials of Starting Your Own Design Firm.* New York: John Wiley & Sons, Inc., 2003.

Piven, Peter, with William Mandel. *Architect's Essentials—Ownership Transition.* New York: John Wiley & Sons, Inc., 2002.

Pressman, Andy. *Architecture 101.* New York: John Wiley & Sons, Inc., 1997.

Valence, Jean. *Architect's Essentials of Professional Development.* New York: John Wiley & Sons, Inc., 2003.

INDEX

401373